CHRISTIAN
NON-RESISTANCE

A Da Capo Press Reprint Series

CIVIL LIBERTIES IN AMERICAN HISTORY

GENERAL EDITOR: LEONARD W. LEVY
Brandeis University

CHRISTIAN NON-RESISTANCE

IN ALL ITS IMPORTANT BEARINGS

By Adin Ballou

Appendix by William S. Heywood

DA CAPO PRESS · NEW YORK · 1970

A Da Capo Press Reprint Edition

This Da Capo Press edition of
Christian Non-Resistance
is an unabridged republication of the
second edition published in Philadelphia
in 1910.

Library of Congress Catalog Card Number 70-121104
SBN 306-71980-0

Published by Da Capo Press
A Division of Plenum Publishing Corporation
227 West 17th Street, New York, N.Y. 10011

Manufactured in the United States of America

CHRISTIAN NON-RESISTANCE
IN ALL ITS IMPORTANT BEARINGS

ILLUSTRATED AND DEFENDED

BY

ADIN BALLOU

Whoso readeth let him understand

SECOND EDITION

ALSO

AN APPENDIX—In Two Parts

By WILLIAM S. HEYWOOD

1. Biographical Sketch of the Author

2. The Higher Patriotism

UNIVERSAL PEACE UNION

PHILADELPHIA, PA.

1910

CONTENTS

CHAPTER I.—EXPLANATORY DEFINITIONS.

CHAPTER II.—SCRIPTURAL PROOFS.

CHAPTER III.—SCRIPTURAL OBJECTIONS ANSWERED.

CHAPTER IV.—NON-RESISTANCE NOT CONTRARY TO NATURE.

CHAPTER V.—THE SAFETY OF NON-RESISTANCE.

CHAPTER VI.—GENERAL OBJECTIONS ANSWERED.

CHAPTER VII.—NON-RESISTANCE IN RELATION TO GOVERNMENT.

APPENDIX.

INTRODUCTION.

By William S. Heywood.

The Treatise upon Christian non-resistance, which is reproduced on the following pages, constituting the more essential part of the present volume, was first published in the year 1846, more than half a century ago. It was at a time when a great wave of philanthropic thought and feeling seemed to be sweeping over the land and world, especially over the so-called Christian world, recasting and to some extent displacing previously existing conceptions of truth and duty, by bringing more distinctly to view the practical and humanitary features of the Gospel of Christ, relegating to a subordinate place those of a merely speculative and dogmatic character so long dominant in the church, and demanding that the principles and spirit of the Gospel of Christ be uncompromisingly applied to human life in all its multiform phases, manifestations and relations—not only to private but to public concerns—to concerns affecting alike personal character and conduct and also the character and conduct of communities, neighborhoods, townships, States and nations, both in regard to forms of organization and modes of administration—to their attitude toward and treatment of each other under all possible conditions and circumstances.

The work was received with heartfelt approval and gratification by some of the foremost philan-

thropists and radical reformers of both this country
and England, as expressed in numerous personal
letters to the author and through the medium of
the public press, and, when occasion permitted, was
commended by them to the attention and favorable
judgment of all lovers of truth and humanity whom
their testimonies might reach. Mr. Garrison, the
distinguished leader of the Anti-Slavery movement
in the United States, gave it most earnest greet-
ing, at the outset, in the columns of his paper, The
Liberator, as a brief extract from his pen will show:
"We hail the appearance of this work with great
satisfaction. It treats of a subject more vital perhaps than any other that ever challenged the attention of mankind—vital to human safety, vital to
the attainment and establishment of true liberty,
vital to the prosperity of nations, vital to the reconciliation of a hostile world: a subject, too, grossly misapprehended by some, maliciously misrepre-
sented by others, and clearly understood by very
few. It is such a work as we have long desired
to see, and from the pen of one who is, in all respects, qualified to undertake it and carry it through
in the best manner.

"We have no desire to deal in laudation, but simply to express our conviction of the value of the
work and of the competency of Adin Ballou to
state, illustrate and defend the great doctrine it
inculcates. With a mind strictly logical, and a
spirit deeply imbued with gentleness and peace—
aided by rare good sense, great self-possession and
a resolute dispositon to be in the right—*for right's*

sake, he brings to his task the best qualities of both head and heart.

"The work is soberly and frankly addressed to the reason, conscience and higher sentiments of mankind—not to their propensities, passions and carnal ambitions and desires. In the circulation of this little volume the friends of Peace should take a lively interest. At this particular crisis, when the spirit of war and violence is so madly raging in the land, its distribution, as far and wide as possible, is most earnestly to be desired."

The book very soon arrested the attention and won the approbation of the more active friends of humanity in Great Britain, and two years later, in 1848, two widely known philanthropists of Edinburgh, Scotland, caused it to be republished for special circulation in the United Kingdom. The English edition was a verbatim reprint of the original, with the exception of portions of two chapters relating to local political affairs, but which were without pertinency or force under a system of government differing from that of the United States. The parties responsible for the re-publication of the book beyond the sea commended it to the favorable attention of its readers in the following language: "We have been impressed with the excellence of the matter contained in the work, and with the sound Scriptural arguments of the talented author on the highly important question discussed by him; and we trust that the present edition will be generally acceptable to the friends of the Peace Cause. We have carefully perused the volume, and, having weighed the sentiments which it contains, desire to express our firm conviction that they are entirely in accordance with pure Christianity, evidently proceeding from a mind richly imbued with the spirit of love to God and man, desirous of promoting the advancement of the Redeemer's kingdom on the earth."

In the sincere belief, shared by a considerable number of the friends of universal peace, that the importance of the exposition of the doctrine of Christian non-resistance given by Adin Ballou in the work under notice, is not over-estimated by the writers of the foregoing paragraphs, and that the work has in no proper sense "outlived its usefulness"; a new edition is now offered to the general public and urged upon the thoughtful and conscientious consideration of all well-wishers of their kind, with the well-assured conviction and most ardent hope that, by setting forth most clearly and uncompromisingly the essential barbarism and iniquity, not only of the great war system of the world and the death-dealing exploits of the battlefield, but of all forms of injurious and brutal force, under whatever pretext called into exercise between man and man, it will contribute much to the growth of that public sentiment which seems to be tending in the right direction, promising, as it does, to rise at an early day into an imperative demand for the entire abolition of war and of all the armaments and preparations for war of every kind and name, and prove to be, henceforth, as hitherto, an efficient instrumentality in promoting "Peace on earth and good will among men"—a cause most dear to its author's heart, to the advocacy and advancement of which he devoted much of his thought, energy and time during a long, active and eminently useful life.

It is to be presumed that among the readers of this volume there will be many who, while assenting to the general doctrine which it inculcates and admitting the principal points of the argument of the author in its support, will yet feel unable to agree with him in all the practical applications which he makes of it; especially in regard to political action under the provisions of a constitution and form of government claiming and exercising from time to time the power and the right to declare war and carry on the work of human slaughter; failing to recognize or allow that the responsibility involved in such action is so great and so inclusive as he assumes and maintains to be the case, nevertheless, it has been deemed wise and just to the author, in this new edition of his work, to reprint the original, verbatim, giving his views in full as they came from his pen, without excision or emendation, leaving the reader to make such qualifications or set such limitations, in the respects indicated, as in loyalty to his own highest conviction of truth and duty, he feels bound to do.

Supplementary to the subject-matter treated in the earlier pages of this work, constituting its characteristic feature, may be found an appendix, in two parts; the first being a "Biographical sketch of the author," which will be of interest, no doubt, to those readers otherwise uninformed in regard to his earthly life and the manifold labors in which he was engaged, the other an address before the

Universal Peace Union upon a theme concerning which there is great confusion and oftentimes much question, when considered in connection with the practical bearings of the doctrines of Christian non-resistance; the purpose of the address being to show that as "there are victories of peace no less renowned than those of war," so is there a patriotism disassociated from all scenes of carnal strife enacted on the bloody, death-inflicting battlefield no less honorable and praiseworthy than that thus associated, as is so often the case—a love and service of one's country, calculated to promote and secure, in an eminent degree, the highest prosperity, welfare, happiness and truest glory of a country; and yet strictly accordant with the principles and sentiments which this work is designed to expound, illustrate and apply to the various interests and activities of human life.

PREFACE.

Here is a little book in illustration and defence of a very unpopular doctrine. The author believes it to be as ancient as Christianity, and as true as the New Testament. But it is a doctrine little understood and almost everywhere spoken against. He therefore entreats his readers to divest themselves as much as possible of prejudice, and patiently examine what he has here written. He does not expect every one to be pleased with what he has presented in this volume, not even those who approve of it as a *whole*. But he desires friends and opposers to be candid, just and generous; to treat the work as they would have one of their own (on any important subject) treated. He wishes no personal strain of panegyric from those who may think well of his Treatise. Let all glory be given to the Supreme Source of wisdom and goodness. On the other hand, he hopes that those who may think ill of it will be manly enough not to condemn it merely on account of its authorship. Let it be approved or condemned solely on its own intrinsic merits or demerits.

It is soberly and frankly addressed to the reason, conscience and higher sentiments of mankind—not to their propensities and lower passions. May it be read and responded to accordingly. The honest inquirer will ask: Is it in accordance with divine

truth and righteousness? Search and see. Perhaps
the controversial critic will look for its errors, fal-
lacies, inconsistencies and assailable points. If there
are any such, let them be detected and exposed.
This ought to be done; but let those who undertake
it prove themselves workmen that need not be
ashamed. Let them be sure that they understand
the subject, that they understand precisely what is
contended for in this work, and that they are com-
petent to refute its fundamental positions by good
and sufficient arguments. It is so plain, discriminating and unequivocal in the style of its statements
and reasonings, that serious misapprehension or
misrepresentation of its meaning will hardly be excusable. It does not court controversy, but if subjected to it will be entitled to fair and honorable
treatment.

It is a book for the future rather than the present,
and will be better appreciated by the public half a
century hence than now. But a better future is
even now dawning and it is needed to help develop
the coming age of love and peace. A great transi-
tion of the human mind has commenced and the
reign of military and penal violence must ultimately give place to that of forbearance, forgiveness and
mercy. Such a work as this will meet a deepfelt
want of many minds scattered up and down Christendom. So strongly was the author persuaded of
this fact by various indications, that he felt impelled
by a sense of duty to prepare this Manual as a supply for that want. Providentially the worthy friend,
who assumes the pecuniary responsibility of its pub-
lication, generously came forward to facilitate the

object, and thus by a concurrence of effort, it has made its appearance. It is now sent forth on its mission of reconciliation. The author feels a comfortable assurance that the blessing of the Most High God will accompany it wherever it goes, that it will diffuse light among many that sit in darkness and promote in some humble degree that glorious regeneration of the world for which the good men of all ages have constantly prayed and hoped.

A. B.

Hopedale, Mass., April, 1846.

Engraved by H.W. Smith

Adin Ballou

CHRISTIAN NON-RESISTANCE.

CHAPTER I.

Explanatory Definitions.

Different kinds of Non-Resistance—The term Non-Resistance –The term Force, etc.—The term injury, etc.—The
term Christian Non-Resistance; its derivation—The key
text of Non-Resistance—Necessary applications of Non-
Resistance—What a Christian Non–Resistant cannot consistently do—The principle and sub-principle of Non-Resistance—The conclusion.

DIFFERENT KINDS OF NON-RESISTANCE.

What is Christian Non Resistance ? It is that original, peculiar kind of non-resistance, which was enjoined and exemplified by Jesus Christ, according to
the Scriptures of the New Testament. Are there
other kinds of non-resistance ? Yes. 1. Philosophical non-resistance of various hue; which sets at
nought divine revelation, disregards the authority of
Jesus Christ as a divine teacher, excludes all strictly
religious considerations, and deduces its conclusions
from the light of nature, the supposed fitness of
things and the expediency of consequences. 2. Sentimental non-resistance, also of various hue; which is

held to be the spontaneous dictate of man's higher
sentiments in the advanced stages of his development,
transcending all special divine revelations, positive
instructions, ratiocination and considerations of expediency. 3. Necessitous non-resistance, commonly
expressed in the phrase, "passive obedience and non-
resistance," imperiously preached by despots to their
subjects, as their indispensable duty and highest virtue; also recommended by worldly prudence to the
victims of oppression when unable to offer successful
resistance to their injurers. With this last mentioned
kind Christian non-resistance has nothing in common.   With philosophical and sentimental non resistance it holds much in common; being, in fact, the divine original of which they are human adulterations,
and embracing all the good of both without the evils
of either.   This treatise is an illustration and defence
of Christian non-resistance, properly so designated.

THE TERM NON-RESISTANCE.

The term non-resistance itself next demands attention.   It requires very considerable qualifications.   I
use it as applicable only to the conduct of human beings towards human beings—not towards the inferior
animals, inanimate things, or satanic influences.   If
an opponent, willing to make me appear ridiculous,
should say—" You are a non-resistant, and therefore
must be passive to all assailing beings, things and influences, to satan, man, beast, bird, serpent, insect,
rocks, timbers, fires, floods, heat, cold and storm," —
I should answer, not so; my non resistance relates
solely to conduct between human beings.   This is an
important limitation of the term.   But I go further,
and disclaim using the term to express absolute passiv-

ity, even towards human beings. I claim the right
to offer the utmost moral resistance, not sinful, of
which God has made me capable, to every manifestation of evil among mankind. Nay, I hold it my duty
to offer such moral resistance. In this sense my very
non-resistance becomes the highest kind of resistance
to evil. This is another important qualification of
the term. But I do not stop here. There is an uninjurious, benevolent physical force. There are cases in
which it would not only be allowable, but in the highest degree commendable, to restrain human beings by
this kind of force. Thus, maniacs, the insane, the delirious sick, ill natured children, the intellectually or
morally *non-compos mentis*, the intoxicated and the
violently passionate, are frequently disposed to perpetrate outrages and inflict injuries, either on themselves or others, which ought to be kindly and uninjuriously prevented by the muscular energy of their
friends. And in cases where deadly violence is inflicted with deliberation and malice aforethought, one
may nobly throw his body as a temporary barrier between the destroyer and his helpless victim, choosing
to die in that position, rather than be a passive spec-
tator. Thus another most important qualification is
given to the term non-resistance. It is not non-resistance to animals and inanimate things, nor to satan,
but only to human beings. Nor is it moral non-resistance to human beings, but chiefly physical. Nor is
it physical non-resistance to all human beings, under
all circumstances, but only so far as to abstain totally
from the infliction of personal injury, as a means of
resistance. It is simply non-resistance of injury with
injury—evil with evil.

Will the opposer exclaim—"This is no non-resist-

ance at all; the term is mischosen !'' I answer. So
said the old opposers of the Temperance Reformation,
respecting the term "total abstinence." They began
by insisting that the term must be taken unqualifiedly,
and pronounced total abstinence an absurdity. It
was replied—"we limit its application to the use of
ardent spirits and intoxicating liquors.'' "Then
you exclude these substances from the arts and from
external applications, do you ?'' rejoined the opposers.
"No,'' replied the advocates of the cause, " we mean
total abstinence from the internal use—the drinking of
those liquors.'' " But are they not sometimes necessary for medical purposes ?'' said the opposers, "and
then may they not be taken internally?'' "Certainly,
with proper precautions," was the reply; "we mean
by total abstinence, precisely this and no more—the
entire disuse of all ardent spirits and intoxicating
liquors, as a beverage." "That,'' exclaimed the ob-
jectors, (despairing of a *reductio ad absurdam,*) " is
no total abstinence at all; the term is mischosen !''
Nevertheless, it was a most significant term. It had
in it an almost talismanic power. It expressed
better than any other just what was meant, and
wrought a prodigious change in public opinion and
practice. The term non-resistance is equally significant and talismanic. It signifies total absinence
from all resistance of injury with injury. It is thus
far non-resistance—no farther.

The almost universal opinion and practice of mankind has been on the side of resistance of injury with
injury. It has been held justifiable and necessary, for
individuals and nations to inflict any amount of injury
which would effectually resist a supposed greater injury. The consequence has been universal suspicion,

defiance, armament, violence, torture and bloodshed.
The earth has been rendered a vast slaughter-field—a
theatre of reciprocal cruelty and vengeance—strewn
with human skulls, reeking with human blood, resounding with human groans, and steeped with human tears. Men have become drunk with mutual revenge; and they who could inflict the greatest amount
of injury, in pretended defence of life, honor, rights,
property, institutions and laws, have been idolized as
the heroes and rightful sovereigns of the world. Non-
resistance explodes this horrible delusion; announces
the impossibility of overcoming evil with evil; and,
making its appeal directly to all the injured of the human race, enjoins on them, in the name of God, never
more to resist injury with injury; assuring them that
by adhering to the law of love under all provocations,
and scrupulously suffering wrong rather than inflicting it, they shall gloriously "overcome evil with
good," and exterminate all their enemies by turning them into faithful friends.

THE TERM FORCE, ETC.

Having thus qualified and defined the term non-
resistance, it would seem proper to do the same with
several others, frequently made use of in the discussion of our general subject. One of these terms is
force. Non-resistants, like others, have been in the
habit of using this, and similar terms too loosely; thereby giving needless occasion for misunderstanding, on
the part of the uninformed, and misrepresentation on
the part of interested opposers. The word force, is
thus defined by Walker, "strength, vigor, might,
violence, virtue, efficacy, validness, power of law,
armament, warlike preparations, destiny, necessity,

fatal compulsion.'' Now if we should use the word force, as the contrary of non-resistance, without any qualification, the idea would be conveyed that non-resistance was identical with absolute passivity, and that it necessarily excluded all kinds and degrees of force, under all circumstances whatsoever. The generic meaning of the term force, is ''strength, vigor, might,'' whether physical or moral. Thus we may speak of the force of love, the force of truth, the force of public opinion, the force of moral suasion, the force of non resistance. Or we may speak of the force of gravitation, the force of cohesion the force of repulsion, &c. Or in relation to the muscular force of human beings, we may speak of benevolent force, kind force, uninjurious force; meaning thereby, various applications of muscular strength for the purpose of preventing human beings committing on themselves or others some injury; in which prevention no personal injury is inflicted, but real kindness and benefit done to all parties concerned. As non resistance is not identical with absolute passivity but allows, implies and requires various kinds and degrees of moral and physical ''strength,'' according to circumstances, the term force must not be used as its converse unless it be with such qualifications, or in such a connection, as will give it some one of its conventional significations, so that it shall mean violence, warlike force, positive vengeance, destructive force —in fine, INJURIOUS FORCE. Injurious force of all kinds and degrees, between human beings, is incompatible with non-resistance. Such are the qualifications with which the term force will be used in this work.

The term moral force will be understood from the preceding remarks, as synonymous with moral power

—the effective influence of moral "strength, vigor, might." Physical force, as distinguished from moral force, is a term used to express the idea of material force, the action of one body on another, compelling the weaker to yield to the stronger by mere animal strength or mechanical power. As moral force may be either good or evil, injurious or uninjurious, according to its kind, its object, its spirit, or its manner of application; so may physical force be good or evil, injurious or uninjurious, according to the same considerations. When a licentious man corrupts the mind of an innocent youth by bad examples, bad counsel, bad maxims, and other evil influences, in which there is no physical force, he exerts a most injurious moral force. He demoralizes the principles and habits of one, whom he ought to encourage and confirm in virtue. When a good man converts a sinner from the error of his ways, by good examples, counsels, maxims and other purifying influences, he exerts a most beneficent and salutary moral force. So when a man by physical force destroys or impairs the life, intellect, moral sentiment, or absolute welfare of a human being, he uses an injurious physical force. But in restraining a madman from outrage, or holding a delirious sick person on the bed, or compelling an ill-natured child to desist from tearing out the hair of a weaker brother, or interposing his body and muscular strength to prevent rape, or any similar act, wherein he does no one a real injury, while he renders to some or all the parties concerned a real benefit, he uses a rightful, uninjurious, physical force.

THE TERM INJURY.

I use this term in a somewhat peculiar sense, to sig-

nify any moral influence or physical force exerted by
one human being upon another, the legitimate effect
of which is to destroy or impair life, to destroy or impair the physical faculties, to destroy or impair the intellectual powers, to destroy, impair or pervert the
moral and religious sentiment, or to destroy or impair
the absolute welfare, all things considered, of the person on whom such influence or force is exerted,
whether that person be innocent or guilty, harmless,
or offensive, injurious or uninjurious, sane or insane,
compos mentis or *non-compos,* adult or infant.   Some
of the lexicographers define an "injury" to be "hurt,
harm or mischief, unjustly done to a person;" thereby
implying that any hurt, harm or mischief done to one
who deserves nothing better, or can be considered as
justly liable to it, is no injury at all. I reject entirely
every such qualification of the term. I hold an injury
to be an injury, whether deserved or undeserved, whether intended or unintended, whether well meant or ill
meant, determining the fact in accordance with the
foregoing definition.   But, says the inquirer—" what
if it can be proved justifiable, by the law of God, to
inflict personal injury in certain cases on the offensive
and guilty ? "   Then, of course, it will be proved that
non-resistance is a false doctrine. " What if it can be
proved that the infliction of small injuries may prevent much greater evils ? "   Then it will be proved
that we may do evil that good may come, which will
forever keep the world just where it is.   " What if it
can be shown that the person who inflicts an injury
honestly intended it for a benefit ? "   That will only
prove him honestly mistaken, and so undeserving of
blame.   " What if a man inflicts death or any other
injury, according to established human laws, but does

it without malice, or revenge, or any malevolent intent?" Then he does an anti-Christian act, without
conscience as to its real nature. The act must be condemned; he must be credited for his motives; due allow-
ance must be made for his misapprehension of duty;
and light poured into his mind to superinduce a better conscience, that he may be brought to act the
Christian part. But in no case must we lose sight of
the inquiry, whether an injury has been done. And in
determining this, we must not ask whether the recip-
ient were guilty or innocent, whether the thing done
were well or ill intended, whether it were done in a
right or a wrong spirit. If it be in fact an injury, it is
contrary to the doctrine of Christian non-resistance;
and no person knowing it to be such can repeat it under any pretext whatsoever, without violating the law
of God. This is the sense and signification of the
terms injury, injurer, injurious,&c., as used in these
pages. The objector may here interpose critical
queries, with a view to test the soundness of my definition. He may suppose that a man's leg, hand or
eye, is so diseased as to require amputation in order
to save his life. But such member is one of his physical faculties, which must not be destroyed or im-
paired, because that would be an injury. I answer.
The diseased member is already lost. The question
is not whether the friendly surgeon shall destroy or
impair it; but only whether he shall amputate it, in
order to preserve the life and remaining faculties. No
injury, but an absolute benefit is proposed. This case
is clear. But suppose the minister of the law is ordered to amputate a sound leg, hand or eye, as a punishment, or for an example to deter others from the
commission of crime. This is absolute injury, done

under good pretexts indeed, but on that account none
the less an injury. Again, a child dangerously sick requires some medical application, very disagreeable,
yet indispensable to his recovery, which can only be
applied by physical force. Or an insane adult is in
the same circumstances. Or a person infected with
hydrophobia, and subject to terrible paroxysms of the
disease, needs to be confined; and yet for want of
judgment, even in his intervals, refuses to be. Or a
man subject to violent impulses of propensity or passion, rendering him dangerous to all around him when
excited, needs to be excluded from general society, or
otherwise watched and restrained by keepers in order
to prevent serious mischief to others; and yet he re-
sents and resists all entreaties to submit to such re-
striction. Or a wicked man is exceedingly alarmed,
disturbed and offended by a truthful exposure of his
iniquitous proceedings, or by the faithful remonstrances and rebukes of some good man. Now in all
such cases the will must be crossed, the personal freedom abridged, and the feelings pained. Must it not
be an injury to coerce, restrain, expose and reprove
such persons, however necessary to their and the public good, and however kindly executed? Is it not generally more intolerable to be crossed in one's will, and
wounded in one's feelings, than to be beaten, maimed
and otherwise maltreated? Answer. It is not man's
imaginations, thoughts and feelings, that determine
what is or is not injurious to him. Love itself may
"heap coals of fire on a man's head." Truth may
torment his mind. The most benevolent restraint
may be painful to his feelings. He may be made, for
a while, quite unhappy by crossing his evil will. He
may prefer to be smitten and mutilated, rather than

be exposed in his secret iniquities, or endure the faithful reproof of the upright. Such persons often prefer an injury to a benefit. They are not, for the time being, in a state of mind to understand and choose what is best for them. Therefore their wills, feelings and opinions are not the indices of their own good—much less that of others. Is it good for a capricious, obstinate child to be indulged in opposing a necessary medical application? Is it good for an insane or delirious, sick adult to have his own will, even to the commission of murder and self-destruction? Is it good for a man to have unlimited freedom, when he will almost certainly make it a curse to himself and others, by gross involuntary outrage, or uncontrollable passion? Is it good for a wicked man, under specious hypocritical disguises, to perpetrate the most atrocious mischief, unexposed and unreproved? These things are not good for mankind. On the contrary, it is good for them to be crossed, restrained, coerced and reproved, by all uninjurious moral and physical forces, which benevolence prompts and wisdom dictates. To cross their wills, and pain their feelings, by such means, under such circumstances, is not an injury, but a substantial good, to them and to all who are connected with them. It may be said—"these things cannot be done uninjuriously. It would be impracticable." Cannot unreasonable children be nursed, delirious adults controlled, dangerously distempered people prevented from doing themselves and others harm, outrageous *non-compos* persons restrained, hypocrites exposed, and sinners reproved without inflicting injury on them! Then can nothing good be done without doing evil. Imperfection is indeed incidental to all human judgment and conduct; and therefore it is probable that some mistakes and some accidental injuries might happen. But the reason and common sense of mankind, once fairly pledged to the true principle of action, would seldom fail to discharge all these duties to general satisfaction. Still it may be asked: "What is to be done if uninjurious force should prove inadequate? May life be sacrificed, limbs broken, the flesh mangled, or any other injuries allowed in extreme cases?" Never. The principle of non-injury must be held inviolable. It is worth worlds and must be preserved at all hazards. What cannot be done uninjuriously must be left undone. But these extreme cases are mostly imaginary. The truth is, that what cannot be done uninjuriously can scarcely ever be done at all. Or if done, had better have been let alone. Experience in the case of the insane has already proved that incomparably more can be done by uninjurious forces, scrupulously and judiciously employed, than by any admixtures of the injurious element. Presuming that my definition and use of the terms injure, injury, injurer, injurious, &c., cannot be misunderstood, I pass on.

THE TERM CHRISTIAN NON-RESISTANCE.

Whence originated the term Christian non-resistance? Non-resistance comes from the injunction, "resist not evil," Matt. 5: 39. The words "resist not," being changed from the form of a verb to that of a substantive, give us non-resistance. This term is considered more strikingly significant than any other of the principle involved, and the duty enjoined in our Saviour's precept. Hence its adoption and established use. It is denominated Christian non-resistance, to distinguish it, as the genuine primitive doctrine, from mere philosophical, sentimental and necessitous non-resistance. Literally, then, Christian non-resistance is the original non-resistance taught and exemplified by Jesus Christ; the bearings, limitations and applications of which are to be learned from the Scriptures of the New Testament.

And what are those bearings, limitations and applications? I have already given an imperfect view of them in the previous definitions. But I will be more explicit. What I aim at is to carry the obligations of non-resistance just as far and no farther than Jesus Christ has done. It is easy to go beyond, or to fall short of his limits. Ultra radicals go beyond him. Ultra conservatives fall short of him. Even those of both these classes, who profess to abide implicitly by his teachings, construe and interpret his language so as to favor their respective errors. The ultra radicals seize on strong figurative, hyperbolic, or intensive forms of expression, and make him seem to mean much more than he could have intended. The ultra conservatives ingeniously fritter away and nullify the very essence of his precepts, in such a manner as to make him seem to mean much less than he must have intended. There is, however, a general rule for such cases, which can scarcely fail to expose the errors of both classes, in respect to any given text. It is this: "Consider the context; consider parallel texts; consider examples; consider the known spirit of Christianity." Any construction or interpretation of the recorded language of Christ, or of his apostles, in which all these concur, is sound. Any other is probably erroneous.

THE KEY TEXT OF NON-RESISTANCE.

Now let us examine Matt. 5: 39. "I say unto you,

resist not evil,"&c. This single text, from which, as
has been stated, the term non-resistance took its rise,
if justly construed, furnishes a complete key to the
true bearings, limitations and applications of the doctrine under discussion. This is precisely one of those
precepts which may be easily made to mean much
more, or much less, than its author intended. It is in
the intensive, condensed form of expression, and can
be understood only by a due regard to its context.
What did the divine Teacher mean by the word "evil,"
and what by the word "resist?" There are several
kinds of evil. 1. Pain, loss, damage, suffered from
causes involving no moral agency, or natural evil. 2.
Sin in general, or moral evil. 3. Temptations to sin,
or spiritual evil; and 4. Personal wrong, insult, outrage, injury—or personal evil. Which of these kinds
of evil does the context show to have been in our
Saviour's mind when he said, "resist not evil?" Was
he speaking of fires, floods, famine, disease, serpents,
wild beasts, or any other mere natural evil agents?
No. Then of course he does not prohibit our resisting such evil. Was he speaking of sin in general?
No. Then of course he does not prohibit our resisting such evil by suitable means. Was he speaking of
temptations addressed to our propensities and passions, enticing us to commit sin? No. Then of
course he does not prohibit our resisting the devil,
withstanding the evil suggestions of our own carnal
mind, and suppressing our evil lusts. Was he speaking of personal evil, injury personally inflicted by man
on man? Yes. "Ye have heard that it hath been
said, an eye for an eye and a tooth for a tooth; but I
say unto you that ye resist not evil," i. e. personal
outrage, insult, affront—injury. The word "evil,"

necessarily means, in this connection, personal injury or evil inflicted by human beings on human beings.

But what did Jesus mean by the words "resist not?" There are various kinds of resistance, which may be offered to personal injury, when threatened or actually inflicted. There is passive resistance—a dead silence, a sullen inertia, a complete muscular helplessness—an utter refusal to speak or move. Does the context show that Jesus contemplated, pro or con, any such resistance in his prohibition? No. There is an active, righteous, moral resistance—a meek, firm remonstrance, rebuke, reproof, protestation. Does the connection show that Jesus prohibits this kind of resistance? No. There is an active, firm, compound, moral and physical resistance, uninjurious to the evil doer, and only calculated to restrain him from deadly violence or extreme outrage. Was Jesus contemplating such modes of resisting personal injury? Does the context show that he intended to prohibit all resistance of evil by such means? No. There is a determined resistance of personal injury by means of injury inflicted; as when a man deliberately takes life to save life, destroys an assailant's eye to save an eye, inflicts a violent blow to prevent a blow; or, as when, in retaliation, he takes life for life, eye for eye, tooth for tooth, hand for hand, &c.; or, as when, by means of governmental agencies, he causes an injurious person to be punished by the infliction of some injury equivalent to the one he has inflicted or attempted. It was of such resistance as this, that our Saviour was speaking. It is such resistance as this that he prohibits. His obvious doctrine is: Resist not personal injury with personal injury. I shall have occasion to press this point more conclusively in the next chapter, when presenting my Scriptural proofs. Enough has been said to determine the important bearings and limitations of the general doctrine. It bears on all mankind, in every social relation of life. It contemplates men as actually injured, or in imminent danger of being injured, by their fellow men ; and commands them to abstain from all personal injuries either as a means of retaliation, self-defence, or suppression of injury. If smitten on the one cheek, they must submit the other to outrage, rather than smite back. If the life of their dearest friend has been taken, or an eye or a tooth thrust out, or any other wrong been done to themselves or their fellow men, they must not render evil for evil, or railing for railing, or hatred for hatred. But they are not prohibited from resisting, opposing, preventing, or counteracting the injuries inflicted, attempted or threatened by man on man, in the use of any absolutely uninjurious forces, whether moral or physical. On the contrary, it is their bounden duty, by all such benevolent resistances, to promote the safety and welfare, the holiness and happiness of all human beings, as opportunity may offer.

NECESSARY APPLICATIONS OF NON-RESISTANCE.

The necessary applications of the doctrine, are to all cases in human intercourse where man receives aggressive injury from man, or is presumed to be in imminent danger of receiving it; i. e., to all cases wherein the injury of man upon man, is either to be repelled, punished or prevented. There are four general positions in which human beings may stand to resist injury with injury. 1. As individuals; 2. As a lawless combination of individuals; 3. As members of allowable

voluntary associations; and 4. As constituent supporters of human government in its State or National
sovereignty. Standing in either of these positions,
they can resist injury with injury, either in immediate self-defence, in retaliation or by vindictive punishments. As individuals, they may act immediately
by their own personal energies, or they may act
through their agents—persons employed to execute
their will. Connected with a lawless combination,they
may act directly in open co-operative violence, or
clandestinely, or through select agents, or in a more
general manner through their acknowledged leaders.
As members of allowable voluntary associations, they
may exert a powerful influence, without any deeds of
violence, by means of speech, the press, education,re-
ligion, &c., to delude, corrupt, prejudice and insti-
gate to evil the minds of mankind one toward another.
Thus designedly to stimulate, predispose and lead
men to commit personal injury, under pretence of
serving God and humanity, is essentially the same
thing as directly resisting injury with injury by physical means. The mischief may be much greater, the
moral responsibility certainly no less. As constituent
supporters of human government, (whether civil or
military, or a compound of both,) in its State or National sovereignty, men are morally responsible for
all constitutions, institutions, laws, processes and
usages which they have pledged themselves to support,
or which they avowedly approve, or which they depend upon as instrumentalities for securing and promoting their personal welfare,or in which they acqui-
esce without positive remonstrance and disfellowship.
Thus if a political compact, a civil or military league,
covenant or constitution, requires, authorizes, pro-

vides for or tolerates war, bloodshed, capital punishment, slavery,or any kind of absolute injury, offensive
or defensive, the man who swears,affirms or otherwise
pledges himself to support such a compact, league,
covenant or constitution, is just as responsible for
every act of injury done in strict conformity thereto,
as if he himself personally committed it. He is not responsible for abuses and violations of the constitution.
But for all that is constitutionally done he is responsible.   The army is his army, the navy his navy, the
militia his militia, the gallows his gallows, the pillory
his pillory, the whipping post his whipping post, the
branding iron his branding iron,the prison his prison,
the dungeon his dungeon, and the slaveholding his
slaveholding.   When the constitutional majority declare war, it is his war.   All the slaughter, rapine,
ravages, robbery, destruction and mischief committed
under that declaration, in accordance with the laws of
war, are his.   Nor can he exculpate himself by plead-
ing that he was one of a strenuous anti-war minority in
the government. He was in the government. He had
sworn, affirmed or otherwise pledged himself, that the
majority should have discretionary power to declare
war.   He tied up his hands with that anti-Christian
obligation, to stand by the majority in all the crimes
and abominations inseparable from war.   It is therefore his war, its murders are his murders, its horrible
injuries on humanity are his injuries.   They are all
committed with his solemn sanction.   There is no escape from this terrible moral responsibility but by a
conscientious withdrawal from such government, and
an uncompromising protest against so much of its
fundamental creed and constitutional law, as is decidedly anti-Christian. He must cease to be its pledged
supporter, and approving dependent.

WHAT A CHRISTIAN NON-RESISTANT CANNOT CONSISTENTLY DO.

It will appear from the foregoing exposition, that a true Christian non-resistant cannot, with deliberate intent, knowledge or conscious voluntariness, compromise his principles by either of the following acts.

1. He cannot kill, maim or otherwise absolutely injure any human being, in personal self defence, or for the sake of his family, or any thing he holds dear.

2. He cannot participate in any lawless conspiracy, mob, riotous assembly, or disorderly combination of individuals, to cause or countenance the commission of any such absolute personal injury.

3 He cannot be a member of any voluntary association, however orderly, respectable or allowable by law and general consent, which declaratively holds as fundamental truth, or claims as an essential right, or distinctly inculcates as sound doctrine, or approves as commendable in practice, war, capital punishment, or any other absolute personal injury.

4. He cannot be an officer or private, chaplain or retainer, in the army, navy or militia of any nation, state, or chieftain.

5. He cannot be an officer, elector, agent, legal prosecutor, passive constituent, or approver of any government, as a sworn or otherwise pledged supporter thereof, whose civil constitution and fundamental laws, require, authorize or tolerate war, slavery, capital punishment, or the infliction of any absolute personal injury.

6. He cannot be a member of any chartered corporation or body politic, whose articles of compact oblige or authorize its official functionaries to resort for com-

pulsory aid in the conducting of its affairs, to a gov
ernment of constitutional violence.

7. Finally, he cannot do any act, either in person
or by proxy; nor abet or encourage any act in others;
nor demand, petition for, request, advise or approve
the doing of any act, by an individual, association or
government, which act would inflict, threaten to inflict, or necessarily cause to be inflicted, any absolute
personal injury, as herein before defined.

Such are the necessary bearings, limitations and
applications of the doctrine of Christian non-resistance.
Let the reader be careful not to misunderstand the
positions laid down. The platform of principle and
action has been carefully founded, and its essential
peculiarities plainly delineated. Let it not be said
that the doctrine goes against all religion, government, social organization, constitutions, laws, order,
rules, and regulations. It goes against none of these
things *per se.* It goes for them in the highest and
best sense. It goes only against such religion, government, social organization, constitutions, laws, order,
rules, regulations and restraints, as are unequivocally
contrary to the law of Christ; as sanction taking "life
for life, eye for eye, tooth for tooth;" as are based on
the assumption, that it is right to resist injury with in
jury, evil with evil.

THE PRINCIPLE AND SUB-PRINCIPLE OF NON-RESIS-
TANCE.

This chapter may be profitably concluded with a
brief consideration of the doctrine under discussion
with respect to the principle from which it proceeds,
to the sub-principle which is its immediate moral basis,
and to the rule of duty in which all its applications

are comprehended. What is the principle from which it proceeds? It is a principle from the inmost bosom of God. It proceeds from ALL PERFECT LOVE that absolute, independent, unerringly wise, holy love, which distinguishes the Divine from all inferior natures, and which, transfused into the natural sentiment of human benevolence, superinduces the highest order of goodness. Of this it is said—"Love worketh no ill to his neighbor; therefore love is the fulfilling of the law." Or as the amiable John expressed it—"He that dwelleth in love, dwelleth in God, and God in him." This love is not mere natural affection, nor sentimental passion, but a pure, enlightened, conscientious principle. It is a divine spring of action, which intuitively and spontaneously dictates the doing of good to others, whether they do good or evil. It operates independently of external influences, and being in its nature absolutely unselfish, is not affected by the merit or demerit of its objects. It does not inquire, "Am I loved? have I been benefitted? have my merits been appreciated? shall I be blessed in return? Or, am I hated, injured, cursed and contemned?" Whether others love or hate, bless or curse, benefit or injure, it says, "I will do right; I will love still; I will bless; I will never injure even the most injurious; I will overcome evil with good." Therefore its goodness is not measured by or adjusted to the goodness of others, but ever finds in itself a sufficient reason for doing good and nothing but good to all moral agents. Jesus, in whom flowed the full current of this divine love, the sublime efflux of the heavenly nature, laying hold of the great commandment, "Thou shalt love thy neighbor as thyself," drew it forth from the ark of the Mosaic Testament,

all mildewed and dusky with human misapprehension,
and struck from it the celestial fire. The true principle was in it, but men could not clearly perceive it,
much less appreciate its excellency. He showed that
the "neighbor" intended was any human being, a
stranger, an enemy, a bitter foe—any one needing
relief, or in danger of suffering through our selfishness,
anger or contempt—the greatest criminal, the veriest
wretch of our race. Hence, knowing that the entire
wisdom of this world had justified injury to injurers,
hatred to enemies, and destruction to destroyers, he reversed the ancient maxims, abrogated the law of retaliation, and proclaimed the duty of unlimited forbearance, mercy and kindness. Imperfect religion, worldly minded philosophy, and vindictive selfishness had
concurrently declared " there is a point beyond which
forbearance ceases to be a virtue." He swept
away this heartless delusion with a divine breath,
and sublimely taught obedient and everlasting adherence to the law of love, as well toward offenders, injurers and enemies, as toward benefactors,
lovers, and friends. " I say unto you, take not life
for life, eye for eye, and tooth for tooth. Smite
not the smiter to save thine own cheek. Give to him
that asketh, and turn not the borrower away. Love
your enemies, bless them that curse you, do good to
them that hate you, and pray for them which despitefully use you and persecute you; that ye may be the
children of your Father in Heaven. For he maketh
his sun to rise on the evil and the good, and sendeth rain
on the just and on the unjust. For if ye love, and
salute, and do good to them that love you, what are
ye better than the publicans ?" Be like your Father
in Heaven. Such is the true light radiated from

the bosom of the Infinite Father, and reflected on this benighted world from the face of Jesus Christ. What are the puerile sentimentalisms of effeminate poets, or the gossamer elaborations of the world's philosophers, or the incantations of solemn but vindictive religionists, compared with the divine excellency of Truth, as it distilled in the language of the Messiah.

All-perfect, independent, self-sustaining, unswervable love—DIVINE LOVE—is the principle from which Christian non-resistance proceeds. What is the sub-principle which constitutes its immediate moral basis? The essential efficacy of good, as the counteracting force with which to resist evil. The wisdom of this world has relied on the efficacy of injury, terror, EVIL, to resist evil. It has trusted in this during all past time. It has educated the human race to believe that their welfare and security depended mainly on their power to inflict injury on offenders. Hence it has been their constant endeavor to possess a sufficiency of injurious means to overawe their enemies, and terrify their encroaching fellow-men. Their language has been, "keep your distance; touch not my property; insult not my honor; infringe not my rights, assail not my person; be just and respectful; yield to my convenience, and be my friend; or I will let slip the dogs of war; you shall feel the weight of my vengeance; I will inflict unendurable injuries on you death itself, torture, imprisonment in a loathsome dungeon, pains and penalties, shall be your portion. I will do you incomparably greater evil, than you can do me. Therefore be afraid, and let me alone." And so perfectly befooled are the children of this world, with faith in injury as their chief ultimate se-

curity, that scarcely one in a thousand will at first
thought allow the non-resistance doctrine to be anything better than a proclamation of cowardice on one
side, and of universal anarchy, lawlessness and violence on the other.   As if all mankind were so entirely controlled by the dread of deadly, or, at least
tremendous personal injury, that if this were relinquished a man's throat would be instantly cut, his
family assassinated, or some horrible mischief inflicted.
Very few know how entirely they trust for defence
and security in this grim and bloody god of human injury.   They have enshrined him in the sword, the
gibbet and the dungeon. They worship him in armies,
navies, militia organizations, battle-ships, forts, arsenals, penal statutes, judicial inflictions, pistols, daggers
and bowie knives.   And if we propose to lay all these
evils aside, and go for nothing but uninjurious, beneficent treatment of transcending mankind never,
even with the most outrageous, the limits of firm, but
friendly personal restraint, lo, they cry out with
alarm, "these have come hither that turn the world up-
side down !"   " Torment us not before the time !"
"Great is Diana of the Ephesians!" "Great is the sword,
the halter, the salutary power to kill or injure sinners at
discretion!   What would become of human society, if
war, capital and other injurious punishments should
be abolished !"   On this altar they have sacrificed
human beings enough to people twenty such planets
as the earth, with no other success than to confirm and
systematize violence throughout the whole habitable
globe.   And yet INJURY is their god, and at his gory
altar of revenge and cruelty they are resolved forever
to worship, amid the clangor of deadly weapons, and
the groans of a bleeding world.

THE CONCLUSION.

But the Son of the Highest, the great self-sacrific-
ing Non-Resistant, is our prophet, priest and king.
Though the maddened inhabitants of the earth have
so long turned a deaf ear to his voice, he shall yet be
heard. He declares that good is the only antagonist
of evil, which can conquer the deadly foe. Therefore
he enjoins on his disciples the duty of resisting evil
only with good. This is the sub-principle of Christian non-resistance. "Evil can be overcome only
with good." Faith, then, in the inherent superiority
of good over evil, truth over error, right over wrong,
love over hatred, is the immediate moral basis of our
doctrine. Accordingly we transfer all the faith we
have been taught to cherish in injury, to beneficence,
kindness, and uninjurious treatment, as the only all-
sufficient enginery of war against evil doers. No
longer seeking or expecting to put down evil with evil,
we lift up the cross for an ensign, and surmounting it
with the glorious banner of love, exult in the divine
motto displayed on its immaculate folds, " RESIST NOT
INJURY WITH INJURY. " Let this in all future time
be the specific rule of our conduct, the magnetic
needle of our pathway across the troubled waters or
human reform, till all men, all governments and all
social institutions shall have been moulded into moral
harmony with the grand comprehensive commandment of the living God "—" THOU SHALT LOVE THY
NEIGHBOR AS THYSELF. " Then shall Love (God by
his sublimest name) " be all in all. "

> The earth, so long a slaughter-field,
> Shall yet an Eden bloom;
> The tiger to the lamb shall yield,
> And War descend the tomb:
> For all ; hall feel the Saviour's love,
> Reflected from the cross—--
> That love, that non-resistant love,
> Which triumphed on the cress.

CHAPTER II.

Scriptural Proofs.

Matt. 5: 38—41, a proof text—Evasive constructions of the text—Reason for noticing these evasions—Second proof, Matt. 5: 43—48—Third proof, forgiveness—Further important proofs—Apostolic testimonies—General view of the evidence—The primitive Christians—Testimony of Celsus and Gibbons.

The preceding chapter presents a clear statement and thorough explication of the doctrine of Christian non-resistance. This will present the Scriptural proofs of its truth. It is affirmed to have been taught and exemplified by Jesus Christ. If this can be demonstrated, all who acknowledge Him their Lord and Master should feel bound to receive the doctrine as divine. In determining such a question, the New Testament must be our principal text book. From its records, fairly construed, we are to learn what Jesus Christ taught, what his examples were, and what is the essential spirit of his religion. The evangelists and apostles shall be our witnesses in the case.

MATTHEW, 5: 38—41, A PROOF TEXT.

In Matthew's report of the Sermon on the Mount, Jesus thus speaks:—" Ye have heard that it hath been said, an eye for an eye, and a tooth for a tooth: but I say unto you, that ye resist not evil; but whosoever shall smite thee on thy right cheek, turn to him the other also. And if any man will sue thee at the law, and take away thy coat, let him have thy cloak also.

And whosoever shall compel thee to go a mile, go
with him twain. " Matt. 5: 38—41. What is the
exact meaning of this language, and what does it
teach? To whom does Jesus refer as having said,
" an eye for an eye, and a tooth for a tooth?"   To
Moses and his expounders.   Read the following passages.   Speaking of injury done to a woman in preg-
nancy:—" And if any mischief follow, then thou shalt
give life for life, eye for eye, tooth for tooth, hand for
hand, foot for foot, burning for burning, wound for
wound, stripe for stripe. "   Ex. 21: 23—25.   " If a
man cause a blemish in his neighbor; as he hath done,
so shall it be done to him; breach for breach, eye for
eye, tooth for tooth; as he hath caused a blemish in a
man, so shall it be done to him. " Lev. 24: 19, 20. In
the case of a false witness: "And the judges shall make
diligent inquisition: and, behold, if the witness be a
false witness, and hath testified falsely against his
brother then shall ye do unto him, as he had thought
to have done unto his brother; so shalt thou put the
evil away from among you.   And thy eye shalt not
pity; but life shall go for life, eye for eye, tooth for
tooth, foot for foot. "   Deut. 19: 18—21.   Here we
have a comprehensive view of the personal injuries
authorized to be inflicted on injurers under the Mosaic code, from capital punishment down to the infliction of a stripe.   And we have a strong expression of
the design of those inflictions: " So shalt thou put
the evil away from among you. "   Now did Jesus refer to these precepts of Moses, and to the enforcement
of them ?   Who can doubt it?   And if so, did he intend to confirm or to abrogate them?   Certainly to
abrogate them.   For his words express positive opposition of sense:—" BUT I say unto you, that ye resist

not evil. " How ? As they do who take "life for life, eye for eye, tooth for tooth, " &c. " But whosoever shall smite thee on thy right cheek, turn to him the other also. " Instead of smiting back and giving wound for wound, or going to the magistrate to get thy assailant punished, as the olden sayings authorize, endure to be smitten again and again. If under color of the law thy coat be taken from thee; withold not thy cloak. Sue not back to recover thy spoiled goods. If men force thee to go whither they will, become their prisoner without turbulence. Resist not injury with injury. Inflict not evil in opposing evil. It has been so commanded in time past, as a means of suppressing and preventing evil among men; "but I say unto you, that ye resist not evil doing with inflictions of evil. " Nothing can be plainer, than that, so far as Moses and his expounders enjoined the infliction of penal personal injuries in resistance of injuries, and for the suppression of evil doing, Jesus Christ prohibits the same. He enjoins his disciples never to resist evil with such inflictions. They are forbidden to render evil for evil, either directly as individuals. on their own responsibility, or as prosecutors at law. Is this a just and unobjectionable construction of the Saviour's language? If it is, the doctrine of Non-Resistance is already established, by a single quotation. But this will be contested.

EVASIVE CONSTRUCTIONS OF THE TEXT.

It will be said that the words of Christ, in the passage quoted, are extremely figurative and intensive in their form of expression; that there is danger of taking them too literally; and they must be duly qualified. I grant it, and have construed them accordingly. I ascertained first their reference to the sayings of Moses, and then determined the prohibition to be exactly commensurate with the Mosaic require-ment. That resistance of evil which Moses sanctioned and enjoined Jesus obviously repudiates and forbids. The prohibition is made precisely co-extensive in all its bearings with the allowances and injunctions of the olden code. This is the only fair construction which can be given to the great Teacher's language. Should any one affirm that Jesus prohibits all kinds and degrees of resistance to evil, he could sustain his affirmation only by insisting on the literal expression, and would make the Saviour contradict himself, his own example, and the common sense of mankind. Should any one affirm, on the other hand, that Jesus did not intend to abrogate and prohibit all the personal and judicial inflictions of evil on offenders, authorized by the fore-cited sayings of Moses, he would find himself in an equally perplexing dilemma. I have seen distinguished opposers in this latter dilemma.

EVASION FIRST.

One says, "I doubt if Jesus referred to the sayings of Moses, quoted from Exodus, Leviticus, and Deuteronomy. He must have referred to certain perverse Rabbinical glosses on the precepts of the law, and to common sayings among the people pleaded in justification of frequent and extreme revenge." Is there any proof of this? No; it is mere supposition. But if it were true, why did not Jesus give some intimation that he was prohibiting only abuses. And withal, what glosses or common sayings could go beyond the original sayings themselves? They express the *lex talonis* in its fullest extent; "life for life, eye for eye, tooth for tooth, hand for hand, foot for foot, breach for breach, wound for wound, stripe for stripe." It would be hard glossing, or overstraining such sayings. This plea is futile.

EVASION SECOND.

Another insists that Christ was only inculcating the importance of executing legal penalties, and of using lawful inflictions of injury against assailants, in a right spirit. "He does not prohibit the act, but only a vindictive, revengeful spirit in performing it. Life ought to be taken for life, and various evils inflicted on evil doers, as a just punishment; and self-defence ought to be maintained, even to the infliction of death in extreme cases; but all should be done without revenge, without unnecessary cruelty and in pure love to the offender, as well as with a sacred reverence for the law." In this way Jesus is smoothly construed to have really said nothing at all,— practially nothing that Moses and the ancients had not said. Did they authorize personal hate, malice, revenge and wanton cruelty in executing the penalties of the law? Did they not positively prohibit all such feelings and conduct? "Thou shalt not avenge, nor bear any grudge against the children of thy people." "Thou shalt not hate thy brother in thy heart: thou shalt in anywise rebuke thy neighbor, and not suffer sin upon him." "In righteousness shalt thou judge thy neighbor." Lev. 19th chap. "If there be a controversy between men, and they come unto judgment, that the judges may judge them; then they shall justify the righteous, and condemn the wicked. And i shall be, if the wicked man be worthy to be beaten, that the judge shall cause him to lie down, and to be beaten before his face, according to his fault, by a certain number. Forty stripes he may give him, and not exceed: lest if he should exceed, and beat him above these with many stripes, then thy brother should seem vile unto thee.'' Deut. 25: 1—3. See Deut. 16: 18, 20; 17: 2—12; 19: 15. Ex. 23: 1—8. From these and other passages in the writings of Moses, it will be seen that, notwithstanding the severity of his code, he did not authorize individual hatred, revenge and wanton cruelty in punishing the wicked. To make Christ prohibit only a personal, spiteful, malicious, cruel spirit in executing the punishments of the law, is to make him the mere echo of Moses and his expounders; whereas he goes absolutely against the deed—the act of inflicting evil on the persons of offenders. And by killing the body of the thing, he banishes the spirit of it. Seeming love only renders the infliction of death or torture on offenders the more abhorrent to Christian sensibility. It is too much like a mother kissing, while at the same time she presses her child to death ; or a beautiful damsel, with all her charming airs, embracing, and at the same time slowly thrusting a fine stiletto into the bosom of her admirer. Death is death, torture is torture, injury is injury, how gently and politely soever inflicted. And there is a kind of fittness in having stern hearted, severe-natured persons to execute such sentences.

EVASION THIRD.

Another pleads that Jesus was inculcating the duty of referring all punishments to magistracy and the government ; that he prohibited a resort to pri-

vate revenges ; and only meant to teach his disciples
to seek redress for the injuries done them in courts of
law.   This is a still lamer shift than the other.   The
connection gives no intimation whatever that this was
his design.   On the contrary, he enjoins non resistance alike in respect to personal assult and legal
wrong.   If a man smite thee on thy right cheek, offer
the other.   If he sue thee at the law and take away
thy coat, let him have thy cloak also.   If he make
thee a prisoner, and force thee to go with him, resist
not.   This does not look like teaching men to go to
law for redress of grievances ,or encouraging them to
make magistrates the revengers of their wrongs.   He
does not say '' Ye have heard that it hath been said,
let every man take vengeance on his own offenders,
and redress his own grievances ; but I say unto you
look to the government, complain to the magistrates,
carry all your causes into the courts for adjudication.''
Not a word of this.   And not a word of it is to be
found in any part of the New Testament.   Jesus
Christ never sued or taught his followers to sue men
at the law.   It would have sunk his divine dignity
to contempt had he exhibited such folly.

EVASION FOURTH.

Another presumes he intended to discountenance
all petty vindictiveness, retaliation and litigation,
but not to forbid these things in extreme cases, on a
great scale, and where important interests are at
stake.   This is very accommodating but very fallacious.   Who shall draw the line between the great
and the small, the frivolous and the important, in
these matters ?   The injured party, of course.   It is for
him to say whether the wrongs done him are of suffi-

cient moment to justify litigation, retaliation or personal resistance ; and the consequence is that small offences, insults and injuries, are rare.   Nearly all are too great to be endured.   Jesus gives not the slightest intimation that he is drawing a line of distinction between great and small evils ; and that he forbids his followers to resist ordinary personal injuries. whilst great ones are left to the law or resistance and retaliation.   Such pleadings are only so many attempts of a worldly mind, to procure itself indulgence under the Christian name in practices upon which, root and branch, the Son of God has placed the seal of prohibition.

EVASION FIFTH.

Another presumes to assert that Jesus never intended the precept, "Resist not evil," &c., "for a general rule ; but it was given to his early followers, as their guide when wronged by the tyrants under whom they lived.   To resist then would be of no avail ; it was better therefore patiently to endure." What a despicable expediency does this ascribe to the Saviour !   What a skulking prudence !   Resist not evil when unable to do so !   Submit to irresistable tyranny and outrage ; offer the other cheek ; crawl like spaniels, when you cannot help yourselves ! But fight like dragons when you have a fair prospect of overmatching your enemies !   To a mind capable of drawing such a meaning from the words of Christ, I should think the text would furnish a general rule, i. e. "submit when you must, but resist when you can."   If it were not utterly derogatory to the character of Jesus, and utterly unsupported by a single hint in the context, it might be worth while to at-

tempt its sober refutation.   As it is, the mere statement sufficiently explodes it.

EVASION SIXTH.

Still another argues that Jesus, though he preached
strict non-resistance, as to the duty of his followers
in all strictly religious matters, nevertheless left them
perfectly free in secular matters, to resist, litigate and
make war at discretion.   That is, while attending
purely to religious duties, and propagating Christianity by divinely appointed means, they must suffer all manner of personal abuse, insult, outrage, persecution and violence, without offering the least resistance, either by individual force of arms or prosecutions at law.   But as men of the world, politicians,
merchants, tradesmen, money-getters, &c. they are at
full liberty to follow the dictates of worldly expediency, and to resist even unto death all who threaten
their lives, liberty or property.   This stands on the
same sandy foundation with the others, and cannot be
sustained by one single decent looking reason.   Indeed, its bare statement ought to be its sufficient
refutation.

EVASION FINAL.

Finally, another declares that he does not know
what Jesus did really mean to teach, in the passage
under consideration; but he is sure it cannot have
been the prohibition of life-taking, penal inflictions
on criminals, defensive war, or personal self-defense
under severe assault.   Because Jesus himself had before declared in the same discourse:—"Think not
that I am come to destroy the law and the prophets;
I am not come to destroy, but to fulfil.   For verily I

say unto you, till heaven and earth pass, one jot or tittle shall in no wise pass from the law, till all be fulfilled. Whosoever, therefore, shall break one of these least commandments, and shall teach men so, he shall be called least in the kingdom of heaven; but whosoever shall do and teach them, the same shall be called great in the kingdom of heaven. For I say unto you, that except your righteousness shall exceed the righteousness of the scribes and pharisees, ye shall in no case enter into the kingdom of heaven." Matt. 5: 18—20. And what is the deduction from these words? It is, that if Moses commanded men to take "life for life, eye for eye, tooth for tooth, hand for hand," &c., Jesus does not abrogate or invalidate such commandment, and cannot have intended any such thing, whatever else he meant; since one jot or tittle of the least of the commandments in the law and the prophets was not to be destroyed, or left unfulfilled. In answer to this, I may remark that it is rather a cavil than a candid objection, and would sound much better from the lips of an infidel, than from those of a professed Christian. It is alleging an apparent self contradiction of Jesus. He says, "Ye have heard that it hath been said (*i. e.*, by Moses and his expounders,) an eye for an eye, and a tooth for a tooth; but I say unto you that ye resist not evil (thus); but whosoever shall smite thee on thy right cheek (rather than smite him) turn unto him the other also." Then on the contrary he says, "Whosoever therefore, shall break one of the least of these commandments, (even the one which requires eye to be taken for eye, and tooth for tooth,) and shall teach men so, shall be called least in the kingdom of heaven," &c. Thus the opposer urges a self-contradiction. Well, if there be a contradiction, and it weigh anything at all in the case at issue, it is not worth as much for non-resistance as against it? Is not Jesus as good authority against himself for the abrogation of the commandment, as for its confirmation? Certainly. But if it would invalidate his testimony, then it only furnishes food for the infidel. Such is not the object; for I have heard this identical cavil from the lips of a venerable Hopkinsian clergyman. What then does it avail? If it proves any thing against my construction of Matt. 5: 38—41, it certainly proves a great deal too much. It would carry us back, and bind us hand and foot to Judaism, with its every "jot and tittle." It would re-enact the whole ceremonial as well as moral and penal code of the Mosaic dispensation! Circumcision, sacrifices and all the commandments, least as well as greatest, would be made binding on us. No Christian would admit any thing like this for a moment. Many commandments have been abrogated: Jesus and Paul are explicit on this point. But it does not follow that any one has been absolutely destroyed, or left unfulfilled. Many have emerged from the shadow into the substance, from types and figures into the reality. Others have been lost in the letter, and more than preserved in the spirit. All have done their work, or are still doing it in the essence of Christianity. Did not Jesus mean to be understood in this sense, when he declared he had not "come to destroy the law or the prophets," but "to fulfill them," &c.? Was it to preserve them in the mere letter and form—in the type and shadow—or rather in their essence—in the absolute reality of their spiritual excellence? Clearly, the latter. When he abolished the oath, did he abolish the truth? Did he re-

lax the obligations of men to speak the truth ?   Did
he weaken the sanctions of truth ?   No; he enhanced
them: He exalted the truth. In prohibiting his disciples from all inflictions of injury in resistance of
evil, did he absolve them from one iota of the law of
love—the obligation to love their neighbors as them-
elves—the doing unto others as they would that
others should do unto them ?   Did he weaken that
great law ?   Did he not exalt and perfect its power
and sanctions ?   If his professed followers should
faithfully obey his instructions, in respect to this
heavenly treatment of offenders, would they become
worse, or would offenses increase ?   Let the tongue of
blasphemy alone presume to say it ?   We know the
contrary.   In a word, we know that this self-same
doctrine of Christian non-resistance, as we deduce it
from the passage before us, is the righteousness of the
law and the prophets in its perfection and true glory;
and therefore is in strict harmony with the doctrine
taught in the 18th, 19th, and 20th verses.   The cavil
is silenced.

REASON FOR NOTICING ALL THESE EVASIONS.

I have been particular to notice these various constructions of our Lord's words, these attempts to avoid
the legitimate force of Matt. 5: 38—41, and to disal-
low it as a proof text of the doctrine before us; not because I thought them really worthy of it in them
selves; but because I have known them all urged and
relied on by clergymen and reputable professing
Christians, of various sects, in their struggle to withstand the truth.   It is remarkable how very incon-
grous all these anti-non-resistant constructions, objections and cavils are, Yet I have heard them put

forth with great confidence, even by different clergy-men of the same general sect, and repeatedly pleaded with apparent sincerity and earnestness as a sufficient invalidation of our leading proof text. It is impor-tant to explode them, in order to secure the convic-tion of an order of minds, at once conscientious and in-telligent, but liable to be misled by the confident spe-cial pleadings of those from whom they have been ac-customed to receive their religious opinions. When we pretend to prove a doctrine, we ought not only to quote passages which sound well to the ear, but to de-monstrate that those passages cannot fairly be con-strued in any other sense than that in which we take them. To have demonstrated Matt. 5: 38—41 to be an undeniable proof text of our doctrine is no small achievement in this department of my work. This once established, I can accomplish the rest with little difficulty. What I insist on, then, is, that I have ad-duced one fundamental proof from the highest scrip-ture authority. If this cannot be invalidated; if it must be admitted; if the passage cannot fairly be con-strued to mean any thing else than I have shown, the probability is that I shall find ample corroborative proof all the way through the New Testament. I therefore proceed to make a further quotation from the same chapter and discourse.

SECOND PROOF, MATT. 5: 43—48.

" Ye have heard that it hath been said, thou shalt love thy neighbor and hate thine enemy: But I say unto you, love your enemies, bless them that curse you, do good to them that hate you, and pray for them which despitefully use you and persecute you. " Ib. 5: 43, 44. This is plainly in the same strain, and of the same import with the other. It is clear, explicit, significant and forcible. By whom the saying, "thou shalt love thy neighbor and hate thine enemy," had been literally uttered, I cannot with certainty learn. Probably it had long since passed into a common maxim. But in its nature and origin it was kindred with the preceding saying, "an eye for an eye and a tooth for a tooth." It derived its principal sanction from the Mosaic injunctions respecting capital criminals and doomed national enemies. Read the following passages. "If thou shalt hear say in one of thy cities, which the Lord thy God hath given thee to dwell there, saying, certain men, the children of Belial, are gone out from among you, and hath withdrawn the inhabitants of their city, saying, let us go and serve other gods, which ye have not known; then shalt thou inquire, and make search, and ask diligently; and behold, if it be truth, and the thing certain, that such abomination is wrought among you: Thou shalt surely smite the inhabitants of that city with the edge of the sword, destroying it utterly, and all that is therein, and the cattle thereof, with the edge of the sword. And thou shalt gather all the spoil of it into the midst of the street thereof, and shalt burn with fire the city, and all the spoil thereof every whit, for the Lord thy God: and it shall be a heap forever; it shall not be built again." Deut. 13: 12—16. "But of the cities of these people, which the Lord thy God doth give thee for an inheritance, thou shalt save alive nothing that breatheth. But thou shalt utterly destroy them; namely the Hittites, and the Amorites, the Canaanites, and the Perrizites, the Hivites, and the Jebusites, as the Lord thy God hath commanded thee." Deut. 20: 16, 17. "Thou

shalt make no covenant with them, nor show mercy
unto them." Ib. 7:2.   In accordance with these
sentiments David utters the following language:
" Plead my cause, O Lord, with them that strive with
me: fight against them that fight against me. Take
hold of shield and buckler, and stand up for my help.
Draw out also the spear, and stop the way against
them that persecute me: say unto my soul, I am thy
salvation. * * *   Let them be as chaff before the
wind: and let the angel of the Lord chase them.   Let
their way be dark and slippery: and let the angel of
the Lord persecute them. " Psal. 35: 1—8.

With equal abhorrence of idolatry, and of all the
crimes of those who are holden to be outlaws and
doomed enemies under the former Testament, but in
striking contrast with the authorized hatred and vengeance exercised towards them, Jesus says, " love,
bless, do good to, and pray for them, even though
they be your bitter foes and persecutors. "   He in-
cludes among enemies, haters and persecutors, all injurers, whether personal, social, religious or national.
His words are equally irreconcilable with all hatred,
all persecution, all cruelty, all war, all injury which
one man, one family, one community or one nation,
can do to another.   The truly Christian individual could not devise, execute or abet any injury
against an offending fellow man. What then would a
truly Christian family, neighborhood, community,
state or nation do ?   Could they act any other than
the non-resistant part toward their foes and injurers ?
If they loved, blessed, benefitted, and prayed for the
worst of aggressors and offenders, what a spectacle
would be presented !   What a conquest would be
achieved over all evil doers !   Does not Jesus enjoin.

this sublime love and heavenly practice? Can he mean any thing less than appears upon the beautiful face of his words? What professed Christian can erect the gibbet, or light the faggot, or draw out the rack, or contrive any injurious punishment, or gird on any weapon of war, or give his sanction to any cruelty, by individuals or society, and yet plead that he is in the spirit and practice of this his Lord's commandment? Dees that man love his enemies, bless those who curse him; do good to those that hate him and pray for his injurers, who hangs, or shoots, or tortures, or stones them, or holds himself sworn to inflict any such evils? But let us hear the Saviour urge his own precepts. "That ye may be the children of your Father which is in heaven; for he maketh his sun to rise on the evil and on the good, and sendeth rain on the just and on the unjust. For if ye love them (only) which love you, what reward have you? Do not even the publicans the same? And if ye salute your brethren only, what do ye more than others? Do not even the publicans so? Be ye therefore perfect, even as your Father which is in heaven is perfect." Verses 45—48. Your Father loves his enemies, blesses those that curse him and does good to them that hate him. Else the sun would not shine as it does on the evil, nor the rain distil on the unjust, nor salvation descend from heaven for the lost. Imbibe the spirit of your Father. Imitate his goodness to the unthankful and evil. Put on his moral character. Be his children. Be not content barely to love them that love you. Love, forbear with, benefit and seek to save even the guilty and undeserving. Else what higher are ye in the moral scale than the publicans? Salute and befriend, not only your own kindred, friends and intimate associates, but all men, however strange or hostile to you. Aspire continually to be perfectly, independently good to all, as your Father in heaven is. What can be plainer than this? What can be more pure, sublime, spiritually excellent or morally beautiful ! It is Christian non-resistance; or rather that perfect love, of which true non-resistance is a distinguishing fruit. But let us proceed.

THIRD PROOF—FORGIVENESS.

He enjoins the duty of forgiveness on the same general principle. "After this manner, therefore, pray ye." * * * "Forgive us our debts, as we forgive our debtors." "For if ye forgive men their trespasses, your heavenly Father will also forgive you. But if ye forgive not men their trespasses, neither will your Father forgive your trespasses." Matt. 6: 12. 14, 15. "Then came Peter to him, and said, Lord, how oft shall my brother sin against me, and I forgive him ? Till seven times ? Jesus saith unto him, I say not unto thee, until seven times, but until seventy times seven." Ib. 18: 21, 22. See also the illustrating parable to the end of the chapter. "And when ye stand praying, forgive, if ye have aught against any, that your Father also which is in heaven may forgive you your trespasses ; but if ye do not forgive, neither will your Father which is in heaven forgive your trespasses." Mark 11: 25, 26. "Judge not, and ye shall not be judged: condemn not, and ye shall not be condemned: forgive, and ye shall be forgiven." Luke 6: 37.

The idea in all these passages is, that the injured party claims a right to punish the injurer on account of some actual offence. Jesus is not speaking of mere envious grudges, causeless resentment, or ill will. He pre supposes a real injury done, which, according to the common law, "an eye for an eye " &c., or, in other words, according to strict natural justice, might rightfully be punished by the infliction of an equivalent evil on the offender. He does not palliate the offence, nor deny the ill-desert of the guilty party, nor require that his wrong should be considered right. He addresses the injured party, the rightful complainant, and commands him to forgive his injurer; *i. e.* not to exact the infliction of the deserved punishment ; not to hold the offender punishable on his account, but to leave him as an object of pity, even though he be one of dread, uninjured—a subject of the same kindness as if he had committed no offence. He is to inflict no evil upon him on account of his trespass. This is human forgiveness, as enjoined by Jesus on all his followers. To enforce this he declares that our Father in heaven will forgive the forgiving, but will not forgive the unforgiving. He reminds us that we have all sinned against our Father, and are justly punishable at his hands ; that the only ground of our acceptance with him, and of his continued benefactions, is his grace, not our merit ; and that we are perpetually entreating him to bless us in spite of our evil deserts. Therefore he enjoins that we forgive our fellow men their trespasses against us, as we beseech God to forgive us the sins we have committed against him. He requires that we do unto others as we would that God should do unto us. He commands us to refrain from punishing our offenders, and still to do them good, as we would that God should continue to forbear with and do us good, notwithstanding

our sins. And if we freely forgive while we pray to
be forgiven, this will attest our sincerity, and fit our
spirits for the reception of the divine forgiveness.
God will accept and commune with us: for we shall
then present no insuperable bar to his inflowing love
and mercy. But if, while we sue for mercy, we exercise none towards the guilty ; if while we pray for forgiveness, we meditate vengeance against our offenders;
if while we ask to be treated infinitely better than we
deserve, we hold those who have trespassed against
us punishable at our hands according to their deserts, we at once betray our own insincerity, offer
mockery to God, and present an impassable bar of
hardheartedness to his love and mercy. He is essentially a forgiving Father, but he will not, indeed cannot communicate his forgiveness to us. Our spirit is
in opposition to his spirit ; we do not worship him in
spirit and in truth ; we stand self-excluded from his
presence—alike unforgiving and unforgiven. We
cannot be at peace with him, nor worship him ac-
ceptably, nor taste the richness of his grace, so long
as we desire to punish our offenders. It is only in
the spirit of human forgiveness that we can receive
and enjoy the divine forgiveness. Such is the doctrine of Jesus. How blessed a doctrine is it to the
broken-hearted, merciful and meek ? How terrible
a one to the iron-hearted, who delight in rigorous
human punishment ! Here the whole superstructure
of piety and religion is baptised in the waters of non-
resistance. We cannot even pray in a punishing
spirit, without insulting a forgiving Father, and im-
precating on our heads all the deserts of our own
transgression. If we forgive not, but persist in
punishing them that trespass against us, and yet

pray to be forgiven of God as we forgive, we only call
on God to be as severe and punitive towards us, as
we are towards our fellow men. How tremendous a
thought is this! Yet who can evade it. Jesus has
brought it as a live coal from off the alter of God, and
laid it on our consciences. Can the utmost ingenuity
of man avoid the conclusion which these precepts of
Christ, respecting forgiveness, are thus shown to warrant? I think not. Yet millions of professing
Christians, authorize, aid and abet war, capital
punishment and the whole catalogue of penal injuries.
Still they daily pray God to forgive their trespasses
as they forgive ! ! The language of the prophet Isaiah,
in his 58th chapter, seems not inapplicable to them.
"Cry aloud, spare not ; lift up thy voice like a trumpet, and show my people their transgressions, and the
house of Jacob their sins. Yet they seek me daily
and delight to know my ways, as a nation that did
righteousness, and forsook not the ordinance of their
God ; they ask of me the ordinances of justice ; they
take delight in approaching to God." See the subsequent verses. This drawing near to God with the
lips, while the heart is far from him, is as common as
it is reprehensible. And in no respect is it more so,
than in meditating and executing punishment for offenses against ourselves, whilst in humble supplication we plead for the divine forgiveness of our own
transgressions.

FURTHER IMPORTANT PROOFS.

Another important class of proof texts, corroborative of those already cited, is the following: "My
kingdom is not of this world. If my kingdom were
of this world, then would my servants fight that I
should not be delivered to the Jews ; but now is my

kingdom not from hence." Jno. 18: 36.   Compare
this with Matt. 10: 16.   "Behold, I send you forth
as sheep in the midst of wolves: be ye therefore wise
as serpents, and harmless as doves."   Also with Luke
22: 24—26.   "And there was also a strife among
them, which of them should be accounted the greatest.   And he said unto them, The Kings of the Gentiles exercise lordship over them; and they that exercise authority upon them are called benefactors.
But ye shall not be so : but he that is greatest among
you, let him be as the younger; and he that is chief,
as he that doth serve."   In the same group we may
include the following : "And they went, and entered
into a village of the Samaritans, to make ready for
him.   And they did not receive him, because his
face was as though he would go to Jerusalem.   And
when his disciples James and John saw this, they said,
Lord, wilt thou that we command fire to come down
from Heaven, and consume them, even as Elias did ?
But he turned and rebuked them, and said, Ye know
not what manner of spirit ye are of.   For the son of
man is not come to destroy men's lives, but to save
them."   Luke 9 : 52-56,   "Then came they and laid
hands on Jesus, and took him.   And, behold, one of
them which were with Jesus, stretched out his hand,
and drew his sword, and struck a servant of the high.
priest, and smote off his ear.   Then said Jesus unto
him, put up again thy sword into his place : for all
they that take the sword shall perish with the sword.
Thinkest thou that I cannot now pray to my Father,
and he shall presently give me more than twelve
legions of angels."   Matt. 26 : 50—53.   See also Jno.
8: 3—11, the case of the woman taken in adultery, and
brought to Jesus to see whether he would adjudge her

to be stoned to death, according to the law of Moses. After her accusers had declined excuting the penalty, Jesus said—"Neither do I condemn thee, (*i. e.* to death) go and sin no more."

These and similar passages are impressive practical comments on the positive doctrinal precepts of the Saviour. His kingdom is not of this world, and therefore excludes all military and warlike defences. His ministers are sent forth unarmed, like sheep in the midst of wolves. They are therefore to be wise as serpents, and harmless as doves, All things must be conducted on the non-resistant principle. There must be no political strife for the highest place ; no patronizing lordship ; no Gentile love of dominion ; but they that really occupy the highest place, must prove themselves worthy of it, by an entire willingness to take the lowest ; by governing only through the influence of useful service. Government must doff its worldly insignia, its craft and its prerogative to punish, and be vested in real worth—unglorified, unpampered, and undistinguished by exclusive privileges. This is Christian government. He and his followers might be treated inhospitably, as by the Samaritans, but no injury must be returned—not even though by a miracle fire could be commanded from heaven. No such spirit might be indulged. Because the Son of man came not to destroy men's lives, but to save them. Therefore non-resistance of evil with evil must be the invariable rule of action for his disciples forever. They must never destroy men's lives, but endeavor to save them. Even the holy one, at his betrayal into the hands of a mob, might not be defended with the sword by a Peter, because, "All they that take the sword shall perish with the sword."

"The wrath of man worketh not the righteousness of God." Evil cannot be overcome with evil.

How is it possible to contemplate such clear, striking mutually sustaining irrefragable evidence of the scriptural truth of Christian non-resistance, without feeling the whole soul penetrated with profound conviction. But still the tide rises and flows on.

APOSTOLIC TESTIMONIES.

The Apostles, having been gradually delivered from their early traditionary and educational predispositions for a temporal and military kingdom, renounced all carnal weapons, and drinking in the heavenly inspiration, reiterated the non-resistance doctrine of their Master: " Be not conformed to this world; but be ye transformed by the renewing of your mind, that ye may prove what is that good and acceptable, and perfect will of God. " " Bless them which persecute you; bless, and curse not." "Recompense to no man evil for evil. " "Dearly beloved, avenge not yourselves; but rather give place unto wrath; for it is written—vengeance is mine; I will repay, saith the Lord. Therefore, if thine enemy hunger, feed him; if he thirst, give him drink: for in so doing thou shalt heap coals of fire on his head. Be not overcome of evil, but overcome evil with good." Rom. 12: 2, 14, 17, 19—21. " Dare any of you, having a matter against another, go to law before the unjust, and not before the saints. " " Now, therefore, there is utterly a fault among you, because ye go to law one with another; why do ye not rather take wrong ? Why do ye not rather suffer yourselves to be defrauded !" 1 Cor. 6: 1, 7. " For though we walk in the flesh, we do not war after the flesh. For the weapons of our warfare are not carnal, but mighty through God, to the pulling down of strong holds; casting down imaginations, and every high thing that exalteth itself against the knowledge of God, and bringing into captivity every thought to the obedience of Christ. " 2. Cor. 10: 3—5. "The fruit of the Spirit is love, joy, peace, long-suffering, gentleness, goodness, faith, meekness, temperance; against such there is no law. And they that are Christ's have crucified the flesh, with the affections and lusts. If we live in the Spirit, let us also walk in the Spirit. " Gal. 5: 22—25. " Be ye angry and sin not; let not the sun go down upon your wrath. " " Let all bitterness, and wrath, and anger, and clamor, and evil speaking be put away from you, with all malice. " Ephes. 4: 26, 31. " Put on therefore, as the elect of God, holy and beloved, bowels of mercies, kindness, humbleness of mind, meekness, long suffering. " Col. 3: 12. "See that none render evil for evil unto any man; but ever follow that which is good, both among yourselves and to all men. " 1 Thes. 5: 15. "Let us run with patience the race set before us, looking unto Jesus. the author and finisher of our faith; who for the joy that was set before him, endured the cross, despising the shame, and is set down at the right hand of the throne of God. " " For consider him that endured such contradiction of sinners against himself, lest ye be wearied and faint in your minds ! " " Follow peace with all men, and holiness, without which no man shall see the Lord. " Heb. 12: 1, 2, 3, 14. " My beloved brethren, let every man be swift to hear, slow to speak, slow to wrath: for the wrath of man worketh not the righteousness of God. " James 1: 19, 20. " From whence come wars and fightings among you?

Come they not hence, even of your lusts that war in your members?" "Submit yourselves therefore to God. Resist the devil, and he will flee from you." Ib. 4: 1, 7. "This is thank-worthy, if a man for conscience towards God, endure grief, suffering wrongfully. For what glory is it, if when ye be buffeted for your faults, ye shall take it patiently? But if, when ye do well, and suffer for it, ye take it patiently, this is acceptable with God. For even hereunto were ye called; because Christ also suffered for us, leaving us an example, that ye should follow his steps: who did no sin, neither was guile found in his mouth: who when he was reviled, reviled not again; when he suffered, he threatened not; but committed himself to him that judgeth righteously." 1 Peter. 2: 19 —23. "And who is he that will harm you, if ye be followers of that which is good? But if ye suffer for righteousness sake, happy are ye; and be not afraid of their terror, neither be troubled." "For it is better, if the will of God be so, that ye suffer for well-doing than for evil doing. For Christ also hath once suffered for sins, the just for the unjust." Ib. 3: 13, 14, 17, 18. Also, Ib. 4: 13—19. "He that saith he abideth in him, ought himself also to walk, even as he walked. He that saith he is in the light, and hateth his brother, is in darkness even until now, * * * and walketh in darkness, and knoweth not whither he goeth, because that darkness hath blinded his mind." 1 Jno. 2: 6, 11. "He that loveth not his brother abideth in death. Whosoever hateth his brother is a murderer, and ye know that no murderer hath eternal life abiding in him." Ib. 3: 14, 15. "No man hath seen God at any time. If we love one another, God dwelleth in us, and his love is perfected in us." "If a man say I love God, and hateth his brother, he is a liar; for he that loveth not his brother whom he hath seen, how can he love God whom he hath not seen?" Ib. 4: 12, 20.

GENERAL VIEW OF THE EVIDENCE.

Is it possible to read these quotations without an irresistable conviction of their perfect harmony with the teachings of the Saviour on this great subject? Can we doubt that they all proceeded from the same Divine source? And now what was the example of Jesus? What was the practice of the Apostles, after the resurrection of Christ, when fully endued with power and grace from on high? Did they ever slay any human being? Ever threaten to do so? Ever make use of any deadly weapon? Ever serve in the Army or Navy of any nation, state or chieftain? Ever seek or accept any office, legislative, judicial or executive, under the existing governments of their day? Ever make complaint to the magistrates against any offender or criminal, in order to procure his punishment? Ever commence any prosecution at law, to obtain redress of grievances? Ever apply to the civil or military authority to protect them by force of arms when in imminent danger? Or ever counsel others to do any one of these acts? Did they ever express, by word or deed, their reliance on political, military or penal power to secure personal protection or to carry forward the christianization of the world? I answer confidently, NO. But let every one be fully persuaded in his own mind. Let the New Testament be thoroughly searched with reference to these questions. If it shall be found that I am correct, let the opposers of non-resistance make up their minds to yield. For if precept and practice, spirit and example, go together throughout the Scriptures of the New Testament, the case is decided beyond controversy.   I am aware of the objections urged with so much desperation from such texts as that which speaks of the scourge of small cords, that which mentions the direction of Jesus to buy swords, Paul's appeal to Cæsar, his notification of the chief captain when the forty men conspired to slay him, the thirteenth chapter of Romans, &c. Neither of these, nor all of them together, will serve the objector's purpose, as I shall demonstrate in the next chapter.   On the other hand, we are able to show a series of examples, indeed a life, conformable to the doctrine of non-resistance.   And we are also able to show that this doctrine practically prevailed among the primitive Christians for a considerable time subsequent to the apostolic age.

Look at Jesus in the temptation.   He was offered all the kingdoms of the world.   But on what condition ? Provided only he would fall down and worship the Tempter.   Is not this essentially the condition on which his followers have ever been offered worldly political power ?   There is a spirit which animates and characterizes carnal human government.   It is the destroying spirit—the angel of injury, the old serpent of violence.   This is the grand controlling power underneath the throne, the *dernier resort*, the ultimate indispensable reliance of all mere worldly authority.   And he is accounted a fool who supposes there can be any such thing as government among mankind without it.   Consequently its solemn acknowledgment is now, as ever, the condition on which men must take the sceptre, or assume the seals of office.   He who would rule, must first worship this gen-

ius of violence—must swear to support his authority
with sword and penal vengeance. Jesus chose the
pain and shame of the cross, in preference to the
fame and glory of universal empire on such a condition. It was no inducement with him, that all the
world should take his name, and verbally confess him
Lord, while at heart and in practice they served the
evil spirit. He would not be a king of nations, when
he could not be a king of hearts and consciences. He
would not do evil that good might come; because his
kingdom was not of this world, but was essentially
one of righteousness and peace. So he spurned a 1 offered sceptre, and left it in hands which he knew
would ere long baptize him in his own non-resistant
blood. For the same reason, when he perceived the
determination of the people to proclaim him a king,
he promptly placed himself beyond their reach. Nor
would he be a "judge and a divider," among the
people. Nor when he alone stood up in innocence to
pass a rightful condemnation on the adulterous woman, would he pronounce the deadly sentence or raise
the destroying stone   When a violent multitude, led
on by his betrayer, came to seize him in the prayerful
solitude of Gethsemane, he raised not a weapon of defence. But he rebuked his mistaken disciple for
drawing the sword, healed the wound he had inflicted,
and taught him that all who take must perish with
the sword. So he suffered himself to be "led as a
sheep dumb before the shearers," and "as a lamb to
the slaughter." They stripped him of his raiment,
attired him in a mock royal robe, crowned him with
thorns, smote him, spit upon him, sentenced him
without cause to death, nailed him to the cross between two malefactors, tormented him in his agonies,

and followed him to the verge of life with all the ven-
em of a murderous hate. Yet never a word of threatening, reviling, cursing or bitterness escaped him.
With a meek and sorrowful dignity he bore all; and
at the moment when he could have summoned legions
of angels to his rescue, and to the destruction of his
foes, lo, he uttered that last victorious prayer:—
"Father forgive them, for they know not what they
do." The mourning heavens in silence heard. Then
came the expiring groan—not to seal the just perdi-
tion of a murderous world, but as the awful amen of
the New Covenant, and the signal of complete triumph
over hatred, sin and death !

THE PRIMITIVE CHRISTIANS.

If we enter among the evangelists and apostles of
the Crucified, and inquire how they lived and died,
what will be the response? "God hath set forth us
the apostles last, as it were appointed unto death : for
we are made a spectacle unto the world, and to angels,
and to men," "We both hunger and thirst, and are
naked, and are buffeted, and have no certain dwelling place." "Being reviled, we bless ; being persecuted, we suffer it ; being defamed, we entreat ; we
are made as the filth of the world, the offscouring of
all things." Stephen was stoned to death, calling on
the Saviour to receive his spirit, and with the holy
prayer on his lips. "Lord lay not this sin to their
charge." James was slain with the sword, Peter
crucified, Paul beheaded, and innumerable martyrs
brought to seal their testimony with their blood.
But in those days they suffered all things for the sake
of the cross, and inflicted nothing. Always heroic
for the truth, yet meek, patient and non-resistant,

they exemplified in a wonderful manner the depth and strength of their Christian principles. Never do we find them aspiring to places of power ; never dis· tinguishing themselves in the army ; never wheedling and coaxing the worldly great to shed on them the renown of their official influence ; never engaged in rebellions, riots, tumults, or seditions ; never trusting in carnal weapons for the security of their persons, not even in the most barbarous and ruffian-like society ; never cursing, reviling, or insulting even their persecutors. Such were the apostles and primitive Christians. They had learned of Jesus ; and non-resistance, for the first two centuries, was the practical orthodoxy of the church. Justin Martyr, early in the second century, declared the devil to be the author of all war. Tertullian denounced the bearing of arms, saying, shall he who is not to avenge his own wrongs, be instrumental in bringing others into chains, imprisonment, torment, death?" Lactantius declares :—"It can never be lawful for a righteous man to go to war, whose warfare is in righteousness itself," "We find," says Clarkson, "from Athenagoras and other early writers, that the Christians of their times abstained, when they were struck, from striking again; and that they carried their principles so far, as even to refuse to go to law with those who injured them." The language of those primitive Christians was in this strain :—One says, "It is not lawful for a Christian to bear arms." Another— "Because I am a Christain, I have abandoned my profession of a soldier." A third—"I am a Christain, and therefore I cannot fight?" A fourth, Maximillian:—"I cannot fight, if I die; I am not a soldier of this world, but a soldier of God." And in his fidelity he died by the hands of military tyranny.

TESTIMONY OF CELSUS AND GIBBON.

Celsus, a heathen philosopher, wrote an elaborate work against the Christians, about the middle of the second century. One of his grave allegations was in the following words:—"You will not bear arms in the service of the empire when your services are needed, and if all the nations should act upon this principle, the empire would be overrun by the barbarians."

Gibbon, the popular English historian of the declining Roman empire, a skeptic as to Christianity, incidentally comfirms the fact that the early Christians were unequivocal non-resistants. "The defence of our persons and property they knew not how to reconcile with the patient doctrine, that enjoined an unlimited forgiveness of past injuries, and commanded them to invite fresh insults. Their simplicity was offended by the use of oaths, by the pomp of magistracy, and by the active contention of public life ; nor could their humane ignorance be convinced that it was lawful, on any occasion, to shed the blood of their fellow creatures, either by the sword of justice or that of war, even though their criminal and hostile attempts should threaten the whole community." * * * * "They felt and confessed that such institutions [life-taking, &c.] might be necessary for the present system of the world, and they cheerfully submitted to the authority of their Pagan Governors. But while they inculcated the maxims of passive obedience, they refused to take any active part in the civil administration, or military defence of the empire." Vol. I p. 24. "The humble Christians were sent into the world as sheep among wolves, and since they were not permitted to employ force, even in the defence of their religion, they deemed that they should be still more criminal, if they were tempted to shed the blood of their fellow creatures in disputing the vain privileges or the sordid possessions of this transitory life. Faithful to the doctrine of the apostle, who in the reign of Nero had preached the duty of unconditional submission, the Chirstians of the first tnree centuries preserved their conscience pure and innocent of the guilt of secret conspiracy or open rebellion. While they experienced the rigor of persecution, they were never provoked either to meet their tyrants in the field, or indignantly to withdraw themselves into some remote and sequestered corner of the globe." Vol. II. p. 200.

Can there be any doubt that Jesus Christ, his apostles and the primitive Christians held, taught and exemplified the doctrine for which I am contending? Is not the scriptural proof of its truth abundant, positive, unequivocal and irresistible? It seems to me that it is. I therefore commend what has been submitted to the deliberate consideration of all candid minds, whose veneration for and attachment to the Scriptures give their testimony the least weight in determining such a question.

CHAPTER III.

Scriptural Objections Answered.

Obj. 1. You throw away the Old Testament—Voice of the New Testament—Voice of the Old Testament— Obj. 2 The scourge of small cords—Obj. 3. The two swords—Obj. 4. The death of Ananias and Sapphira— Obj. 5. Human government—Thirteenth of Romans —How the apostles viewed the then existing governments—Submission to, not participation in governments enjoined on Christians—In what sense the powers that be are ordained of God—Pharaoh God's "minister"—Also the monarch of Assyria—Also Nebuchadnezzar—The Roman government—Respects wherein government is ordained of God—Paul's conduct in relation to government —Conclusion.

I devote the present chapter to the consideration of Scriptural Objections. Our doctrine is obviously sustained by the most abundant and convincing proofs from the scriptures of the New Testament. It forces a degree of conviction on many minds by no means prepared for the great practical change involved, or even for a cordial assent to the doctrine itself. Hence they fall back behind certain apparently formidable objections, urged by more determined opponents from the scriptures. They demand that these should be satisfactorily answered. It is only fair that it should be done.

OBJECTION I.—YOU THROW AWAY THE OLD TESTA-
MENT.

"You quote exclusively from the scriptures of the

New Testament, to prove the non-resistance doctrine. Those of the Old Testament are unequivocally against it. They afford abundant precepts and examples in justification of war, capital punishment, and various forms of penal restraint on criminals. Is not the whole Bible the word of God? Do you throw away and trample under foot the Old Testament? If your doctrine were of God, it would be equally proveable from both Testaments. "

ANSWER. It is true that I have quoted exclusively from the scriptures of the New Testament, to prove the doctrine of Christian non-resistance. And I grant that those of the Old Testament, with a few unimportant exceptions, are unequivocally against it, *i. e.*, taken independently of the Christian revelation. I also admit the whole Bible, properly considered and interpreted, to be in a general sense the word of God. But I do not admit the Old Testament to be as clearly, fully and perfectly the word of God as the New Testament; nor to be of equal authority with the latter, on questions of doctrine and duty; nor to be the rule of faith and practice for Christians. It is to be held in reverence as the prophecy and preparative of the New Testament—the fore-shadow of better things to come. If I can prove this to be the true character and office of the Old Testament, I shall thereby silence the objection before us. Not only so, I shall demonstrate that I pay the highest respect to both Testaments; and that those who claim for the Old an equal authority with the New, discredit both. Let us settle this point. The scriptures of the two Testaments shall speak for themselves. What they say of each other must determine the matter.

VOICE OF THE NEW TESTAMENT.

We will commence with the New Testament. "God, who at sundry times, and in divers manners, spake in time past unto the fathers by the prophets, hath in these last days spoken unto us by his Son, whom he hath appointed heir of all things, by whom also he made the worlds." Heb. 1: 1, 2. "Wherefore, holy brethren, partakers of the heavenly calling, consider the Apostle and High Priest of our profession, Christ Jesus; who was faithful to him that appointed him, as also Moses in all his house. For this man was counted worthy of more glory than Moses, inasmuch as he that builded the house, hath more honor than the house." "Moses verily was faithful in all his house as a servant, for a testimony of those things which were to be spoken after. But Christ as a Son over his own house, whose house are we, &c., Ib. 3: 1, 2, 3, 5, 6. "For if perfection were by the Levitical priesthood, (for under it the people received the law,) what further need was there that another priest should arise after the order of Melchisedec, and not be called after the order of Aaron? For the priesthood being changed, there is made of necessity a change of the law." "There is verily a disannulling of the commandment going before, for the weakness and unprofitableness thereof. For the law made nothing perfect, but the bringing in of a better hope did; by the which we draw nigh to God." "By so much was Jesus made the surety of a better Testament." Ib. 7: 11, 12, 18, 19, 22. "But now hath he obtained a more excellent ministry than they, by how much also he is the mediator of a better covenant, which was established upon better promises. For if that first

Covenant had been faultless, then should no place have been sought for the second. For, finding fault with them, he saith, Behold the days come, saith the Lord, when I will make a new covenant with the house of Israel, and with the house of Judah; not according to the covenant that I made with their fathers, in the day when I took them by the hand, to lead them out of the land of Egypt, &c. * * * After those days, saith the Lord, I will put my laws into their mind, and write them in their hearts; and I will be to them a God, and they shall be to me a people, " &c. " In that he saith, a new covenant, he hath made the first old. Now that which decayeth and waxeth old is ready to vanish away. " Ib. 8: 6, 13. See Ib. 10: 1, 2. " Wherefore then serveth the law? It was added because of transgressions till the seed should come to whom the promise was made. " " But before faith came we were kept under the law, shut up unto the faith which should afterwards be revealed. Wherefore the law was our school-master to bring us unto Christ, that we might be justified by faith. But after that faith is come, we are no longer under a school-master. " Gal. 3: 19, 23, 25. " Whereby, when ye read, ye may understand my knowledge in the mystery of Christ, which in other ages was not made known unto the sons of men, as it is now revealed unto his holy apostles and prophets by the Spirit. " Ephes. 3: 4, 5. " Not that we are sufficient of ourselves to think any thing as of ourselves; but our sufficiency is of God; who also hath made us able ministers of the New Testament; not of the letter, but of the spirit: for the letter killeth, but the spirit giveth life. But if the ministration of death, written and engraven in stones, was glorious, so that the children of Israel could not steadfastly behold the face of Moses for the glory of his countenance; which glory was to be done away; how shall not the ministration of the Spirit be rather glorious?" "For even that which was made glorious, had no glory in this respect, by reason of the glory which excelleth." "Seeing then that we have such hope, we use great plainness of speech, and not as Moses, who put a veil over his face, that the children of Israel could not steadfastly look to the end of that which is abolished. But their minds were blinded; for until this day, remaineth the same veil untaken away in the reading of the Old Testament; which veil is done away in Christ. But even unto this day, when Moses is read, the veil is upon their heart." 2 Cor. 3: 5—8, 10—15. "Having, therefore, obtained help of God, I continue unto this day witnessing both to small and great, saying none other things than those which the prophets and Moses did say should come. That Christ should suffer, and that he should be the first that should rise from the dead, and should show light unto the people, and to the Gentiles." Acts 26: 22, 23. "Forasmuch as we have heard, that certain which went out from us have troubled you saying, Ye must be circumcised and keep the law; to whom we gave no such commandment." "For it seemed good to the Holy Ghost, and to us, to lay upon you no greater burden than these necessary things: That ye abstain from meats offered to idols, and from blood, and from things strangled, and from fornication: from which if ye keep yourselves, ye shall do well." Ib. 15: 24, 29. "And by him all that believe are justified from all things, from which ye could not be justified by the law of Moses." Ib. 13: 39. "For Moses truly said unto.

the fathers, a Prophet shall the the Lord your God
arise up unto you of your brethren, like unto me; him
shall ye hear in all things, whatsoever he shall say
unto you.   Yea, and all the prophets from Samuel,
and those that follow after, have likewise foretold of
these days. " Ib. 3: 22, 24.   " Do not think that I
will accuse you to the Father; there is one that ac-
caseth you, even Moses, in whom ye trust.   For had
ye believed Moses, ye would have believed me: for he
wrote of me.   But if ye believe not his writings how
shall ye believe my word. "   John 5: 45—47.   " We
have found him of whom Moses in the law and the
prophets did write. "   John 3: 45   " These are the
words which I spake unto you, while I was yet with
you, that all things must be fulfilled which were
written in the law of Moses, and the prophets, and in
the Psalms, concerning me. "   Luke 24: 44   " The
law and the prophets were until John; since that time
the kingdom of God is preached, and every man
presseth into it. "   Ib. 16: 16.   " Among those that
are born of women, there is not a greater prophet than
John the Baptist; but he that is least in the kingdom
of God is greater than he. "   Ib. 7: 28, " There was a
man sent from God, whose name was John.   He was
not that Light' but sent to bear witness of that Light,
the true Light which lighteth every man that cometh
into the world. "   " John bore witness of him, and
cried, saying, This was he of whom I spake, He that
cometh after me is preferred before me: for he was before me. "   " For the law was given by Moses, but
grace and truth came by Jesus Christ.   No man hath
seen God at any time; the only begotten Son, which is
in the bosom of the Father, he hath declared him. "
John 1: 6—8, 15, 17, 18.   " John answered and said.

A man can receive nothing, except it be given him from heaven.'' ''He [Christ] must increase, but I must decrease. He that cometh from above, is above all.'' For God giveth not the Spirit by measure unto him.'' John 3: 27, 31, 34.

Such is the testimony of the New Testament Scriptures. The objector professes to hold them, at least, equally authorative with those of the Old Testament, and to receive the entire Bible as the word of God. Now, does he implicitly believe what is declared in the forecited passages? Does he believe that ''Christ was counted worthy of more glory than Moses;'' that Moses was ''a servant, but Christ a son over his own house:'' that ''perfection was not by the Levitical priesthood:'' that Christ is the great ''High Priest after the order of Melchisedec:'' that ''the priesthood being changed, there is made of necessity a change of the law:'' that the old ''law made nothing perfect:'' that Jesus was made the surety of a better Testament —the mediator of a better covenant: that the old covenant was faulty, that it waxed old and was ready to ''vanish away:'' that the law was a mere ''schoolmaster to bring mankind to Christ:'' that the New Testament is not of ''the letter which killeth, but of the spirit which giveth life:'' that the law was ''a ministration of death,'' whose ''glory was to be done away:'' that the Christian dispensation ''excelleth in glory:'' that the end of the Mosaic dispensation was to be ''abolished:'' that a veil remaineth untaken away from a certain Judaizing class of minds in reading the Old Testament, ''which veil is done away in Christ:'' that Moses and the prophets wrote of Christ: that Moses wrote of him when he announced the future coming of a prophet, whom the people should

"HEAR IN ALL THINGS:" that the law and the prophets were until John the Baptist, and then the kingdom of God was preached: that John was greatest among prophets previously born, and yet inferior to the least in the gospel kingdom: that Christ was before and above John—from heaven and above all—endowed with the Spirit beyond measure—the true "light of the world?" If he believes all this, what becomes of his objection? If he believes it not, what becomes of the New Testament?

VOICE OF THE OLD TESTAMENT.

And what says the Old Testament? Does it contradict the testimony of the New? Does it represent itself as the perfect and final revelation of God respecting divine truth, human duty and destiny? Does it claim a higher mission, or more permanent authority, than is ascribed to it in the New? Does not Moses predict Christ, and enjoin that he shall be heard in all things? Do not the prophets foreshow the coming of the Messiah, and the establishment of a new covenant, superior to that of Sinai? Do not all the types and shadows of the old dispensation presuppose a new and more glorious one? Is there any need of my quoting texts from the Old Testament Scriptures to this effect? No; the objector will not demand it. He will spare me the labor. For he must admit the obvious truth. To doubt it would be to doubt the divine inspiration of both Testaments, and thus to do the very thing he so much deprecates—discredit the whole Bible. If then, the New Testament claims to supersede the Old, and the Old, by prophecy, type and shadow, announced beforehand the coming in of a more glorious dispensation than itself, viz. the New, the point is settled forever. The New Testament supersedes the Old on all questions of divine truth and human duty. In affirming this, I only affirm what both Testaments unequivocally declare respecting themselves and each other. To question it is virtually to question the credibility of both. To affirm the contrary is to charge falsehood on both. Instead, therefore, of throwing away the Old Testament, I receive its testimony and render it a just reverence. By looking to the New Testament and accepting it as my rule of faith and practice, I rendered the most honorable obedience to the teachings of the Old. Whereas they who turn back from the perfection of the New to the imperfection of the Old—from the substance to the shadow—from sunlight to lamplight, to determine their Christian duty, trample on both Testaments, and invalidate the whole Bible. They believe neither; they obey neither.

In this view of the subject, the Old Testament, being in its nature and design a prophecy and foreshadow of the New, is not against but for non-resistance; notwithstanding the anti-non-resistant character, for the time, of its particular precepts and examples. Because it is, on the whole, for Christ and the supreme authority of his teachings, non-resistance included. It is for the New Testament with all its peculiarities, and for the excellency of the glorious gospel. Who can gainsay this? Hence, for professed Christians to quote its precepts and examples as applicable to the present dispensation, is not only a gross perversion, but a kind of pious fraud—not to be tolerated for a moment. That man can be no friend to the Old Testament, who drags it into overbearing conflict with the New. He is the enemy of both.

Nor is he the friend of Moses, who claims equality for him with Jesus Christ.   It is no better than an attempt to turn a faithful herald into a rival of the king his master, whose approach he is commissioned to announce and prepare for.   Yet there have never been wanting those who have set up Moses in superiority to Jesus.   Moses predicted, and instituted preparations for the coming of a Prophet whom the Lord God should in due time raise up.   That Prophet was Christ.   And what did Moses enjoin respecting the reverence to be paid to Christ ?   "Him shall ye hear in all things whatsoever he shall say unto you." Well, the predicted one came into the world and spake as man never before had spoken.   But he corrected some, modified others, and absolutely abrogated several of the sayings of Moses.   Moses, for the hardness of the people's hearts, had authorized them to divorce their wives for ordinary causes of dislike. But Jesus imperatively forbade them to do so, except for one cause—fornication.   Moses sanctioned sacred and judicial oath-taking, and enjoined the most faithful performance of all vows.   "But 1 say unto you swear not at all," is the injunction of Jesus.   Moses said—"life shall go for life, eye for eye, tooth for tooth," &c.   "But I say unto you, that ye resist not evil" thus, is the mandate of the new Prophet.   This very superiority of Jesus to Moses became an offence to the Jews.   "Whom makest thou thyself ?" said they contemptuously.   "We know that God spake unto Moses: as for this fellow, we know not from whence he is."   But Jesus said—"if ye had believed Moses ye would have believed me; for he wrote of me." Yet he became to them a stumbling stone, and a rock of offence.   They would not hear him in all things,

even though solemnly enjoined by Moses to do so.
The same stumbling still happens among professing
Christians. When the plain non-resistant precepts of
Jesus are urged upon them, and are demonstrated to
be prescriptive requirements of the gospel, they are
accounted hard sayings. The old law of retaliation
is so sweet, and inflictions of evil are so convenient,
as means of resisting evil, that though unable to
avoid the obvious non-resistant construction of the
language in which those precepts are expressed, they
retire behind the authority of Moses, and deny that
Jesus abrogated his sayings. They do not know what
Jesus really meant, but they affect to be certain that
he left war, capital punishment, penal inflictions and
personal resistance, just where Moses did. Though
Jesus expressly refers to the saying of Moses—"life
for life, eye for eye, and tooth for tooth " -and re-
vokes it, still they adhere to it. And this they do
under pretence of extraordinary reverence for the
word of God— the whole Bible; alleging that non-resistants contemn Moses and the Old Testament, in the
very act of receiving Jesus and the new covenant for
what those precursors announced they should be.
But the accusation returns upon their own heads.
They are the contemners of Moses and the Old Testament. For if they believed Moses and the prophets,
they would believe in Jesus and the New Testament,
as more excellent, glorious and authorative than their
forerunners. But as it is, they receive neither the Old
nor the New Testaments as the Word of God, in any
such sense as each separately, and both mutually,
purport to be. Is it to be believed, then, that if they
could summon Moses from the world of spirits, he
would commend them for their adherence to his war

like and punitive precepts, regardless of Christ's non-resistant precepts? Would he thank them for over-bearing and nullifying the laws of Jesus, by perpetuating and enforcing his code? Would he not rebuke them for their unbelief and rebellion of soul? Would he not, like Elias, say, "he that cometh after me is mightier than I, whose shoes I am not worthy to bear?" "He must increase, but I must decrease. He that is of the earth is earthly; he that cometh from heaven is above all." "Hear him in all things." I consider the objection under notice fairly answered.

OBJECTION II.—THE SCOURGE OF SMALL CORDS.

"And Jesus went up to Jerusalem, and found in the temple those that sold oxen, and sheep, and doves, and the changers of money, sitting. And when he had made a scourge of small cords, he drove them all out of the temple, and the sheep, and the oxen; and poured out the changer's money, and overthrew the tables; and said unto them that sold doves, take these things hence; make not my Father's house a house of merchandize. And his disciples remembered that it was written, the zeal of thy house hath eaten me up." Jno. 2: 13—17. Is not this transaction of Jesus directly contrary to your doctrine of non-resistance?

ANSWER.—Whether the conduct of Jesus on this occasion was inconsistent with my construction of his non-resistance precepts, depends very much on the particular facts of the case. Did Jesus injure, or threaten to injure, any person whom he expelled from the temple? Did he impair the life or health of any human being? Did he wantonly destroy property? Did he commit any injurious act on the body, mind, or rightful estate of any person concerned? If he did,

his conduct was inconsistent with what I have defined
to be Christian non-resistance. If he did not, it is perfectly reconcilable with my doctrine. That he displayed an extraordinary zeal for the religious honor of
the temple is certain. That by some remarkable means
he caused a considerable number of persons traffick-
ing within the temple suddenly to remove from the
same, with their animals and other effects is granted.
That those persons had no right to occupy the temple
for such purposes, and ought to have voluntarily removed upon the remonstrance of Jesus, will, I trust,
be admitted on all sides. The precise point of inquiry
is, did Jesus inflict any injury on the persons, estate
or morals of those who were caused to remove by his
interference? If it is to be presumed that he inflicted
blows on the men with his scourge of small cords, and
that he violently upset tables covered with coin, scat-
tering it in all directions, I should have to admit that
he injured, more or less, those whom he drove out of
the temple. But I want some proof that he touched
a single person with his scourge, and that in over-
throwing the money changers' tables he exhibited a
single undignified gesture. He urgently and authori-
tatively commanded the intruders to remove those
things thence, and probably assisted in pouring their
money into such vessels as were at hand, and in re-
moving the fixtures they had constructed for their
convenience. In all this he was earnest and determined, no doubt. But was he violent, outrageous, or
punitive? Are we to imagine him rushing furiously
among the sacreligious, smiting right and left whom-
soever he might reach with his scourge; knocking one
thing one way, and another the other way; tearing up
and breaking to pieces benches, tables and seats, like

the leader of a mob ! ! Some minds seem to imagine such proceedings as these, and of course conclude that many grievous cuts of the scourge remained on the persons of the expelled, and that money and other property was wantonly destroyed or wasted, or at least lost to the owners. But as I have an equally good right to imagine how Jesus acted on the occasion, I shall presume that he did nothing unworthy of the principles, the character and spirit which uniformly distinguished him. When he saw the temple occupied by such a mixed multitude of pretended worshippers; some really devout, some hypocritically observing their formalities, and many others, who, while professing to be promoting the service of God, were intent only on acquiring gain—crowding their cattle, fowls, and money changing tables hard upon the sanctuary—so that the lowing of oxen, bleating of sheep, cooing of doves, clinking of coin, and vociferations of the keepers, mingled confusedly with the prayers, hymns, recitations and responses of the devotees, his soul was filled with grief, loathing and abhorrence. A divine zeal fired his mind, to testify against and suppress this gross confusion and sacrilegious disorder. Taking up from the pavement a few of those rushes, or pieces of small cord made of rushes, which chanced to lie about him, he fastened them together in the form of a scourge or switch, and holding it up as an emblem of the condemnation in which the multitude had involved themselves, he commenced rebuking them for corrupting the divine worship, and mocking the Almighty with such a medley of prayer and traffic. Waxing warmer in his denunciations, he assumed a high moral and religious tone of authority, and commanded the temple to be instantly cleansed of all those nuisances. The people amazed and overawed by the truth, justice, earnestness and uncompromising energy of his rebukes, shrunk backward from his presence, yielded to the impulse which his moral force imparted to them, almost involuntarily obeyed his directions, and in a short time were actively engaged in the work of removal. Jesus, waving the emblem of condemnation and reproach, but without harming either man or beast, followed up the retreating throng, urging forward the cattle, expediting the clearing and taking down of the money changer's tables, and pouring forth with increasing fervor his rebukes and admonitions into the ears of the people, till the work was consummated. I take for granted that in this whole proceeding, spiritual and moral power was the all-controlling element; that Jesus used very little physical force, and that little uninjuriously; that he acted in all respects worthily of his authority, dignity, spirit and mission as the Son of God; that there was nothing of the mobocrat, fanatic, or police officer in his manner; and that he did no injury to any human being,—nothing but good to all parties concerned. This is what I imagine respecting this affair. There is no positive proof one way or the other; as to the particular facts, we are left to form the best judgment we can in view of the probabilities. These are all on the non-resistant side of the question. It is unnatural, absurd, and altogether improbable to suppose, that Jesus drove out so large a number of persons, by actually scourging, or threatening to scourge their bodies. That he severely scourged their minds with just reproof, of which his rush scourge was a significant emblem, I willingly admit. And in this there is nothing inconsistent with non-resistance, as I have defined it. I insist, then, that it was neither mobo-cratic, military, political, or any mere physical force, by which Jesus cleansed the temple; but divine, spiritual and moral power. Therefore, I throw the laboring oar upon the objector, and demand that he adduce some evidence, other than mere inference or conjecture, that the Saviour struck a single person with his scourge, or otherwise absolutely injured any human being. When something like this shall be proved, I will confess the force of the objection. Until then, I shall consider it sufficiently answered.

OBJECTION III.—THE TWO SWORDS.

According to the 22d chapter of Luke, Christ directed his disciples to provide themselves swords. "He that hath no sword, let him sell his garment, and buy one." Swords could be of no other use than as weapons of war, or of self-defence. How can this be reconciled with your doctrine of non-resistance?

ANSWER.—There is one other use, to which the sword might possibly be put. It might be employed on a memorable occasion as the significant emblem of in- i irious resistance, for the purpose of emphatically inculcating non-resistance. I will attempt to demonstrate that this was the special use to which Jesus intended to apply it in the case before us. He gave this direction to buy swords at the last passover, just before his betrayal in the garden of Gethsemane. When he had given it, his disciples presently responded,— "Lord, behold, here are two swords. And he said unto them, it is enough," v. 38. How could two swords be enough to arm twelve men for war or self-defence? This single fact shows that such was not the design of Jesus. He had a more sublime purpose.

When Judas gave the traitorous kiss, and the multitude approached to seize Jesus, his disciples demanded, saying, " Lord, shall we smite with the sword ? And one of them smote a servant of the high priest, and cut off his right ear. " v. 49, 50.   Matthew (26: 52) informs us how Jesus disposed of the sword. " Then said Jesus unto him, put up again thy sword into his place: for all they that take the sword shall perish with the sword. " So saying, he touched the wounded ear, and restored it, suffering himself to be borne away by his enemies without resistance.   Thus the sequel proved that he caused swords to be provided for that occasion, (two only being enough) for the sole purpose of emphatically, finally, and everlastingly prohibiting the use of the instrument, even by the innocent in self-defence.   Ever after this, those apostles, and for a long time the primitive Christians, conscientiously eschewed the use of the sword.   These three facts prove my assertion. 1. Two swords were enough. 2. The moment one of these was wielded in defence of betrayed innocence, it was peremptorily stayed, the wound caused by it healed, and the sublime mandate given, " Put up thy sword again into his place; for all they that take the sword shall perish with the sword. "   And 3. The apostles and primitive Christians obeyed the injunction, never afterwards making the least use of such deadly weapons.   This objection then ends in solid confirmation of the non-resistance doctrine, and may be appreciated accordingly.

OBJECTION IV.—DEATH OF ANANIAS AND SAPPHIRA.

The sudden death of Ananias and his wife Sapphira, for deception practised on the apostles, in keeping back a portion of their estate for private use, while pretending to consecrate the whole to the use of the church, seems to have been virtually an infliction of capital punishment. Is this reconcileable with your non-resistance?

ANSWER.—The death of those persons is not represented as the act of the apostles, or as in any manner procured or occasioned by them. It is recorded as the visitation of God, without any curse, imprecation or wish of men. This will more fully appear from the record itself. "But a certain man named Ananias, with Sapphira, his wife, sold a possession, and kept back part of the price, his wife also being privy to it, and brought a certain part, and laid it at the apostles' feet. But Peter said, Ananias, why hath Satan filled thy heart to lie to the Holy Ghost, and to keep back part of the price of the land? While it remained, was it not thine own? and after it was sold, was it not in thine own power? Why hast thou conceived this thing in thy heart? Thou hast not lied unto men, but unto God. And Ananias, hearing these words, fell down and gave up the ghost." Three hours after, when his wife, not knowing what was done, came in, Peter said unto her, "How is it that ye have agreed together to tempt the Spirit of the Lord? Behold, the feet of them which have buried thy husband are at the door, and shall carry thee out. Then fell she down straight way at his feet, and yielded up the ghost." Acts 5: 1—5, 7—10. Is there any intimation in this account, that Peter, or any of the other apostles, assumed judicial authority over those persons? Or that they assumed any power, human or divine, over their lives? Or that they caused, occasioned, imprecated or desired their death? Certainly not. The case then is not one on which the objection can pertinently rest. I therefore dismiss it.

OBJECTION V.—HUMAN GOVERNMENT—13TH OF
ROMANS, &c.

Human government is recognised in the New Testament, as the ordinance of God, for good to mankind.
Rulers are declared to be a terror, not to good works,
but to the evil ministers of God, and revengers "to execute wrath upon him that doeth evil;" who bear not
the sword in vain, and ought to receive tribute, custom and honor at the hands of Christians," not only
for wrath but also for conscience' sake. " Paul
pleaded his citizenship as a Roman to obtain an honorable discharge from prison, and on another occasion
to save himself from the scourge. He applied for
military protection to save his life from the forty con-
spirators, and appealed to Cæsar to obtain justice in
his defence against the accusations of the Jews. See
Romans 13: 1—7. Acts 16: 37. Ib. 22: 24—29. Ib.
23: 17. Ib. 25: 10—12. Titus 3: 1. 1 Peter 2: 13,
14, and other passages. Now, as human government,
in all its various forms, with its military and penal
terrors, is the ordinance of God for good to mankind;
as its rulers are declared to be the ministers of God
for the protection of the innocent and the punishment
of the guilty; and as its requirements are to be respected with submission, it follows that Christians, in
stead of non participating therein, on account of war,
capital punishment and penal inflictions, ought to
share in its responsibilities, and be its firmest supporters,—always conscientiously endeavoring to render it in the highest degree efficient for its divinely
appointed purpose. Here then is an insuperable objection to your doctrine of non-resistance—certainly
so, as respects government, war, capital punishment,
&c.

ANSWER. This is by far the most plausible and se-- ductive objection, now urged against Chistian non-re- sistance. It deceives and misleads more good minds, and is harder to be answered than any other. And yet it is essentially fallacious and invalid. This I will endeavor to demonstrate. Government is the bond of social order. It is that directing and regu- lating authority which keeps individuals in their prop- er relations to each other and the great whole. The intelligent Christian must contemplate it in three several characters. 1. Government *per se*; 2. Gov- ernment *de jure*; and 3. Government *de facto*. Gov- ernment *per se* is authority exercised to maintain and promote moral order. Moral order, of course, pre- supposes rational social beings. When such beings are in a state of true moral order they are right-mind- ed, and being right-minded, gradually reduce all things physical to the right condition. Mind gov- erns matter and moral authority governs mind. Mor- al order involves all other order. Imperfect moral order leaves all things in a state of imperfect order. Moral disorder draws after it all manner of physical disorder. Therefore, all depends on a supreme mor- al authority, or government. This must be inherent- ly divine. It is original and self-existent in God only. Government *per se*, then, is essentially divine ; it is of and from God. It is not original in any created be- ing. Wherever it exists, it is derivable from God. If so, there is, strictly speaking, no such thing as hu- man government. Man is always subordinate to God, and can have no right to enact any law, or to exer- cise any governmental power contrary to the divine law and government. If human nature possessed original, independent governing authority, men could

rightfully repeal, or nullify the divine law. Now
they cannot. Consequently all law and government
absolutely contrary to the law and government of God
is morally null and void. But all law and government, in accordance with the divine law and government, is morally binding on every human being.
This presents government in its second character;
government *de jure*, or of absolute right. Tnat all
human governments ought to be conformed to the
standard of the divine none will deny. If they were
thus conformed, they would cease to be human in
their spirit and character. They would become mere
incarnations and elaborations of the divine. But as
the word human, when joined to the word government, may imply nothing more than a human manifestation, is a well regulated social organization, I will
not discard its use, my meaning being understood. I
will say, then, that Christian non-resistance, so far
from conflicting with government *per se*, or human
government *de jure*, *i. e.*, human government strictly
subordinate and conformed to the divine government,
holds the first supremely sacred, and the last as its
grand desideratum. And on this very account it requires the disciples of Christ to keep themselves dis-
entangled from all such human governments as are
fundamentally repugnant to the divine government,—
all such as are not *de jure*, according to the law of God
declared by Jesus Christ. This brings into view the
third character, in which non-resistants are obliged to
contemplate government; viz: government *de facto*, as
it is in fact. And what has human government ever
been in fact, from the beginning to this day? Has it
been identical with the divine government? Has it
been radically government *de jure*, according to the

law of the living God ? Is the present government of the United States, with all its captivating professions, and really good things, fundamentally a Christian government ? Who will dare to say so ? What then was human government *de facto* in the apostolic times? The government of Herod, Pilate, Nero and the Roman Cæsars, under whom oppression, injustice, tyranny and cruelty rioted on human rights, deluged the habitable globe with blood, crucified the son of God, and made myriads of martyrs?

Now, a preliminary question to be settled is, whether the Apostle Paul in the 13th chapter of Romans, speaks of government *per se*, or of government *de jure* or of government *de facto*. If only of the first or second, then is there no incompatibility of his words with non resistance, and the objection falls to the ground. But if he speaks of human governments and rulers, such as they were in the Roman empire, further investigation will be necessary to set the subject in a true light. I will take for granted that he was speaking of the governments and rulers under whom Christians then lived ; for I can suppose nothing else.

HOW THE APOSTLES VIEWED THE THEN EXISTING GOVERNMENTS.

Taking this ground, we wish to know precisely how he and other apostles viewed those governing powers, and how they counselled the disciples of Christ to feel and act with regard to them. If Christ and His apostles regarded the Cæsars and their subordinate kings, governors and magistrates, as moved and approved of God, as His conscious ministers, in carrying on the government of those times; if they really held the then existing governments of the earth to be ordained of

God, in the same sense that their own spiritual, religious and moral authority was, then is the objection
before us unanswerable. Then, of course, I must admit that it is the duty of Christians to share in the responsibility of any government under which they may
live, and to support its requirements in all things,
war, capital punishment, persecution, idolatry, slavery
and whatever else it may exact. It would then be
God's own law and voice—to be obeyed implicitly in
all things. There could be no limitations or exceptions. Did the apostles teach such doctrine as this?
If they did, how happens it that they and the primitive Christians kept themselves so scrupulously aloof
from the governments of their times? No : the objector will not contend for any such unqualified en
dorsement of human government by the apostles He
will disclaim such extreme conclusions. He will admit the gross corruption, tyranny and wickedness of
those very governments which Paul declares to have
been "ordained of God." He will admit more than
I shall stop to demand, of horrible impiety, iniquity
and persecution on the part of those very rulers, whom
the apostle declares to be the "ministers of God—
avengers to execute wrath on evil doers." He will
not argue that such governments as those of the
Herods, the Pilates and the Neroes, were "ordained of
God," in the same sense that the Church of Jesus
Christ was. Nor that those bloody minded rulers and
their agents were "ministers of God," consciously and
approvedly, as were the apostles. He knows that
Paul never intended to be so understood. Here, then,
is the mischievous little catch of the objection.
Words and phrases are taken in a false sense. There
is a sense in which it is true that "there is no power

but of God;'' in which "the powers that be are ordained of God;" in which "rulers," even the worst of
them, "are not a terror to good works, but to the
evil;" in which they are "the ministers of God for
good" to the righteous, and "avengers to execute
wrath" on men of violence. But what is this sense?
Let us investigate the matter.

SUBMISSION TO, NOT PARTICIPATION IN, GOVERN-MENT ENJOINED ON CHRISTIANS.

It is clear that Christians are everywhere in the
New Testament enjoined to render respect and submission to human governments, kings, rulers and
magistrates. They are forbidden to resist "the
powers that be," or their ordinances, by any act of
wanton disobedience, insurrection, sedition or violence,
whatsoever. They are commanded to obey them in all
things not involving disobedience to God, and then to
do their duty patiently, suffering whatever persecution, penalties or violence government may inflict upon them. But it is equally clear that Christians are
now here in the New Testament enjoined to enter
into political combinations; nor to accept offices
of trust and emolument, civil or military, under any
human government; nor to apply to courts of law
for redress of injuries committed upon them; nor to
seek personal protection from the civil or military
power. All this being assumed, we wish to ascertain whether Christians are enjoined to pay re
spect, submission and tribute to governments and
their administrative officers, otherwise than to bodies
of men, or individuals not governmentally organized
constituted and empowered. It would seem that they
are. They are to render respect, submission, tribute

and custom to governments and rulers as such. There
must then be reasons for paying this peculiar defer-
ence and homage. What are they? Paul presents
them in the passage referred to, Romans 13: 1—7.
But there is a difficulty in determining precisely what
he means by such terms and phrases as "ordained of
God." "ordinances of God," "ministers of God."
What is the true sense of these expressions? Let us
see if we can determine.

IN WHAT SENSE "THE POWERS THAT BE ARE OR-
DAINED OF GOD."

It cannot be in the sense, that he requires them to
be just what they are, and to do just what they do.
It cannot be in the sense that they can do no wrong,
commit no sin, and deserve no punishment. It cannot be in any such sense as that kings, counsellors,
rulers and magistrates are not moral agents, or are in
any manner absolved from the common obligations of
other men, to love God with their whole heart, to love
their neighbors as themselves, to forgive the trespasses
of their offenders, to love their enemies, bless those
that curse them and do good to them that hate them.
It can be in no such sense, as would change the law of
God, reverse right and wrong, or screen them from
condemnation in anything sinful. It must be in some
general sense, a sense which implies merely their
necessity in the nature of things, and that they are
overruled in the providence of God for the good of
mankind. In this sense they certainly are ordained of
God; and in this sense kings, presidents, governors and
rulers are ministers of God, *i. e.*, instruments in the
grand economy of his providence for the good of well
doers, and the punishment and restraint of evil doers.

And this is as true of the most corrupt, perverse, tyrannical rulers, as of the more worthy. It was as true of Pharaoh, Nebuchadnezzar, Nero and Robespierre, as of Melchizedec, David, Antoninus and Washington. Hence we must make a great difference between a consciously inspired and approved minister of God, and those "ministers of God" that "bear not the sword in vain," that are a "terror to evil doers," and that are "avengers to execute wrath."   Because these latter have frequently no consciousness that they are instruments in the divine hand, that he is using them to any holy purpose, or that he approves of their conduct.   On the contrary they are frequently conscious of setting at defiance his law and judgments, and of trampling under foot every thing divine and human which appears to stand in the way of their selfishness, ambition, revenge and lust.

PHAROAH GOD'S MINISTER.

Thus it is written concerning Pharoah: " For this same purpose have I raised thee up, that I might show my power in thee, and that my name might be declared through all the earth. "   But Pharaoh had no consciousness of all this.   It entered not into his motives.   He acted entirely according to his own perverse and wicked inclinations.   And God punished him just as if nothing but evil was to result from his tyrannical reign.   Yet in the great providential sense he was " ordained of God, " was the servant or minister of God for good to Israel, and for the punishment of the cruel Egyptians.   He knew not the use God was putting him to; he intended not the good which he was made to promote; and therefore received according to the evil which he did intend.   Yet probably the whole human race is now in a better condition for his having oppressed the children of Israel, and thereby hastened their exodus from Egypt. The results have been good, by reason, not of his righteous motives, but of an all-wise, overruling providence which made the tyrant unconsciously a minister of its beneficent purposes.

THE MONARCH OF ASSYRIA GOD'S MINISTER.

So it was with the Assyrian government and its monarch. "O Assyrian, the rod of mine anger, and the staff in their hand is mine indignation. I will send him against a hypocritical nation, and against the people of my wrath will I give him a charge, to take the spoil, and to take the prey, and to tread them down like the mire of the streets. Howbeit he meaneth not so, neither doth his heart think so." "Wherefore it shall come to pass, when the Lord hath performed his whole work upon Mount Zion, and on Jerusalem, I will punish the fruit of the stout heart of the king of Assyria, and the glory of his high looks. For he saith, by the strength of my hand have I done it, and by my wisdom, for I am prudent." "Shall the axe boast itself against him that heweth therewith? shall the saw magnify itself against him that shaketh it?" Isaiah 10: 5—7, 12—15. Thus was the Assyrian government ordained of God, in the apostle's sense, and the king thereof made to be "God's minister," servant, instrument. He was made to be so, not only without any consciousness, but against his own proud, ambitious and vindictive will. And like Pharaoh before him he was judged according to the evil he intended, and not according to the good which God obliged him, unwittingly, to subserve. He was made a rod of correction to hypocritical Israel, in the divine hand "a terror to evil doers," even while being himself a gigantic evil doer. He "bore not the sword in vain, " "howbeit he meant not so. " Query. Would this have been a good reason why the prophets and pious portion of Israel should go and connect themselves with his government or army! Yet it was a good reason why they should persevere in declaring the truth, in promoting righteousness, and in patiently awaiting the deliverances of divine providence.

NEBUCHADNEZZAR GOD'S MINISTER.

Nebuchadnezzar affords another instance of the same ordination and overruling of God. "Behold, I will send and take all the families of the north, and Nebuchadnezzar, my servant [my minister,] and will bring them against this land, " &c. "And it shall come to pass, when seventy years are accomplished, that I will punish the king of Babylon, and that nation saith the Lord, for their iniquity, " &c., Jer. 25: 9, 12. Was Nebuchadnezzar God's minister for good to Jeremiah and the faithful, but 'an avenger to execute wrath on the wicked Israelites? Was he one who bore not the sword in vain—and who was a terror to evil doers? Such God made him to be. But was he conscious of it? Was it his motive? Did he work righteousness? Was he not really a very wicked man? Did not God condemn and punish him? Would it have been commendable, in Jeremiah and the upright few among the Jews, to have gone over and become soldiers in his army? They did, indeed, peaceably go out and surrender to him, and counselled their countrymen to submit to his government, on the very ground that God had determined to humble them for their great national sins, and had in his providence given Nebuchadnezzar power to subdue them.   But they never held up the invading monarch as righteous, and approved in the sight of God.

THE ROMAN GOVERNMENT.

If we descend to Paul's time and contemplate the Roman government, its Cæsars and their governors of provinces, should we not be obliged to view them in the same light?   We might, indeed, find many laws, institutions, measures, and particular acts of administration worthy of. commendation, which no good man would wish depreciated. But how much of the tyrannical, oppressive, cruel and utterly abominable would rise up before us, to awaken our disgust and abhorrence?   What shall we think of the emperor Nero, under whom Paul, Peter and thousands of Christians were put to death, whose name has become universally infamous for cruelty, persecution and brutality ! Yet he was a "minister of God"—"a terror to evil doers,"—"an avenger to execute wrath,"—one who "bore not the sword in vain"—to whom tribute should be paid, honor rendered, and unresisting submission offered.   Paul, Peter, and the Christian martyrs, all acted accordingly.   And though he persecuted them unto death, it was doubtless true, that God in his providence made him, in spite of his wickedness, a minister to them for good; causing all things to work together for good to them, as the true lovers of righteousness.   How else shall we understand the apostle's doctrine, or interpret the persecutions inflicted on them by " the powers ordained of God," and by rulers like Nero and his deputies, the

" ministers of God ? " We cannot for a moment regard these "powers" as approved of God, nor those
tyrant monsters as his conscious " ministers, " the or-
acles and conscientious doers of his will. And yet, in
the general sense, the great providental sense, all
Paul says of them is true. Nor is his declaration of
this truth useless or unimportant? It is necessary for
the comfort, support and right conduct of Christians
amid the uproar, tumult and apparent confusion of
governmental affairs. They must see by faith the
hand of their Father guiding the helm of events, restraining the wrath of man, and overruling the most
powerful agencies of human society for good. Otherwise they would often despair of the world's redemption, and be thrown into the foaming currents of retaliation, revolution, violence and war. But now they
may do their duty without fear, in full confidence
that " the Lord God omnipotent reigneth " in righteousness over all governments, monarchs, kings, rulers, and magistrates; judging them according to their
own proper motives and works, but overruling their
most perverse doings for the particular good of the
just, and the general good of the universe.

RESPECTS WHEREIN GOVERNMENT IS ORDAINED OF GOD.

I come then to the following conclusion: 1. That
government of some sort supplies a fundamental want
of human nature, and must exist wherever men exist.
In this respect it is ordained of God. 2. That human
governments *de facto* are barbarisms, corruptions, per
versions and abuses of the true government *de jure*,
which God through Christianity aims to establish
among mankind; and are therefore the nearest ap-

proaches which the mass of men in their present low
moral condition are capable of making to the true
ideal. In this respect government is ordained of God.
3. That the worst of governments are preferable to absolute anarchy—being the least of two evils, and rendering the condition of man on the whole more toler-
able. In this respect "the powers that be are ordained of God." 4. That human governments generally proclaim and sanction some great truths and duties, execute some justice, and intentionally maintain
more or less wholesome order; that they are in many
respects positively good in motive and deed, thus far
conforming to the divine government. In this respect
they are ordained of God. 5. Wherein human governments and their administrators are fundamentally
tyrannical, selfish, oppressive, persecuting, unprincipled and morally abhorrent, they are overruled in
the hand of God, as unwitting instrumentalities for
the punishment and restraint of violence, and for
quickening and purifying the moral sense of the
righteous, to superinduce in them a holier, more devoted and mightier activity in the great work of human reformation. In this respect the powers that be
are ordained of God, and rulers are ministers of God
for good to the just, but of wrath to the children of
wrath. Therefore Christians are to respect, submit,
and render homage to the governments and rulers under whom they live, however anti-Christian and even
persecuting; taking care to obey them in all well-doing, to conform to their requirements in all matters,
not conflicting with the divine requirements, differing from them as peaceably as possible, suffering their
wrongs patiently in hope, withstanding them only for
righteousness' sake in things absolutely sinful, and

then enduring their penalties with non resistant meekness and submission. But at the same time they are to be true to the kingdom of God, faithful in their allegiance to the great law of Christ, never departing from it for the sake of assuming the reins of any human government, or obtaining its honors, emoluments, advantages, approbation or protection If they can enter into any government and carry their Christianity with them unadulterated and untrammelled, let them enter. If not, it is their imperative duty to remain out of it, peaceable, unoffending subjects. Their mission is a higher and nobler one than that of the worldly politician, statesman or ruler. They must not, desert, betray or dishonor it. If they continue faithful they will gradually draw up human government to the divine standard. If they lower themselves down, by renouncing or compromising their principles, for the sake of participating in any fundamentally anti-Christian government, hoping thereby to elevate the moral tone of such government, they will infallibly be disappointed. They will sink themselves, and with them the government will sink still lower than before. They must everlastingly insist on the principles and precepts of Jesus Christ; and whatever will not come to those, leave to its own genius and doom. God will take care of all the rest. " For there is no power but of God, " and subject to his own sovereign disposal. The Christian has nothing to care for but to be a Christian indeed, allowing himself never to be transformed into any thing, or committed to any undertaking essentially inconsistent with his sublime profession.

If I have taken a correct view of this important, but difficult subject, I have fairly removed the pending objection, so far as it rests on the 13th chapter of Romans, and similar passages. I am confident this view is substantially correct; and I do not believe the opposers of Christian non-resistance can give any other view which will harmonize decently, either with the plain tenor of the Scriptures, or with their own doctrine, respecting the natu re and functions of civil government. It remains only that I touch on that part of the objection which asserts that Paul in certain cases resorted to human government, idolatrous, warlike and despotic as it then was, to secure immunity, protection and justice.

PAUL'S CONDUCT IN RELATION TO GOVERNMENT.

This is a misapprehension, or at least a false view of the facts. Did Paul ever commence a prosecution at law for the redress of injuries perpetrated on his person, property or rights? Did he ever apply to the civil or military authorities for personal protection, when at large, pursuing his usual avocations? Never. Such a case is not on record The cases cited all occurred when he was a prisoner, in charge of the government officers. The first instance is mentioned Acts 16: 37. Paul and Silas had been thrown into prison and cruelly beaten by order of the magistrates of Phillippi. The next morning those magistrates sent directions to the jailor to let them go. "But Paul said unto them, they have beaten us openly uncondemned, being Romans, and have cast us into prison; and now do they thrust us out privily? nay, verily; but let them come themselves and fetch us out." The result was, that the magistrates, knowing that they had proceeded unlawfully, were glad to acknowledge their error, and discharge the prisoners in an

honorable manner. This was all Paul demanded.
He and Silas had done nothing, even according to the
laws of the land, to merit such vile treatment; and
knowing that they had a right, as Roman citizens, to
redress, they meant that the magistrates and the public should understand the facts. They, however,
brought no action for redress, but were content to forgive their injuries, if only they might be regarded as
the injured party, and as such reputably discharged.
This is just what every Non-Resistant ought to do under like circumstances. It would have been unworthy of the gospel, for Paul and Silas to have crept
off in a private manner, leaving the people to infer
that they were culprits, allowed to escape by mere indulgence. Christianity is as bold, faithful, and heroic
in asserting its rights, and sustaining its just repu-
tation, as it is non-resistant in respect to returning injury for injury. It is never mean and skulking,
but always open, frank, dignified and godlike.

The next instance cited is mentioned in the 22d
chapter, of Acts. The Jews had raised a mob, and
rushed on Paul to kill him. While they were
cruelly beating him, the chief captain came upon
them with his soldiers, and made Paul his prisoner,
causing him to be bound with two chains, and to be
conducted to the castle. Having reached the stairs
of the castle, he asked permission to address the excited multitude. He was permitted, and was heard
for a short time with great attention. But on declaring that God had commissioned him to preach the gospel to the Gentiles, the whole throng broke out into
the most furious invectives, saying, "Away with such
a fellow from the earth; for it is not fit that he should
live. And as they cried out, and cast off their clothes,

and threw dust into the air, the chief captain commanded him to be brought into the castle, and bade
that he should be examined by scourging; that he
might know wherefore they cried so against him.''
This was an extraordinary state of things. An innocent man falsely accused and maliciously assailed by
a crowd of bigoted and ferocious Jews, solely on account of his Christianity, was about to be cruelly
scourged, to extort a confession of some suspected
secret. Paul, being a free born Roman citizen, and
knowing himself privileged by that single fact from
such gross outrage, demanded, as they were binding
him with thongs—''Is it lawful for you to scourge a
man that is a Roman, and uncondemned ?'' This stayed the proceedings instantly. ''Take heed,'' said the
centurion to the chief captain, "what thou doest: for
this man is a Roman.'' "Tell me, art thou a Roman?''
said the captain. Paul said "Yea.'' The captain
answered—''With a great sum obtained I this freedom.'' ''But I was free born,'' replied the prisoner.
''Then straightway they departed from him, which
should have examined him: and the chief captain also
was afraid, after he knew that he was a Roman, and
because he had bound him.'' Here was one remarkable excellency of the Roman law and authority:— a
Roman citizen must be treated with a certain degree
of respect, and fairly heard in his own defence, even
though guilty of great crimes. He must be regularly
condemned before being subjected to the treatment of
a felon. This was nothing but a dictate of plain
justice and common sense. But observe, Paul had
not recently gone and purchased his privilege of Roman citizenship, in order to provide against such con-
tingencies as these. He was "free born.'' All he

did was to remind those who were about to violate the
Roman law by scourging him uncondemned, of
his rights.   He threatens nothing; he only throws
them upon their own responsibility.   It was his right
and privilege to be dealt with civilly, till fairly tried.
He pleaded his rights in the most unassuming manner
possible, and left those who had his person in their
power, to act for themselves.   How just, how honorable, how meek, how noble, how non-resistant, was
his conduct!   There is nothing in it which any non-
resistant, in like circumstances, might not and ought
not to copy.

The next instance followed soon after.   It is recorded in the 23d chapter of Acts.   Paul still a prisoner in the castle, had received a partial hearing before the chief priests and their council.   Meantime
forty of his most violent enemies banded together under oath not to eat or drink till they had killed him.
To find an opportunity for their deadly assault, they
agreed to request the chief captain to bring Paul
again before the council for further hearing; intend-
ing while he was imperfectly guarded to rush upon
him and effect their purpose.   Paul's sister's son, getting knowledge of this conspiracy, communicated it to
his uncle, who, thereupon called one of the centurions,
and said: "Bring this young man unto the chief captain, for he hath a certain thing to tell him."   The
young man did his errand to the chief captain, who
kindly sent him away under a charge of silence respecting the matter.   To prevent bloodshed and all
further violence, the chief captain ordered four hundred and sixty of his soldiers to convey Paul during
the night to Cesarea, to Felix the governor.   Thus
was the threatened mischief avoided.   This is what

some understand to be Paul's application for a military force to protect his person. Did Paul apply for protection? Did he demand a military escort? Did he ask anything, or recommend any thing, except barely that the centurion would conduct his nephew to the chief captain, that he might communicate his message? No, nothing. He was a helpless prisoner, guarded by the chief captain's soldiers. It was the duty of that officer to afford him such personal protection as was due to all Roman citizens. Paul knew from his preceding conduct, that the chief captain was desirous of discharging his duty according to law. He was apprised of the deadly conspiracy formed against him. Had he been his own man, non-resistance would have admonished him to escape the danger by flight. But he was a prisoner. He was to be brought within reach of his foes, under treacherous pretences of a desire to give him a further hearing, and then murdered in spite of his Roman guard. What could he, or ought he to have done, either to save his own life, or pay proper respect to the chief captain, less than to cause the simple facts to be communicated? It was his duty. He would have been most criminal had he done otherwise. He meditated no counter attack on the guilty. He sought no means of punishing them. He counselled no measures of violence. He recommended nothing, threatened nothing, demanded nothing. He caused the proper information to be conveyed to the captain, and meekly left all to his discretion. And the captain proved his good sense, as well as pacific disposition, by so disposing of the prisoner as to prevent all violence and danger. In all this matter Paul acted just as any Christian non-resistant, in such circumstances, should act most unexceptionably.

His "appeal to Caesar" followed in the train of these events. It is mentioned in the 25th chapter. What was the nature and design of that appeal? He had been falsely accused, subjected to a long imprisonment, and partly tried for heresy and sedition. His trial was still pending after a two years delay of justice. Festus, the new governor, found Paul still in bonds. The high priest and chief of the Jews, now moved their suit afresh and requested that Paul might be sent to Jerusalem—"lying in wait in the way to kill him." But not succeeding in this plot, the Jews went down to Cesarea to renew their accusations before the governor's judgment seat. Paul reaffirmed his innocence of all their charges, and nothing could be made out against him. Festus, the governor, "willing to do the Jews a pleasure, asked Paul if he would "go up to Jerusalem, and there be judged of these things." "Then said Paul, I stand at Cæsar's judgment seat, where I ought to be judged; to the Jews have I done no wrong, as thou very well knowest. For if I be an offender, or have committed any thing worthy of death, I refuse not to die; but if there be none of these things whereof they accuse me, no man may deliver me unto them. I appeal unto Cæssar." How noble and Christian like this appeal! Jerusalem was no place for an impartial trial. It was only adding insult to injury, to propose under such circumstances pretexts, to take him back among those prejudiced and blood thirsty men. If he must be further tried, he claimed his privilege to appear before a higher and more impartial court—to go to Rome. God had directed him in a vision to do so, for the purpose of proclaiming the gospel in that great city. His defence was in fact nothing but the defence of the

gospel. He therefore appealed to Cæsar. He was
not the accuser, but the accused. He had not come
into court to complain of and procure the punishment
of his enemies. He was not the prosecutor in this
case; but a prisoner, falsely accused, detained in bonds
unjustly, and now laid under the necessity of going
to Jerusalem or to Rome for the conclusion of his
trial. He might have his choice; it was his acknowledged privilege; and he availed himself of it as a
duty to the cause of Christ, no less than as a right.
And in this, as in other instances, he acted just as
he ought to have acted—just as any Christian non-resistant would be bound to act. Neither of the cases
cited implies the slightest inconsistency of conduct
with the doctrine to which they are brought as objections.

CONCLUSION.

Having thus thoroughly canvassed all the important objections to my doctrine, which I recollect ever
to have seen presented out of the Scriptures, I may
now confidently appeal to the understanding and conscience of the Christian reader for a favorable verdict.
Have I not triumphantly demonstrated that the Holy
Scriptures teach the doctrine of non resistance as defined in the first chapter of this work ? Have I not
fairly answered the objections urged from the Scriptures against it ? Is there any doctrine or duty taught
in the Bible, which can be sustained by more convincing testimony ? Or that can be more satisfactorily
freed from objections ? It seems to me that candid
minds, after seriously investigating the subject, can
come to no other conclusion. I know that it is a mo-
mentous conclusion, drawing after it the most radical

change of views, feelings, conduct and character throughout Christendom and the world which can well be imagined. But will it not be a most glorious and salutary revolution? When all who sincerely reverence the Bible, as in any sacred sense the word of God to mankind, shall contemplate the Old Testament as the prophecy and preparative of the new, pointing forward to the perfect development of moral excellence under the reign of Jesus Christ; when they shall see in his precepts, examples and spirit a perfect manifestation of the divine wisdom and goodness; and shall feel that his righteousness, imbibed into the hearts and exhibited in the lives of mankind, is the only remedy for all the world's disorders!

"Fly swifter round, ye wheels of time,
And bring the welcome day. "

CHAPTER IV.

Non-Resistance Not Contrary To Nature.

Nature and the laws of nature defined—Self-preservation the first law of nature—What is the true method of self-preservation?—Demurrer of the objector—The objector still persists; analogy of the animals—Common method of self-preservation certainly false—Five great laws of human nature considered—These laws radically harmonious —Non-Resistance in perfect unison with these laws—A law of universal nature, like begets its like—General illustrations in common life—Special illustrations; 1, Subdued pride and scorn; 2, The man whose temper was broken; 3, The colored woman and the sailor; 4, The hay makers; 5, The two students; 6, Two neighbors and the manure; 7, Impounding the horse; 8, Two neighbors and the hens; 9, Henry and Albert; 10, The subdued hatter; 11, The revolutionary soldier; 12, Ex-President Jefferson and the cooper's shop; 13, Wm. Ladd and his neighbor Pulsifer— Conclusion.

The opposers of Non-Resistance with one voice confidently assert that it is contrary to the known law of Nature and therefore must be false, however plausibly defended from the Scriptures. It is the design of the present chapter to refute this confident assertion, and to demonstrate that Christian non-resistance is in perfect accordance with the laws of Nature considered in all their developments. I shall endeavor to do this with arguments sustained by numerous facts and illustrations drawn from real life.

NATURE AND THE LAWS OF NATURE DEFINED.

What is "Nature?" and what are "the laws of Nature ?'' These terms are in very common use with a certain class of persons. But they are more flippant-ly uttered than definitely understood. Doubtless they may properly be used with considerable latitude of meaning. In the present discussion, however, we must be definite and clear. I shall, therefore, take the term "nature" to mean—the essential constituent elements, properties, qualities and capabilities of any being or thing. The aggregate of these is the nature of any being or thing, whether the particular being or thing considered be ever so simple, or ever so com-plex. Whatever, in or about a being or thing, is not an essential constituent element, property, quality or capability thereof, is not an absolute necessary of it. And what is not generally an absolute necessary of a being or thing, is not a part of its nature, but merely an incidental or factitious appendage. Take human nature, as that particular division of Universal Na-ture which we must consider in this discussion. There are elements, properties, qualities and capabili-ties essential to the constitution of a human being. These are common to the race. We may say of them in general that they are the absolute inherent neces-saries of man—*i. e.* his nature. But there are many incidental and factitious elements, properties, qualities and capabilities in and about individuals and communities of the human race, which are the results of causes and circumstances, either temporary and transient in their operation or ultimately remov-able by human efforts. None of these are the essen-tial constituents of human nature. They may all be reversed or removed without annihilating or pervert-ing nature. Let this be well understood. Next, "the aws of nature." I understand the l aws of nature to be those forms, modes or methods according to which it necessarily operates in its various developments. When any tendency or action of nature is observed to be uniform under given circumstances throughout the sphere of our knowledge, we infer that a certain law or necessity governs it. Consequently, we speak of all things as governed by some law of nature. What to us is uniform and universal, or nearly so, we regard as the result of nature's laws—a certain necessity of tendency and development, which determines the form, mode, or method of its manifestation. These laws are at best but imperfectly understood, and are oftener talked about than well conceived of. They are only secondary causes in a vast chain incomprehensible to finite minds, and which we vaguely trace to a Supreme First Cause—the Self-Existent Divine Nature, God. What we can with any propriety assume to know of those undefinable some-things, termed "the laws of nature," is only the uniformity and universality of their results within the narrow sphere of our observation. It becomes us therefore to be humble and modest in pronouncing on these laws. We know some things perhaps beyond possibility of mistake. Many other things we know partially and imperfectly; concerning which it is our besetting weakness to presume that we know a vast deal more than we really do. Of the great whole we know comparatively next to nothing. Of the whole, even of those natures concerning which we know most, we are extremely ignorant,– as a few thousand years of existence and continued observation would no doubt convince us. But let us reason as well as we can from what we know, and learn what we may in the great future.

SELF-PRESERVATION THE FIRST LAW OF NATURE.

It is reiterated that "self-preservation is the first law of nature." I grant it, and then what follows? "Self-defence against whatever threatens destruction or injury," says the opponent. I grant it, and what next follows? "Generally mutual personal conflict, injury, and, in extremities, death. Hence there are justifiable homicides, wars, injuries and penal inflictions. Nature impels them. Her law of self preservation necessitates them. They are right in the very nature of things; and therefore non-resistance must be as wrong, as it is impracticable. It is contrary to nature, and cannot be brought into practice." Let us examine these bold assertions. I have granted that "self-preservation is the first law of nature." Also that this law prompts to self-defence against whatever threatens destruction or injury. I also admit the fact that generally men, in common with the lower animals, fight, injure, and frequently slay each other in self-defence, or for something supposed to be necessary to self-preservation. In granting this last, I only grant that men are generally very foolish and wicked.

WHAT IS THE TRUE METHOD OF SELF PRESERVATION.

For it remains to be seen whether this general method of self-preservation be the true method. Whether it be not a very bad method. Whether it be not a method which absolutely defeats its own designed object. Let us inquire. If it be the true method, it must on the whole work well. It must preserve human life and secure mankind against injury, more certainly and effectually than any other possible method. Has it done this? I do not admit it. How happens it that, according to the lowest probable estimate, some fourteen thousand milllons of human beings have been slain by human means, in war and otherwise? Here are enough to people eighteen planets like the earth with its present population. What inconceiveable miseries must have been endured by these worlds of people and their friends, in the process of those murderous conflicts which extinguished their earthly existence! Could all their dying groans be heard and their expiring throes be witnessed at once by the existing generation of men; could their blood flow together into one vast lake, mingled with the tears of their bereaved relatives; could their corpses be seen piled up in one huge pyramid; or their skeletons be contemplated in a broad golgotha, would it be deemed conclusive evidence that mankind has practised the true method of self-preservation!! Would it encourage us still to confide in and pursue the same method? Would it suggest no inquiries, whether there were not "a more excellent way?" Should we not be impelled to conclude that this method was the offspring of a purblind instinct— the cherished salvo of ignorance—the fatal charm of deluded credulity—the supposed preserver, but the real destroyer of the human family? If this long-trusted method of self-preservation be indeed the best which nature affords to her children, their lot is most deplorable. To preserve what life has been preserved at such a cost, renders life itself a thing of doubtful value. If only a few thousands, or even a few millions, had perished by the two edged sword; if innocence and justice and right had uniformly triumphed; if aggression, injustice, violence, injury and insult, after a few dreadful experiences, had been overawed;

if gradually the world had come into wholesome order—a state of truthfulness, justice and peace; if the
sword of self defence had frightened the sword of aggression into its scabbard, there to consume in its
rust; then might we admit that the common method
of self-preservation was the true one. But now we
have ample demonstration that they who take the
sword, perish with the sword. Is it supposable that
if no injured person or party, since the days of Abel,
had lifted up a deadly weapon, or threatened an injury against an offending party, there would have
been a thousandth part of the murders and miseries
which have actually taken place on our earth ? Take
the worst possible view; resolve all the assailed and
injured into the most passive non-resistants imaginable, and let the offenders have unlimited scope to
commit all the robberies, cruelties and murders they
pleased; would as many lives have been sacrificed, or
as much real misery have been experienced by the
human race, as have actually resulted from the general method of self-preservatian, by personal conflict
and resistance of injury with injury ? He must be a
bold man who affirms it. The truth is, man has stood
in his own light. He has frustrated his own wishes.
He has been deceived, deluded, betrayed, and all but
destroyed, by his own self conceited, evil imagination. He would not be taught of God. He would
have his own way. He would be a fool, a spendthrift,
a murderer and a suicide. Yet his Father still calls
after him. He offers to make him wise, good and
happy. He offers to teach him the true method of
self preservation. It is found in the non-resistance of
Jesus Christ. But he is wretchedly wedded to his
old idols, and will scarcely hear the voice of his only
true friend. When he will hear, he shall live.

A DEMURRER OF THE OBJECTOR.

Judged of by its fruits the common and much
vaunted method of self-preservation, by injurious resistance, stands hopelessly condemned. "But, " says
the opponent, " you have judged it unjustly. You
have charged upon it the destruction of fourteen
thousand millions of human lives. It is not answerable for a tythe of all this. It is answerable only for
the loss of life, &c., in cases of justifiable homicide,
war, injury and penal infliction. All the rest is
chargeable on the murderous wickedness of wanton
aggressors. Nor do you give it credit for the lives it
has actually preserved, and the injuries it has prevented." Answer. I do not charge injurious resistance with causing all these murders; but I do charge
it with occasioning most of them, and above all with
being no adequate preventive of them,—with not being the true method of self-preservation. It may have
preserved many lives, and prevented much injury in
particular cases, in certain localities, but what has it
done on the whole—on the great scale? And what
has it absolutely failed to do? It has absolutely
failed to preserve human life to any great extent and
to give peace to the world. The whole world is in
arms, after nearly six thousand years close adherence
to this method of self-preservation. It costs the human race more to maintain the various means of this
method, than for religion, government and education
together. There must be a delusion somewhere. If
there were no such method in operation, the worst
that could happen would be the murders, oppressions
and cruelties of unprovoked aggression. These would
be dreadful enough ; but they would be nothing in

comparison with the results heretofore experienced, and would gradually shrink away from the moral majesty of a renovated public sentiment. Besides, it must be remembered that justifiable homicide, war, injury, &c , are pleaded on all sides with equal earnestness. After a few passes with the sword, a few rounds of musketry, a few assaults and retreats, it is all self-defence—all justifiable homicide, violence and destruction. All parties are seeking only to conquer an honorable peace. One party has been wronged in point of honor, another in person, another in property, and another in imagination; all are standing on the defensive; all are for carrying out the first law of nature by the common method. There is no ultimate arbiter but the sword. Injury must be resisted with injury. There was a first aggression, but so many mutual wrongs have succeeded between the parties, that none but God can determine which is most culpable. This is the confusion which attends the operation of the general method of self-preservation. It professes to eschew all aggression, but invariably runs into it. It promises personal security, but exposes its subjects not only to aggravated assaults, but to every species of danger, sacrifice and calamity. It shakes the fist, brandishes the sword, and holds up the rod *in terrorem* to keep the peace, but constantly excites, provokes and perpetuates war. It has been a liar from the beginning. It has been a satan professing to cast out satan, yet confirming the power and multiplying the number of demons which possess our unfortunate race. It does not conduce to self-preservation, but to self-destruction, and ought therefore to be discarded.

THE OBJECTOR STILL PERSISTS—ANALOGY OF THE
ANIMALS.

But our opponent will not yield the point. "It is
the nature (says he) of all animals to fight for their
lives and their rights. It is the nature of man to do
so. He is a fighting character by the laws of his being. He always was so, and always will be, while
there is aggression, assault and abuse in the world.
When all men are willing to leave off giving just
cause of injurious resistance, there will be peace;
never before. You may make the common method
of self-preservation good or bad, a blessing or a curse,
better than nothing or worse than nothing; man will
resist—will fight—will act out his nature, cost what it
may." Answer. Not so. You assume too much.
Your argument goes too far. Can I not prove by
your own reasoning that man is an aggressor, an assailant, an offender, a robber and a murderer by nature? He has been practising all this aggression like
some of the lower animals—the beasts and birds of
prey—ever since the time of Cain. Is this a law of
his nature, as well as the other? Because he always
has done these things, will he, and must he forever
continue doing them? You say injurious resistance,
war and bloodshed will never cease till aggression
ceases. Will aggression ever cease? Can it ever
cease? Is it not a necessary result of the laws of nature? What is the conclusion from such premises but
this,—that man's nature obliges him to aggress and
resist just as he does, and there is no hope that he
will ever cease doing either. None but an atheist
ought to put forth such arguments. I deny that there
is any law or necessity of nature obliging man to in-

jure his fellow man, either offensively or defensively; any more than there is for his being a drunkard, offensive or defensive, to everlasting ages. He can cease to practice both. He can be cured of his war mania. He can be induced to abstain from committing injury by aggression,. and also from committing it in the way of resistance. The question is, whether we shall preach non-resistance to the good, as well as non-aggression to the bad; or whether we shall insist only on non-aggression, leaving the comparatively good to resist injury with injury, so long as aggression shall continue. The good wish the bad to reform. Will they return good for evil, and thereby hasten their reform? or will they return evil for evil, and thereby frustrate that reform? God has ordered the work begun and prosecuted from both ends at once; the bad to cease aggressive injury, and the good defensive injury. Which shall take the lead in the great work of reform ? Shall the good wait till the bad cease from aggression, before they leave off inflicting injury in self-defence? Christianity says no. It bids them be "the salt of the earth," and "the light of the world;" to suffer wrong rather than do wrong, "to overcome evil with good." Is this possible ? Or is there some irresistible necessity in the laws of nature, compelling mankind to maintain an endless conflict of aggression and resistance ? I deny that there is any such necessity.

COMMON METHOD OF SELF-PRESERVATION CERTAINLY FALSE.

It is plain from the foregoing discussion, that the general method of self preservation by injurious and deadly resistance to aggression, is a false method; that

it has failed; that it has defeated its own designed object; that it has constantly run into the very wrongs
it aimed to prevent; that it has made a bad matter incomparably worse; that it is not the dictate of
absolute nature, but a deplorable mistake of the
human judgment as to ways and means; and that
some other method must be substituted for it.   It is
equally plain that nature necessitates aggression as
certainly as it does injurious resistance to aggression;
that in fact it necessitates neither; and that non-resistance, as I have defined it, is no more contrary to nature than non-aggression.   Both aggressive and resistant injury can be unlearned, abandoned and forever eschewed, without annihilating or perverting
any essential constituent, element, property, quality
or capability of human beings.   More than this, men
brought up to that moral excellency will be more
thoroughly and perfectly men than in any inferior
state.   Their whole nature, physical, mental, moral
and religious, will then he more symmetrically and
gloriously developed than now.   If so, non-resistance
cannot be contrary to nature.   Nor, if embraced and
carried into practice, will it fail to ensure the most
universal and complete self-preservation.   It will
prove to be the true method demanded by that first
great law of nature.

I now confidently proceed with the assertion that
Christian non-resistance is in perfect accordance with
the known laws of nature, and absolutely necessary to
harmonize their development by correcting the un-
toward influence of many evil circumstances under
which they have heretofore acted.

FIVE GREAT LAWS OF HUMAN NATURE CONSIDERED.

Let us bring into view the prominent laws of na-

ture. I will mention five of the most fundamental:
They are self-preservation, social affinity, religious
and moral obligation, rational harmony and progression. These may be pronounced universal and eternal.
Under the law of self-preservation, which is substantially identical with self-love, man instinctively desires to exist and be happy. He dreads death; he
guards against injury; he endeavors to keep what
good he already has, and in a thousand ways strive
to acquire more. He is constantly prompted by this
law to take care of himself, and ensure his supposed
highest welfare. But the ways and means are neither
dictated nor indicated by this law. These come from
another law. Hence it not unfrequently happens that
men ignorantly resort to ways and means of preserving and benefiting themselves, which frustrate their
object, and even result in their destruction. Under
the law of social affinity the sexes unite, families are
reared up, friendships contracted, communities, states
and nations formed, and all the social relations, affections, sympathies and bonds superinduced. Man is
necessitated by this law to be a social being, and to
share the good and ill of life with others. But this
law does not necessarily teach him the best method of
social action—the true ways and means of the highest
social usefulness and enjoyment. Hence he often
forms the most unsuitable connections, and contri-
butes to uphold the most perverse social institutions.
But a social being, for better or worse he always was,
and always must be. Under the law of religious and
moral obligation he confesses, worships and serves a
God; feels a sense of dependence, gratitude and duty;
is conscious that there is right and wrong in human
conduct; that he can choose either, but that he is ac-

countable for the choice he makes—for his use or abuse of ability possessed; feels guilty when he does what he supposes to be wrong and approved when he does what he believes to be right. Hence arises a perpetual conflict between the lower and higher portions of his nature. The carnal or mere animal mind goes for unrestrained indulgence. The spiritual continually says, " do right, refrain from all else, however ardently desired. " His propensities would run riot down the broad road to destruction. But his religious and moral sentiments connect him with God and eternity, and forbid him all sensual indulgence which can endanger his spiritual welfare. He must do the will of God; must deny himself; must do right at all hazards. He must not even preserve his life or seek any good for himself by wrong doing. Thus is he checked, straitened, restrained and disciplined. But even this law, grand and powerful as it is, does not at once acquaint him with the true God, nor with the true right and wrong—the perfect righteousness. Hence, millions have worshipped false gods, been superstitiously religious, and verily thought many things were right, which were in fact utterly wrong. Yet man always was, and always must be a religious and moral being, in some way, to some extent. He cannot escape from this law of his nature. Next comes the law of rational harmony or consistency. This ever prompts men to delight in the harmony of things—the consistency and agreement of one thing with another—and of parts of things with their whole. He is uneasy, dissatisfied, disturbed and restless on account of incongruities, contradictions, incompatibilities and hostilities, in himself and all things around him. Hence his intellectual powers, and

specially his reasoning faculties, are constantly on
the stretch to detect and remove the causes of disturb-
ance, the points of contradiction. If he can do nothing else, he finds fault, grumbles and complains about
this or that presumed evil. If farther advanced, he
becomes a reformer and agitates the world. He may
be a reformer in religion, morals, government, education, science, art or whatever comes in his way—theoretical or practical. And if he cannot construct what
ought to be, he will at least destroy or modify what
ought not to be. This restless activity of the human
mind comes from a deep, undefinable, irresistible desire to get rid of contradictions and reduce things to
harmony, to consistency. This is the great desideratum. Contradiction and inconsistency are the infal-
lible indications of falsehood and wrong. For truth
and right must be harmonious. They cannot involve
contradiction and discord, where they alone exist.
Here then is a universal, irresistible law of our nature. It has done much to correct and reform the errors ensuing from human ignorance and depravity
But it has an infinite deal more to do. The fifth law
is that of progression. This follows close on the heels
of the others, or rather co-exists with them. It is this
which impels man to aspire after something higher and
better than the present. Hence he observes, imitates,
learns, inquires, invents, hopes and perseveres, im-
proves, progresses, and will forever progress amid new
wonders and with new achievements of mind world
without end. His nature will not permit him to become stationary.

THESE LAWS RADICALLY HARMONIOUS.

Now all these fundamental laws of our nature must

be radically agreeable to each other. There can be
no essential incongruity or discord among them. And
when they shall have had their perfect work, man must
be a lovely and glorious being. The human family must
be an affectionate, wise, holy, harmonious, happy
family. Look at the legitimate results. The law of
self-preservation or self-love will secure its desired object, just when the law of social affinity makes every
fellow human be a second self—a co-self—never to be
injured. This will take place when the law of religious and moral obligation completely subdues the propensities to the sense of duty, attaches the soul indissolubly to the true God, and renders right identical
with the absolute highest good. And this will be hastened by the intense workings of the law of rational
harmony, which will detect and expose error, reform
abuses, revolutionize false opinions, maxims, institutions, customs and habits, and bring to light in all
things the " most excellent way." There is a true
God, and this law will never let man rest till he finds
him. There is a real right and wrong, the eternal
reality; and this law will at length bring all men to
see and feel it. There is a consistency, an absolute
harmony of things, and this law will turn and over-
turn till it be attained. All this is possible under the
law of progression. By this knowledge will be increased, light will be added to light, truth to truth,
and triumph to triumph. Ignorance, error, folly, sin
will be left behind. Improvement will follow improvement in all that needs improvement, till the jarring
elements be reconciled, and one soft, sweet, supernal
harmony consummate the happiness of the whole creation. This is the glorious result to which the declared will of God, the predictions of his holy pro-

phets and the prayers of saints through all past generations have ever pointed, and do still look forward.
Then will there be no war, no violence, no wrong, no
sorrow.

> " All crimes shall cease, and ancient fraud shall fail;
> Returning Justice lift aloft her scale;
> Peace o'er the world her olive wand extend,
> And white robed Innocence from heaven descend "

There shall be none to hurt or destroy, for all the
earth shall be filled with the knowledge of God.

NON-RESISTANCE IN PERFECT UNISON WITH THESE LAWS.

Now, is the doctrine of Christian non-resistance
contrary to these general laws of human nature? Is
it contrary to the law of self-preservation? Does it
propose to destroy or preserve life; to increase or di-
minish human injury; to make mankind more miserable or to render them infinitely more safe, secure and
happy? It proposes the very thing which the law of
self-preservation demands, viz: the universal inviolability of human life now held so cheap and sacrificed
so recklessly. Is this doctrine contrary to the law of
social affinity? The very reverse. It stretches forth
the hand of love to the children of men, and entreats
them to consider themselves one great brotherhood;
to refrain from murdering and persecuting each other,
to love one another, to bear every thing of one another
sooner than to kill or injure each other? Is not this
just what the law of social affinity demands? Is the
doctrine contrary to the law of religious and moral obligation? It is an integral part of the divine law, declared and exemplified by the Son of God. It is the
keystone in the arch of moral obligation. And to ful-

fil it in practice is the highest obedience to God,—the
purest devotion to eternal right. It is putting duty
before all things. Is it contrary to the law of rational
harmony ? Surely not. It eschews all war, all violence, all injury, all social discord, all combatting of
wrong with wrong, evil with evil, and lays the only
ample foundation, deep on the rock of principle, for
the pacification and harmony of the world. If men
would only restrain themselves from mutual injury,
how soon would they be able to ascertain all important truths, and to correct all essential errors of theory
and practice. But now, instead of discussion and argument, brute force rises up to the rescue of discom·
fited error, and crushes truth and right into the dust.
"Might makes right, " and hoary folly totters on in
her mad career escorted by armies and navies. Is our
doctrine contrary to the law of progression ? It is a
striking fruit and proof of that law. It takes for
granted that man has been a noisy, fretful, buffeted
child long enough; that it is time for him to act like a
reasonable being; that he ought to be, and can be governed by moral power; that he has been carnally
minded long enough, and ought now to become spiritually minded: that he has quarreled, fought and been
flogged enough; that he is capable of acting from higher motives and better principles than resisting evil
with evil; and that he can, if he will only try, "overcome evil with good, " and thus approximate the angelic nature. It is emphatically a doctrine of glorious
moral and spiritual progress—of progress from barbarism to Christian perfection. Nothing can be more
untrue than that non-resistance is contrary to the
laws of nature. It is in perfect accordance with them.
It is only contrary to the false, foolish, perverse, self-

defeating methods, ways and means by which man, in his ignorance and delusion, has heretofore attempted to execute the dictates of those laws. It is at war with man's ignorance, blind self-will, and vicious habits; but not with his welfare, nor the laws of his nature. As well might the inveterate drunkard, bound to the intoxicating cup by long confirmed habit, plead that total abstinence was contrary to nature. It is in fact this very cup which is contrary to his nature; and though often resorted to for preservation and invigoration, it has crowded him to the brink of an untimely grave. Still he clings to it as his life and health. Just so our drunkards of injurious resistance. They can depend on nothing so confidently as the means of deadly resistance for self-preservation and personal security. They imagine that if they were to renounce these, their lives, rights and happiness, would have no protection left. But they will one day learn better.

A LAW OF UNIVERSAL NATURE. LIKE BEGETS ITS LIKE.

I will now introduce another law of nature—a law of universal nature—and including, of course, human beings in its scope. It is this, that like must beget its like—physical, mental, moral, spiritual. Is non-resistance contrary to this law of nature? Does it beget its like? or does it beget resistance? This is a practical question, and will settle the dispute. Either the true spirit of non-resistance begets a corresponding spirit, or it begets a violent and pugnacious spirit? Which is it? Either the practice of non-resistance tends to disarm and relax the fury of the assailing party, or to encourage, excite, and confirm

him in his attack. Which is it? If the latter, it is
contrary to that law of nature which necessitates the
generation of like by like. If the former, it harmon-
izes with that law. And if this be true, it is the very
doctrine necessary to fill the world with peace. It
is worth while then to ascertain the truth on this point.

Let me commence by asking if the very injury I
am endeavoring to get discarded is not generated by
injury? Why does the assailed person inflict injury
on the offender? "To defend himself," it will be
said. But why defend himself by doing injury to the
other party? "Because that, and that only, will effect the object." How is this certain? What puts it
into the heart or the head of the assailed party to repel injury with injury? It is like begetting its like;
injury suggesting, prompting, and producing injury.
No better way is thought of or desired, than life for
life, eye for eye, tooth for tooth, blow for blow, force
for force, injury for injury. "I will do unto him as he
hath done to me. It is good enough for him. He
shall be paid in his own coin. He shall be taught better after his own fashion." This is the feeling and
language of the Resistant. Here is a proof that the
disposition to injure begets a disposition to injure, and
the act of injury induces a counter injury. What, then,
will be the subsequent effect? If a man strike me violently, and I return the blow with equal or greater violence, will not my blow call for a third, and so on,
till the weaker party cries "hold?" This is the law
of nature. Does the opponent plead that the aggressor, being severely repelled, and knowing himself in
the wrong, will retreat and learn to be civil This
will depend on which of the parties can strike the
hardest, and injure the worst. If the aggressor be

the stronger party, he will only fight the harder, till his antagonist is subdued. If, however, he be the weaker party, he will yield from necessity and not from principle—retaining his impotent revenge in his heart, to fester there till a better opportunity. If justice or conscience ¡have anything to do in restraining him, they would work much more mightily on his soul if the injured party should refuse to strike back at all. So the argument in this case turns wholly in favor of my doctrine.

GENERAL ILLUSTRATIONS IN COMMON LIFE.

Let us now look into the common affairs of life, amid scenes familiar to common experience and observation. We see one man with very large combativeness and feeble counteracting predispositions. If this man meets with another of the same character, he is almost sure to fight, quarrel, or at least, violently dispute. He is surcharged and throws off in all directions a sort of phrenomagnetic fluid of war. No sooner does he come in contact with another like himself, than they mutually inflame each other. He carries strife and debate and violence with him whereever he goes. Even many, who are usually civil and peaceable, are presently provoked into a combat with him. He magnetises, to a certain extent, every susceptible being with whom he meets. If he can live peaceably with any, it is those only who from natural predisposition, or moral principle, are non-resistants towards him. These he will make uncomfortable ; but by bearing with him, and suffering some abuse with patience, they can keep him comparatively decent, and may pass their lives near him without any serious outbreak. Who has not seen some such persons?

And who does not know that such can never be cured
by violence and injurious resistance.   They may be
beaten and bruised half to death over and over again,
with no other result than to make them two-fold
more the children of wrath than before.   This kind
of evil is not cast out, except by prayer, fasting and
abstinence from violence.

Here is another man with overweening self-esteem.
He is proud, haughty, disdainful and overbearing in
all his ways.   What happens when two such meet?
Is there not a reciprocal inflammation of the irritable
organs?   Do they not mutually swell, defy and repel
each other?   Each will accuse the other of the same
fault, and denounce such haughtiness as intolerable
never once suspecting that it is a reflection of his own
face in the other which seems so detestable.   Suppose
one of these characters to move among other persons
ordinarily humble and unassuming.   Let him treat
them with marked neglect, scorn or indifference; and
what will be the effect?   Their moderate self-esteem
will be excited.   Their attitude will become more per-
pendicular.   Their heads will poise backward, and
they will begin to mutter, "he feels himself above
common folks; but he shall know that others are something as well as himself.   We are not to be looked
down by his contempt."   Whence this sudden rising
of self-esteem in their minds?   It has been begotten,
or at least excited, by the over-charged battery of the
magnetiser.   Like produces its like.   Reverse the
case.   Suppose a person of great talents, wealth or
weight of personal influence.   This character naturally commands great respect; but he is humble, unassuming and particularly respectful to all around: to
the poor as well as the rich, the unlearned as well as

the learned, and persons in the lower walks of life as well as those in the higher.   How is he beloved and esteemed by the majority of mankind?   "He is not proud," says one.   "He is not above any one," says another.   "I always love to meet him and be with him," says another, "because he is so kind, unassuming and friendly with every body."   Even the envious and grumbling are half disarmed when they come in contact with such a person.   Like begets its like, as before.

Yonder is a man excessively given to acquisitiveness.   He must always have the best end of a bargain. He must skin something from every one with whom he has dealings, and is sure to get the half cent whenever he "makes change."   He is never pleased but when he is feathering his own nest.   Yet no man complains of tight people more than he.   He seldom meets with a person who in his opinion is entirely willing to do unto others as he would be done unto. What is the difficulty?   This man's selfishness magnetises those with whom he deals.   His acquisitiveness excites theirs and they stand up for their own. They are not going to be cheated by him.   They are determined not to indulge his rapacious avaric . They make it a point not to let him cheat them, filch away their property in a bargain, or extort it in the shape of usury.   They even become tenacious about the half cent when they are settling with him.   And many who would not otherwise stand for a trifle make it a point not to give him the least advantage.   " Let us look out for old hunks, " say they.   The half cent is nothing, but he shall not have it.   Like produces its like.   Hence conflicts and resistance.   Reverse the character.   Suppose a generous whole souled man, always careful to give large measure and weight, always scrupulous not to exact more than his own, and always sure to throw the trifle into his neighbor's scale, rather than even seem to be small in his own favor. How many of the very same persons observed to be sharp and close with the acquisitive dealer, relax their vigilance, become indifferent about small matters, and even insist that they will not always take the half cent of a man so willing to yield it. Is not this nature in every day life?

It is not so with a blackguard and a reviler. He assails a man with hard words, abusive epithets and reviling expressions. Unless the man be particularly on his guard, or naturally of a very mild disposition, or a well principled non-resistant, he will be excited, and ten to one return a broadside as terrible as he has received. His teeth are set on edge and his tongue is fired from beneath. He rails, abuses, reviles and curses too. But let the true Christian receive this storm of envenomed words, and they strike his shield of self composure, only to rattle for a moment like hailstones on its surface, and then fall harmlessly about his feet. A second and a third discharge succeed, but he still remains calm. The assailant is half vexed, quite confounded, and soon grows ashamed of himself. He either quits the field or listens to reason, and perhaps is constrained to beg pardon for his rudeness. At all events he never remembers his abuse of a calm, kind-hearted, firm minded man, without peculiar mortification. And if every man who occupies a place in the better ranks of society would treat him in the same manner, he would ultimately be entirely cured of the bad humor about his tongue. So true is it that "a soft answer turneth away wrath; but grievous words stir up anger."

These familiar workings of this law of nature ought to open the most unwilling eyes to the fact, that non-resistance, instead of being contrary to nature, is in strict accordance with it. And if it is confessedly the object of good men to do away with violence, cruelty, murder, and all the great crimes which blast the happiness of humanity, they ought to know that it never can be done by rendering evil for evil—injury for injury. Like must produce its like, and unless we oppose the injuries of evil-doers with a disposition and treatment the very contrary of theirs, we shall only incite, confirm and educate their evil hearts to worse and worse conduct. We shall only reproduce manifold the very evils we so strenuously resist. Though the injuries we do them are done only in resistance of aggression, still they follow the same law. They produce their like. They breed a fresh brood of injuries. If this be not strictly true in each individual case, it is true on the great whole. The effect, directly or indirectly, sooner or later, will be produced.

SPECIAL ILLUSTRATIONS—FACTS FROM REAL LIFE.

I now propose to offer a series of facts from real life, illustrative of the truths for which I am contending, and in confirmation of my arguments.

SUBDUED PRIDE AND SCORN.

A lady, in one of the neighboring towns to that in which the writer resides, had repeatedly treated a well disposed young man with marked contempt and unkindness. Neither of them moved in the upper circles of society, but the lady, without cause, took numerous occasions to cast reproachful reflections on the young man as beneath her notice, and unfit to be treated with common respect. This lady had the misfortune to meet with a considerable loss in the destruction of a valuable chaise, occasioned by the running away of an untied horse. She had borrowed the horse and vehicle, and was required to make good the damage. This was a serious draft on her pecuniary resources, and she felt much distressed by her ill fortune. The young man, being of a kind and generous disposition, and determined to return good for evil, instantly set himself about collecting money for her relief. Subscribing liberally himself, and actively soliciting others, he soon made up a generous sum, and before she became aware of his movement, appeared before her and placed his collection modestly at her disposal. She was thunderstruck. He left her without waiting for thanks or commendation. She was entirely overcome, wept like a child, and declared she would never be guilty again of showing contempt, speaking reproachfully of, or treating with unkindness, him or any other fellow creature. Was there anything in all this contrary to nature?

THE MAN WHOSE TEMPER WAS BROKEN.

A man of my accquaintance, on hearing some remarks I had made on this subject, observed that he knew, by experience, the doctrine was correct; and though he himself had never practised non-resistance from principle in his general life, he practised it from impulse on one occasion with astonishing success. He was brought up with a childless uncle of his, who was remarkable for violent anger when excited, and for the cruelty with which he beat his cattle, and such boys as he had taken to bring up, whenever they pro-

voked his vengeance. He could bear but little from
boy or brute, and, therefore, was a frequent and furious whipper till considerably past the middle age of
life.   The narrator stated that he was well nigh a
man grown, when on a certain occasion the two went
into the woods with the team, in winter, to take home
fuel. At length, when on their way out of the woods
through an unbeaten path, the sled struck some obstacle concealed under the snow, and the team was
completely set. The uncle, provoked at this inter-
ruption, cried out to his nephew, who held the whip,
to drive on and put the cattle through. He shouted,
and used the lash to order, but in vain, the sled was
fast. "My uncle flew into a most violent rage," said
he, "and seizing a club from the load came furiously
at me with terrible threats, as the author of the
whole mischief. I felt entirely innocent, and for the
moment determined I would not further resist my
uncle's wrath than to exchange my whip for his club,
which was nearly of the size of a common sled stake.
As he rushed upon me, with uplifted weapon, I firmly
grasped it with one hand, reached out my cart-whip
with the other, and said: 'Here, uncle you shall not
beat me with such a thing—take the whip.'   He instantly relinquished the stick of wood, and seizing the
cart-whip, beat me outrageously over the head,
shoulders and back. He then offered me the whip, exclaiming with stern vehemence, — 'now drive that
team home!' I calmly but firmly replied, no; I have
done my best, and shall not try again; drive it yourself, uncle. Upon this he violently assailed the poor
oxen, shouting, screaming, and beating them quite as
mercilessly as he had me, till he fairly gave out from
exhaustion. Pausing for a moment's rest, and com-

ing a little to his reason, he commenced searching for
the obstacle, and soon found that a large sized sapling
had fallen across the path and become firmly bedded
in the subsequent snows.   Having ascertained this,
he directed me to cut off the trunk, in order to its removal.   I commenced, my back and shoulders smart-
ing grievously from their undeserved stripes.   When
partly through, I looked up at my uncle and said—
'uncle do you feel any better for the cruel beating you
have given me?'   He looked pale and conscience-
stricken, and without a word of reply started for
home.   I extricated the load, and without further
difficulty drove the team to its destination.   From
that time, sir, my uncle never broke out into his old
gusts of passion; never struck, scolded or abused me;
never mistreated his cattle; and, going quite to the
opposite extreme, suffered himself to be several times
almost imposed on by a mischievous lad he had tak-
en to bring up, without inflicting a blow, or even expressing anger.   I continued with him several years,
and seeing him, as I thought, grown too lax in correcting the lad just named, I one day asked him what
had so entirely changed his conduct?   He looked me
in the face with a melancholy expression.   Said he—
'do you remember the cruel flogging I gave you when
that load of wood got set in the snow?'   'Too well,'
answered I.   'That broke my temper,' said he.   'I
never had such feelings before.   I have never been
the same man since.   I then solemnly vowed never
to strike another cruel blow on man or beast while I
lived.   And I have scarcely felt a disposition to do
so since.'   Large tears rolled down his cheeks, and
he turned away in silence.   'Many a time have I
thought of that matter,' said the nephew, since my

uncle has gone to the grave. It convinces me your doctrine is the truth.'' How does it impress my reader? Does it indicate that non-resistance is contrary to or consonant with the laws of nature?

COLORED WOMAN AND THE SAILOR.

A worthy old colored woman in the city of New York was one day walking along the street on some errand to a neighboring store, with her tobacco pipe in her mouth, quietly smoking. A jovial sailor, rendered a little mischievous by liquor, came sawing down the street, and, when opposite our good Phillis, saucily crowded her aside, and with a pass of his hand knocked her pipe out of her mouth. He then halted to hear her fret at his trick, and enjoy a laugh at her expense But what was his astonishment, when she meekly picked up the pieces of her broken pipe, without the least resentment in her manner, and giving him a dignified look of mingled sorrow, kindness and pity, said, ''God forgive you, my son, as I do.'' It touched a tender cord in the heart of the rude tar. He felt ashamed, condemned and repentant. The tear started in his eye; he must make reparation. He heartily confessed his error, and thrusting both hands into his two full pockets of ''change,'' forced the contents upon her, exclaiming, ''God bless you, kind mother, I'll never do so again.''

THE HAYMAKERS.

Two neighbors were getting hay from adjoining lots of marsh land. One had the misfortune to mire his team and load so as to require aid from the other. He called to him for assistance with his oxen and men. But his neighbor felt churlish, and loading him with reproaches for his imprudent management, told him to help himself at his leisure. With considerable difficulty he extricated his load from the mire and pursued his business. A day or two after, his churlish neighbor met with a similar mishap. Whereupon the other, without waiting for a request, volunteered with his oxen and rendered the necessary assistance. The churl felt ashamed of himself. His evil was overcome by his neighbor's good, and he never afterwards refused him a favor.

THE TWO STUDENTS.

Two students of one of our Universities had a slight misunderstanding. One of them was a warm-blooded Southron. He conceived himself insulted, and began to demand satisfaction, according to Southern notions of honor. He was met with a Christian firmness and gentleness. The other calmly told his excited fellow-student he could give only Christian satisfaction in any case; that he was not conscious of having intended him either injury or insult, and that if he could be convinced he had wronged him at all, he was willing to make ample reparation. The Southron boiled over with chivalrous indignation for a few moments, discharged a volley of reproachful epithets, and threatened to chastise his cowardly insolence. But nothing could move the other's equanimity. Without the slightest indication of fear or servility, he met his opponent's violence with true heroism, declared that they had hitherto been friends, and he meant to maintain his friendly attitude, however he might be treated, and conjured the threatener to consider how unworthy of himself his present temper, language and conduct were. His manner, look, words, tone, had their effect. The flush of anger turned to a blush of shame and compunction. The subdued Southron stepped frankly forward, reached forth his trembling hand, and exclaimed—"I have spoken and acted like a fool; can you forgive me?" "With all my heart," was the cordial response. Instantly they were locked in each other's embrace; reconciliation was complete; and they were evermore fast friends. The substance of this anecdote was given by a worthy minister of the Baptist persuasion, after one of my lectures on non-resistance; and I think he represented himself as a witness of the scene.

TWO NEIGHBORS AND THE MANURE.

Two of my former neighbors had a slight controversy about a few loads of manure. One of them was the other's tenant. The lessor had distinctly stipulated to reserve all the manure of the stable, and had offset it with certain privileges and favors to the lessee. But as the lessee had purchased and consumed from abroad a considerable amount of hay, he claimed a portion of the manure. He proposed leaving the case to the arbitration of certain worthy neighbors. The other declined all reference to a third party, alleging that they both knew what was right, and ought to settle their difficulties between themselves. But the lessee contrived to have a couple of peaceable neighbors at hand one day, and in their presence renewed with earnestness his proposal to leave out the case to their decision. The other, grieved at his pertinacity, promptly replied: "I have nothing to leave out; I have endeavored to do as I agreed, and to treat you as I would be treated. God Almighty has planted something in all our breasts which tells us what is right and wrong; if you think it right to carry off that manure, do so just when you please; and I pledge myself never to trouble you with even a question about the matter again." This was effectual. The tenant felt his error; all was quiet; the claim expired at the bar of conscience; and non-resistant kindness and decision healed all contention. This was related to me by one of the friends selected as a judge and decider in the case. His peculiar comment was "That was one of the greatest sermons I ever heard."

IMPOUNDING THE HORSE.

" A man approached his neighbor in great anger one afternoon, saying—'Sirrah! I found your horse loose in the road this morning, and put him in the pound, where he now is. If you want him, go and pay the fees and take him out. And I give you notice now, that just as often as I find him loose in the highway, I will impound him at your cost.' 'And I,' said the neighbor, 'looking out of my window, this morning, saw your cows in my corn field. I drove them all out, and turned them into your pasture. I now give you notice that as often as I find them in my cornfield, I will do just so again.' The first was humbled, reconciled, sent to the pound, paid the fees, and restored his neighbor's horse to him with an honorable apology for his ill temper. "—*Anonymous.*

TWO NEIGHBORS AND THE HENS.

A man in New Jersey told Henry C. Wright the following story respecting himself and one of his neighbors: " I once owned a large flock of hens; I generally kept them shut up. But, one spring, I concluded to let them run in my yard, after I had clipped their wings, so they could not fly. One day, when I came home to dinner, I learned that one of my neighbors had been there, full of wrath, to let me know my hens had been in his garden, and that he had killed several of them, and thrown them over into my yard. I was greatly enraged because he had killed my beautiful hens that I valued so much. I determined at once to be revenged, to sue him, or in some way get redress. I sat down and ate my dinner as calmly as I could. By the time I had finished my meal, I became more cool, and thought that perhaps it was not best to fight with my neighbor about hens, and thereby make him my bitter, lasting enemy. I concluded to try another way, being sure that it would be better.

After dinner I went to my neighbor's. He was in his garden. I went out and found him in pursuit of one of my hens with a club, trying to kill it. I accosted him. He turned upon me, his face inflamed with wrath, and broke out in a great fury—'You have abused me. I will kill all your hens, if I can get at them. I never was so abused. My garden is ruined.' 'I am very sorry for it,' said I. 'I did not wish to injure you, and now see that I have made a great mistake in letting out my hens. I ask your forgiveness, and am willing to pay you six times the damage.'

The man seemed confounded. He did not know what to make of it. He looked up at the sky—then down at the earth—and then at the poor hen he had been pursuing, and said nothing. Tell me now, said I, 'what is the damage, and I will pay you six-fold; and my hens shall trouble you no more. I will leave it entirely to you to say what I shall do. I cannot afford to lose the love and good will of my neighbors, and quarrel with them, for hens or anything else.

'I am a great fool!' said the neighbor. 'The damage is not worth talking about; and I have more need to compensate you than you me, and to ask your forgiveness than you mine.' "—*Wright's Kiss for a Blow.*

HENRY AND ALBERT.

"I write chiefly to give you an account of the power of love that took place in the family of an old friend of mine, who is now no more. Besides other children he left two sons, Henry, aged about twenty, and Albert about sixteen. The latter possessed what is called a bad, ungovernable temper, that gave his mother much trouble; and she (probably in a pet) told Henry he must whip him. He did; but Albert resisted, and he received a severe thrashing. But it did not tame him at all, and he vowed that he never would speak to Henry again until he was old enough to have revenge. While he stayed at home (some months, I believe,) he never spoke to Henry. After this he went to sea, and was absent four or five years. But Albert was a boy of many good qualities. He laid up money; and while the vessel was loading and unloading at the ports of the distant countries he visited, he made short excursions into the interior, and made use of his eyes and ears to improve his mind and gain what information he could, and came back an amazingly stout, athletic young man, and apparently greatly improved. He was frank and social with the rest of the family, but not a word did he say to Henry. The latter by this time had become a Methodist preacher, and Albert's conduct towards him grieved him to the heart. After a time Henry went to Albert, and with tears in his eyes, said to him: 'Albert, I cannot possibly live in this way any longer. Your silence I cannot bear another hour. You remember you said, when you had whipped me you would speak to me again; I am now ready to receive your punishment. Let us go to the barn; I will pull off my coat—I promise you that I will make no resistance, and you may whip me as long as you please; and we will then be friends. I never should have struck you, if mother had not requested it. I am sorry that I did.' Albert's stout heart could bear blows in almost any quantity without shrinking, but Henry's love he could not withstand. It melted his proud spirit instantly, and in a moment he was bathed in tears. They embraced each other directly. For a time their love was too great for utterance, but soon Albert expressed his regret for what he had said; and they are now, for aught that I know, two as loving brothers as any in the county. And to God, the God of peace be all the glory —*Letter from Alfred Wells in the Practical Christian.*

THE SUBDUED HATTER

Some nineteen or twenty years ago, when I was in the hatting business, I employed a man by the name of Jonas Pike, from Massachusetts, who was a most excellent workman in the manufacture of hats. But he was one of that kind of journeymen who would have their trains, as they were familiarly called amongst us in that day. Therefore as a natural consequence he was without comfortable clothing the most of the time. After he got a shop he would work very industriously until he had earned from twenty to thirty and sometimes forty dollars worth of clothing ; (for he was always in want of clothing when he commenced work;) and then he would get on one of his trains, and dispose of every article of his clothing that would fetch six cents, expending all for whiskey. When all was gone, and he began to cool off a little, he would be very ugly; sometimes he would fret and scold, and then he would coax and plead, to have me trust him for a hat or something else, that he might sell, and thereby get more whiskey. When I refused him, he would become very angry and threaten to whip me, which I told him he might do as soon as he pleased. But said he: ' I will not do it in your own shop; if I had you out of doors I would thrash you like a sack.' After hearing him repeat these sayings several times, I walked out at the door. I then spoke to him, saying, 'I am now out of the shop, thou canst whip me if thou wishest to do so very much,' at which he stepped out of the shop, came furiously towards me, squaring himself for a box, and struck me a blow on the breast, at which I put my hand upon my cheek, and held it down to him, saying, 'now strike here, Jonas.' He looked at me with surprise and astonishment, then turning round saying at the same time, 'd—n you, if you will not fight, I will let you alone.' He went into the shop, sat down and was quiet. He got sober and went to work, and ever after was affectionate and kind, and very peaceable with me. I employed him several times afterwards to work for me, and he was always very peaceable and obliging.—*Letter from Erastus Hunchett in the Practical Christian.*

THE REVOLUTIONARY SOLDIER.

"A beloved brother, now dead, related to me a circumstance of his life, which I think is worth preserving. He was a soldier in the revolutionary war. After he came here, he became religious, and was convinced that all 'wars and fightings' are contrary to the Gospel of Christ. His zeal in advocating his principles, stirred up the enmity of a wicked man in the neighbourhood, who threatened, when his son came home from the army, he would flog him.

"Sure enough, when the son came home, the old man told such stories to him about this brother, that it excited him to that degree, that he came to the house where my brother lived, in a rage, determined to fight. My brother expostulated with him, and endeavoured, by all the means in his power, to allay his anger, and deter him from his purpose; but all would not do ; fight he must, and fight he would.

" 'Well,' says the brother, 'if we must fight, don't let us be like cats and dogs, fighting in the house; so go out into the field.'

"To this he assented. When they had got into the field, and the young bully had stripped himself for the fight my brother looked him in the face, and said, 'Now you are a great coward.' 'Coward! don't call me a coward.' 'Well, you are one of the greatest cowards I ever saw.' 'What do you mean?' 'I mean as I say; you must be a very great coward to go fighting a man who will not fight you.' 'What, don't you mean to fight me ?' 'Not I ; you may fight me as much as you please, I shall not lift up a finger against you.' 'Is that your principle?' 'Yes, it is; and I mean to be true to it.' The spirit of the young soldier fell; and, stretching out his arm he said, 'Then I would sooner cut off that arm than I would strike you.' They then entered into an explanation, and parted good friends."—*Non-Resistant.*

EX-PRESIDENT JEFFERSON AND THE COOPER'S SHOP.

"The following was related, many years since, by
one of the parties, who was a very respectable citizen
of Montgomery county, Pa., since deceased:

During the presidential term of Thomas Jefferson,
two young men from Pennsylvania took a lease from
him of his merchant mill at Monticello, one of the
stipulations of which was that the landlord should
erect for their use, within a given period, a cooper's
shop. The time for a meeting of Congress soon ar-
riving, the President had to repair to Washington to
attend to his official duties, where he remained a long
time absorbed in national concerns, and the building
of the cooper's shop was entirely forgotten by him.
Not so with his tenants, whose daily wants constantly
reminded them of the provisions contained in the
lease; and finally they determined to erect it themselves, and charge the cost of it to their landlord. On
the return of the President to his mansion, the parties
met to settle a long account current, which had been
running during his absence. The items were gone
over and scrutinized one by one, and all were found
satisfactory but the charge for building the cooper's
shop, to which he objected, alleging that he could
have erected it with his own workmen. Several attempts were made to effect a settlement, but they always failed when they came to the cooper's shop. The
young men became warm and zealous in the affair;
and the parties, instead of getting nearer together,
found themselves at every interview wider apart.

In this state of affairs, the father of the young men,
who was a mild, affable, conciliating gentleman, possess-
ing some knowledge of the world and its ways, arrived
on a visit to his sons, who informed him of their diffi-

·culty with their landlord. He requested them to leave it to him, observing that he thought he could effect an amicable settlement in the case. This course was accordingly acceded to, and in due time he waited on the President with the account. It was scanned and agreed to, except the charge for building the shop, which, he said, with some firmness, he should not allow for reasons stated. His opponent, observing his apparent decision on the subject, very gravely remarked: ' Well, friend Jefferson, it has always been my practice through life, to yield rather than to contend. ' Immediately on this remark being made, the president's chin fell on his breast for an instant, when raising his head in an erect position, he observed in a very emphatic manner, ' a very good principle, Mr. Shoemaker, and I can carry it as far as you can: let the account for the cooper's shop be allowed. ' Thus ended the difficulty, and the parties continued their friendly regard for each other till death separated them. And the cultivation of a similar disposition, ' to follow peace with all men, ' would terminate thousands of difficulties, add much to the happiness of individuals, and tend to promote the general harmony and order of society. ''—*Farmer's Cabinet.*

WILLIAM LADD AND NEIGHBOR PULSIFER.

The late William Ladd, denominated the apostle of the peace cause, used to relate the following anecdote: " I had a fine field of grain growing upon an out-farm, some distance from the homestead. Whenever I rode by I saw my neighbor Pulsifer's sheep in the lot destroying my hopes of a harvest. These sheep were of the gaunt, long legged kind, active as spaniels—they could spring over the highest fence, and no wall could keep them out. I complained to neighbor Pulsifer, and sent him frequent messages, but all without avail. Perhaps they would be kept out for a day or two, but the legs of his sheep were long and my grain rather more tempting than the adjoining pasture. I rode by again—the sheep were all there—I became angry, and told my men to set the dogs on them, and if that would not do, I would pay them if they would shoot them.

"I rode away much agitated, for I was then not so much of a peace man as I am now, and I felt literally full of fight. All at once a light flashed in upon me. I asked myself, would it not be well for you to try in your own conduct the peace principle you are preaching to others? I thought it all over, and settled down my mind as to the best course to be pursued.

"The next day I rode over to see neighbor Pulsifer. I found him chopping wood at his door. 'Good morning neighbor.' No answer. 'Good morning,' I repeated. He gave a kind of grunt like a hog, without looking up. 'I came,' continued I, 'to see you about the sheep.' At this he threw down his axe, and exclaimed in a most angry manner: 'Now arn't you a pretty neighbor to tell your men to kill my sheep! I heard of it —a rich man like you to shoot a poor man's sheep!'

'I was wrong,' neighbor said I, 'but it won't do to let your sheep eat up all that grain; so I came over to say that I would take your sheep to my homestead pasture, and put them with mine; and in the fall you may take them back; and if any one of them is missing you may take your pick out of my whole flock.' Pulsifer looked confounded; he did not know how to take me. At last he stammered out, 'Now Squire, are you in earnest?'' 'Certainly I am,' I answered: 'it is better for me to feed your sheep in my pasture on grass, than to feed them here on grain; and I see the fence cannot keep them out.'

"After a moment's silence—'The sheep shan't trouble you any more,' exclaimed Pulsifer, 'I will fetter them all. But I'll let you know, when any man talks of shooting, I can shoot too; and when they are kind and neighborly, I can be kind too.' The sheep never again trespassed on my lot. 'And, my friends,' (continued Father Ladd, addressing his audience,) 'remember that when you talk of injuring your neighbors, they talk of injuring you. When nations threaten to fight, other nations will be ready, too. Love will beget love—a wish to be at peace will keep you at peace. You can overcome evil only with good, there is no other way.' "—*Democratic Review.*

CONCLUSION.

The foregoing illustrations are from the common affairs of life, and though not involving cases of extreme personal danger and escape, are nevertheless pertinent and important. They show the adaptation of Christian non-resistance to human nature in the ten thousand occurrences of personal difficulty. They demonstrate that it is not contrary to nature, but is peculiarly suited to allay and purify the rising passions of men, that the worst of people are favorably affected by its interposition; that the decent sort might be preserved by it from numberless contentions; and that instead of counteracting the law of self-preservation, it is the highest and surest method of securing the great ends of that law. This will be more fully demonstrated by a continuation of illustrations involving cases of greater peril and deliverance, in the next chapter. In the mean time I can hardly refrain from pressing upon the reader's understanding and conscience, the question, Is not the doctrine contended for, most Christian, most rational, most excellent, most admirably adapted to promote peace on earth and good will among mankind? Is it not just what poor groaning nature needs, to soothe, restore it to health, and carry it forward to its glorious destiny? It will appear more and more sound and lovely the more it is investigated.

> "O, when will man unshackled rise,
>   From dross of earth refined—
> Read mercy in his neighbor's eyes.
>   And be forever kind?"

CHAPTER V.

The Safety Of Non-Resistance.

Raymond the traveller—Agent of the Bible Society in Tex-
as—The young man near Philadelphia—Robert Barclay
and Leonard Fell—Archbishop Sharpe—Rowland Hill—
Two Methodist Non-Resistants—The two New Zealand
chiefs—The Missionary and Arabs—A Christian tribe in
Africa—The Moravian Indians—The Moravians of Grace
Hill—The Shakers—The Indians and the Quaker family
—The Indians and the Quaker Meeting—The Christian
town in the Tyrol—Captain Back, the Quakers, and the
Maylays—Jonathan Dymond—Colony of Pennsylvania.

I have been endeavoring to demonstrate in the
preceding chapter that non-resistance, instead of being contrary to nature, is in perfect accordance with
all her fundamental laws.   I intend in the present
chapter to complete that demonstration by a further
illustration of the superior general safety of non-resistance.   This will be done by anecdotes and historical
facts, showing its actual workings in many cases of
imminent danger.   I do not undertake to prove that
the practice of non-resistance will always preserve the
life and personal security of its adherents, but only
that it generally will.   Jesus, the apostles, and thousands of Christian martyrs were slain notwithstanding their non-resistance.   Doubtless others will be
wronged, outraged, and murdered in time to come,
notwithstanding the same safeguard.   Exceptions do
not disprove a general rule.   As the advocates of
deadly resistance do not contend that it always en-

sures the preservation of life and personal security, so
neither do I contend that Christian non-resistance
will do it. They contend that discretionary resistance is safer than non-resistance; that its general
tendency, despite of incidental failures, is to pre
serve life and render personal safety secure.   I
contend for the exact reverse.   Here is an important
issue.   The deadly resistants affirm the superior safety of their principle of action ; the non-resistants of
theirs.   The parties are in direct contradiction.
Which of them is right?   The resistants have lost, according to Dr. Dick, 14,000,000,000, and according
to Mr. Burke, 35,000,000,000 of human lives, since
their experiment commenced.   Can non-resistants
make a greater loss than this?   Can their principle
of action result in a greater expenditure of life and
happiness?   No.   Under the most unfavorable circumstances they will not lose in the proportion of one
to a thousand, and a few centuries of perseverance in
their principle would totally extinguish the fires of
human violence throughout the earth.   Let us proceed to show that the practice of non-resistance is pre-
eminently safe.

RAYMOND THE TRAVELLER.

Raymond, a celebrated European traveller, bears
the following testimony:

Speaking of the Spanish smugglers, he says: ''These
smugglers are as adroit as they are determined, are
familiarized at all times, with peril, and march in the
very face of death.   Their first movement is a never-
failing shot, and certainly would be an object of
dread to most passengers; for where are they to be
dreaded more, than in deserts, where crime has noth-

ing to witness it, and the feeble no assistance ?   As
for myself, alone and unarmed, I have met them without anxiety, and have accompanied them without fear.
We have little to apprehend from men whom we inspire with no distrust or envy, and everything to expect in those from whom we claim only what is due
from man to man.   The laws of nature still exist for
those who have long shaken off the laws of civil government.   At war with society, they are sometimes
at peace with their fellows.   The assassin has been
my guide in the defiles of the boundaries of Italy; the
smuggler of the Pyrenees has received me with a welcome in his secret paths.   Armed, I should have been
the enemy of both ; unarmed, they have alike respected me.   In such expectation, I have long since
laid aside all menacing apparatus whatever.   Arms
may, indeed, be employed against the wild beast, but
no one should forget that they are no defence against
the traitor ; that they irritate the wicked, and intimi-
date the simple ; lastly, that the man of peace, among
mankind, has a much more sacred defence—his character''.

AGENT OF THE BIBLE SOCIETY IN TEXAS.

"In the early part of the year 1833, or about that
time, an agent of the Bible Society was travelling in
Texas.   His course lay through a piece of woods,
where two men waylaid him with murderous intentions, one being armed with a gun, the other with a
large club.   As he approached the place of their con-
cealment, they rushed towards him; but finding that
no resistance was offered, they neither struck nor
fired.   He began to reason with them; and, presently,
they seemed less eager to destroy him in haste.   After

a short time, he prevailed on them to sit down with
him upon a log, and talk the matter over deliberately; and finally, he persuaded them to kneel with
him in prayer, after which they parted with him in a
friendly manner."—*Calumet.*

THE YOUNG MAN NEAR PHILADELPHIA.

"A few years since, a young man in the vicinity
of Philadelphia, was one evening stopped in a grove,
with the demand, 'Your money, or your life.' The
robber then presented a pistol to his breast. The
young man, having a large sum of money, proceeded
leisurely and calmly to hand it over to his enemy, at
the same time setting before him the wickedness and
peril of his career. The rebukes of the young man
cut the robber to the heart. He became enraged,
cocked his pistol, held it to the young man's head,
and with an oath, said, 'Stop that preaching, or I will
blow out your brains.' The young man calmly replied,—"Friend, to save my money, I would not risk
my life; but to save you from your evil course, I
am willing to die. I shall not cease to plead with
you." He then poured in the truth still more earnestly and kindly. Soon the pistol fell to the ground;
the tears began to flow; and the robber was overcome.
He handed the money all back with the remark, "I
cannot rob a man of such principles."

ROBERT BARCLAY AND LEONARD FELL.

Robert Barclay, the celebrated apologist of the
Quakers, and Leonard Fell, a member of the same So
ciety, were severally attacked by highwaymen in England, at different times. Both faithfully adhered to
their non-resistance principles, and both signally tri-

umphed. The pistol was levelled at Barclay, and a determined demand made for his purse. Calm and self-possessed, he looked the robber in the face, with a firm but meek benignity, assured him he was his and every man's friend, that he was willing and ready to relieve his wants, that he was free from the fear of death through a divine hope in immortality, and therefore was not to be intimidated by a deadly weapon, and then appealed to him, whether he could have heart to shed the blood of one who had no other feeling or purpose but to do him good. The robber was confounded; his eyes melted; his brawny arm trembled; his pistol fell to his side; and he fled from the presence of the non-resistant hero whom he could no longer confront.

Fell was assaulted in a much more violent manner. The robber rushed upon him, dragged him from his horse, rifled his pockets, and threatened to blow out his brains on the spot, if he made the least resistance. This was the work of a moment. But Fell experienced no panic. His principles raised him above the fear of man and of death. Though forbidden to speak, he calmly but resolutely reproved the robber for his wickedness, warned him of the consequences of such a course of life, counselled him to reform, and assured him that while he forgave this wanton outrage on himself, he hoped for his own sake he would henceforth betake himself to an upright calling. His expostulation was so fearless, faithful and affectionate, that the robber was struck with compunction, delivered back his money and horse, and bade him go in peace. Then, with tears filling his eyes, he exclaimed,—"May God have mercy on a sinful wretch," and hastened out of sight.

ARCHBISHOP SHARPE.

" Archbishop Sharpe was assaulted by a footpad on the highway, who presented a pistol and demanded his money. The Archbishop spoke to the robber in the language of a fellow man and of a Christian. The man was really in distress, and the prelate gave him such money as he had, and promised that, if he would call at the palace he would make up the amount to fifty pounds. This was the sum of which the robber had said he was in the utmost need. The man called and received the money. About a year and a half afterwards, this man came again to the palace, and brought back the same sum. He said that his circumstances had become improved, and that, through the "astonishing goodness" of the Archbishop, he had become "the most penitent, the most grateful, and happiest of his species." Let the reader consider how different the Archbishop's feelings were from what they would have been if by his hand this man had been cut off."—*Dymond.*

ROWLAND HILL.

I have seen an impressive anecdote of this distinguished London preacher, which I have failed to find among my papers, notwithstanding considerable search. I have but an imperfect recollection of the details, but the substance was as follows: Mr. Hill was returning from an excursion out of the city. A man suddenly beset him from the wayside, pistol in hand, and demanded his purse. Mr. Hill calmly scrutinized his countenance with a look of compassion, and, while taking out his money, remarked to the robber that he did not look like a man of that bloody calling, and he was afraid some extreme distress had driven him to the crime. At the same time he inquired how much he stood in need of. The man was affected, declared this was his first offence, and pleaded the distress of his family as his only excuse. Mr. Hill kindly assured him of his sympathy, and of his willingness to relieve him. He gave him a certain sum on the spot, and promised him further aid, if he would call at his house. The robber was melted into tears, humbly thanked his benefactor, and hastened towards the city. Mr. Hill, desirous of knowing the whole truth of the matter, directed his servant to follow the man home. This was accordingly done, and it was ascertained that the poor man occupied a miserable tenement in an obscure street, where his wife and children were on the verge of starvation. He was seen to hasten first to a bakery, and then home with a few loaves of bread. His wife received the bread with joy, but with astonishment, expressing her hope that her dear husband had obtained it by none but innocent means. The children cried for joy as they began to satiate their hunger, and the father alone looked sad.

Mr. Hill benevolently took this man under his immediate care, provided a tenement for his family, and made him his coachman. He proved to be a remarkably honest and industrious man: and in a little time became a convert to experimental religion, and connected himself with Mr. Hill's church. For fifteen years he walked with such Christian circumspection as to command the entire confidence of all who knew him. At length he died in the triumphs of hope. His pastor preached an effecting funeral sermon on the occasion, in which for the first time he communicated the affair of the robbery, and took occasion to impress on his auditors the excellency of Christian forbearance, kindness and compassion towards the guilty. Here was a man withdrawn from an awful course of crime, and by divine grace rendered a child of God—an exemplary and beloved brother in Christ. How different might have been the result, had Rowland Hill either resisted him with deadly weapons, or taken the same pains to hand him over to the government, that he did to befriend him ? O how lovely is true righteousness ! How comely is Christian non-resistance ! How safe !

THE METHODIST NON-RESISTANTS.

"The Rev. John Pomphret, an English Methodist minister, always advocated the practical applicability of the 'peace doctrine,'—'If a man will sue thee at the law and take away thy coat, let him have thy cloak also, and if he compel thee to go with him a mile, go with him twain, '—always declaring that if he should be attacked by a highwayman, he should put it in practice. Being a cheese-monger, (he preached to do good, not for wages,) on his return from market one day, after he had received a large amount of money from his customers for the purpose of replenishing his year's stock, he was accosted by a robber, demanding his money, and threatening his life if he refused. The reverend peace-man coolly and kindly replied, ' Well, friend, how much do you want, for I will give it to you, and thus save you from the crime of committing highway robbery ? ' ' Will you certainly give me what I require, ' asked the robber. ' I will, in truth, if you do not require more than I have got, ' replied the non-resistant. ' Then, I want fifteen pounds, ' (about seventy-five dollars.) The required

sum was counted out to him, and in gold, instead of
in bank-bills, which, if the numbers had been observed, the reverend father, by notifying the bank,
could have rendered uncurrent, besides leaving the
robber liable to detection in attempting to pass them,
telling him at the same time why he gave the gold instead of bank-notes; and saying, ' Unfortunate man,
I make you welcome to this sum. Go home. Pay
your debts. Hereafter, get your living honestly. '

"Years rolled on. At length, the good preacher
received a letter, containing principal and interest,
and a humble confession of his sins, from the robber
saying that his appeals waked up his slumbering
conscience, which had given him no rest till he had
made both restitution and confession, besides wholly
changing his course of life. "

Reader ! Conscience is a more powerful principle
than fear: and more difficult to stifle. Precaution
may make the wicked feel safe; but conscience is not
to be thus put off, or its remonstrances hushed by
thoughts of safety. Punishment appeals to physical
fear, which a due precaution against detection quiets;
but cultivate and properly direct the consciences of
children, and urge home moral accountability upon
adults, and an effectual reformation will thereby be
brought about. Reader ! I leave it for you to say,
whether this is not a law of mind.

The Rev. Mr. Ramsay, another Methodist clergyman, was wholly dependent for his living on the quar-
terly collection made by his people, which was barely
sufficient, by the greatest economy, to support his
family. On the night that one of these collections was
taken up, he was obliged to preach six miles distant
from his home, and the night was too stormy to allow

of his return.   During the night, two robbers broke
into his house, called up Mrs. Ramsay and her sister,
(there were no men living in the house,) and demanded
to know where the money was.   Mrs. R., in her night
dress, lit the candle, and leading the way to the bu-
reau that contained the precious deposit, procured the
key, opened the drawer, and pointing out the money
as it lay in a handkerchief, said, ' This is all we have
to live on.   It is the Lord's money.   Yet, if you will
take it, there it is. '   With this remark, she left them
and retired to bed.   The next morning, the money to
a cent was found undisturbed.   Conscience here, as
above, was appealed to, and with the same results.—
Fowler's Phrenological Journal.

THE TWO NEW ZEALAND CHIEFS.

The following highly interesting fact relates to the
conduct of two principal persons in New Zealand; one
of them of the Ngapuhi tribe, and the other residing
at Otumoetai in that island.   We are indebted for
this truly gratifying account of highly elevated feelings (in men, until lately, looked upon as incorrigible
savages,) to the Rev. Messrs. Taylor and Wilson, sta-
tioned among them.   It is extracted from the (Church
of England) Missionary Register, for January, 1841.
Who can but wish that all our countrymen, recently
gone thither, may acquire this truly Christian spirit
in settling disputes, and forget the warlike methods
which, to the disgrace of Christianity, are practiced
in Europe and elsewhere, by the professed followers of
the Saviour of the world, the Prince of Peace?

THE MISSIONARY AND ARABS.

Mr. King, a respectable Missionary in Palestine,
mentions a remarkable instance of the effect of pacific

conduct, which operated to preserve his own life and
the lives of a considerable party, when assailed
by a powerful band of Arabs on the plain of
Esdracion. The party of Mr. King had lost a trunk,
which had been stolen, as they supposed, by some
Arabs. In consequence of this they seized two Arabs,
and bound them together with cords, believing them
to be the robbers. These they took along with them, on
their journey, contrary to the wishes of Mr. King.
Soon the whole party were attacked by a band of
Arabs, who set their brethren at liberty. Great was
the alarm; but one of the party of Mr. King being
about to fire on the Arabs, Mr. King objected, and
others interposed in season to prevent the evil intended. Every part of the Kofila was soon attacked,
and Mr King observes:

"It was no time to parley. All was confusion.
No one knew whether he expected life or death.
The latter, however, seemed to stare us in the face.
Our baggage was at length cut off: there seemed to
be a little cessation on the part of the Arabs, and I
hoped that, contented with our baggage, they would
let us go in peace. But in a moment I saw them
coming on again, and I thought that probably all was
lost, and that, as they had stopped our baggage, they
now intended to take our lives. It was an awful
moment. I could only say, 'Heaven defend us.' I
was in front of the Kofila, and a little distance ahead,
when an Arab Sheik came flying up to me on his
steed with a large club in his hand. Making a halt,
I addressed him, calling him brother ; and said, 'do
me no harm, I have not injured you.'

"I spoke to him words of peace and gentleness.
Upon this he let down his club which he had been

brandishing, halted, listened, and presently turned away; and soon after I saw him driving back some of our pursuers, and the cry of *ayman* (safety) was heard by us ; and I need not say it was a welcome sound to our ears.

"The baggage, too, to my surprise, was soon after permitted to come on. The attack was a gallant one, and made by the Arabs, as if they were determined to carry their point through life or death. And I have no doubt that had one of their party fallen by our hands, it would have been the signal for the slaughter of us all.''

A CHRISTIAN TRIBE IN AFRICA.

The following interesting incident is copied from "Moffat's Southern Africa." It occurred in a remote village of native Africans, the inhabitants of which had received Christian teachers, and were just emerging from a state of barbarism:

"This little Christian band had met on a Sabbath morning, with the people, in the centre of the village, to hold the early prayer meeting, before the services of the day. They were scarcely seated when a party of marauders approached from the interior, whither they had gone for plunder, and not having succeeded to their wishes, had determined to attack this village on their return.

"Moshen (the chief) arose, and begged the people to sit still, and trust in Jehovah, while he went to meet the marauders. To his inquiry what they wanted, the appalling reply was, 'your cattle, and it is at your peril you raise your weapons to resist.' 'There are my cattle,' replied the chief, and then retired and resumed his position at the prayer meeting.

A hymn was sung, a chapter read, and then all kneeled in prayer to God, who only could save them in their distress.

The sight was too sacred and solemn to be gazed on by such a band of ruffians ; they all withdrew from the spot, without touching a single article belonging to the people."

THE MORAVIAN INDIANS.

A small tribe of Indians in the West had been converted by the Moravian Missionaries to their faith, one article of which is that Christians cannot innocently fight, even to save their lives. A while afterwards this little pacific tribe was thrown into extreme alarm and distress by intelligence that a much larger tribe at some distance to the North meditated a hostile incursion upon them. They called on their Moravian teachers for advice. They did not see how they could possibly avoid fighting under such circumstances. They feared they should be utterly destroyed by their enemies unless they resisted. They were affectionately and earnestly exhorted to abide by their principles, and trust in God. They were told of the superior numbers of the hostile tribe, and how uncertain their fate would be, should they presume to make deadly weapons their reliance. They were advised to select a few of their oldest men as a delegation, and to supply them with such presents of choice eatables and other articles, as their circumstances would afford. This venerable delegation, entirely unarmed, except with their baskets of parched corn, fruits, &c., were to advance and meet the enemy at a distance from the village. Meantime those who remained behind were to engage in united supplication to the Father of spirits for his protection. The advice was accepted, faithfully followed, and successfully carried out. The hostile Indians were advancing upon their defenceless prey. The old men, laden with their simple but significant presents, went out to meet them. The invaders, astonished and awed by the spectacle, halted on their tomahawks. When the delegates reached the advanced lines they opened as if by magic, and a passage was freely offered them to the presence of the commanding Sachem. Their age and meekness commanded his instant admiration. He accepted their presents, listened to their counsels of peace, declared his friendship, sent them back with assurances that no injury should be done by his tribe to theirs, and declared that if any attack should be made upon them he and his people would be their protectors. So these truly Christian Indians escaped entirely the threatened injury, and sat down in their cabins, surrounded by bulwarks of security such as nothing but these divine principles and their all perfect Author can establish.

THE MORAVIANS OF GRACE HILL.

During the rebellion in Ireland, in 1793, the rebels, it is stated, had long meditated an attack on the Moravian settlement at Grace Hill, Wexford county. At length, in fulfilment of their threats, a large body of them marched to the town. But the Moravians, true to their principles, in this trying emergency, did not meet them in arms; but assembling in their place of worship, besought Jehovah to be their shield and protector in the hour of danger. The hostile bands who had expected an armed resistance, were struck with astonishment at a sight so unexpected and impressive; they heard the prayers and praises of the Moravians; they listened to supplications in their own behalf; and after lingering in the streets a whole day and night, they with one consent turned and marched away, without having injured a single individual.

THE SHAKERS.

" The Shakers, too, have experienced that protection which pacific principles are sure to afford. About the year 1812, the inhabitants of Indiana were harassed by incursions from the Indians; but the Shakers who lived in that region, although they were without garrisons and without arms, appear to have been entirely secure, while the work of destruction was going on around them. The question was once put to a prominent chief, why the Indians did not attack and injure the Shakers, as well as others. His answer was, ' We warriors meddle with a peaceable people ! That people, we know, will not fight. It would be a disgrace to hurt such a people.' "—*The Friend of Peace*.

THE INDIANS AND THE QUAKER FAMILY.

An intelligent Quaker of Cincinnatti, related to me the following circumstance, as evidence that the principle of non-resistance possesses great influence, even over the savage. During the last war, a Quaker lived among the inhabitants of a small settlement on our western frontier. When the savages commenced their desolating outbreaks, every inhabitant fled to the interior settlements, with the exception of the Quaker and his family. He determined to remain, and rely wholly upon the simple rule of disarming his enemies with entire confidence and kindness. One morning he observed, through his window, a file of savages issuing from the forest in the direction of his house. He immediately went out and met them, and put out his hand to the leader of the party. But neither he nor the rest gave him any notice—they entered his house, and searched it for arms, and had they found any, most probably would have murdered every member of the family. There were none, however, and they quietly partook of the provisions which he placed before them, and left him in peace. At the entrance of the forest, he observed that they stopped and appeared to be holding a council. Soon one of their number left the rest, and came towards his dwelling on the leap. He reached the door, and fastened a simple white feather above it, and returned to his band, when they all disappeared. Ever after, that white feather saved him from the savages; for whenever a party came by and observed it, it was a sign of peace to them. In this instance, we discover that the law of kindness disarmed even savage foes, whose white feather told their red brethren that the Quaker was a follower of Penn, and the friend of their race.—*Montgomery's Law of Kindness.*

THE INHABITANTS OF THE LOOCHOO ISLANDS.

These islands are in the neighborhood of the Chinese Sea. They have been visited by several navigators, and, among others, by Captain Basil Hall. He states that they have neither forts, men-of-war, garrisons, arms, nor soldiers, and appear to be quite ignorant of the art of war. They are kind, hospitable, courteous, and honest, and acquainted with some of the mechanical arts. Well, what has been their fate? Reasoning on the rash premises of our opponents, we should predicate their utter destruction. But have

they been destroyed? Quite the contrary. They
have been preserved in peace, safety and happiness.
"The Olive branch" is planted on their shores, and
they sit beneath it, "no man daring to make them
afraid."—*McCree.*

THE INDIANS AND THE QUAKER MEETING.

I have somewhere met with the following anecdote,
but cannot now recollect where. In western New
York or Pennsylvania, in a period of Indian hostilities, a neighborhood of Friends, who had erected a log
meeting house, regularly assembled after the manner
of their Society. They had been invited and urged
to come within the protection of the army and its fortifications. But they refused to abandon their testimony by expressing any such reliance on the arm of
flesh. They were consequently exposed to the attack
of every wandering horde of warriors on that part of
the frontier. One day, while sitting in silent devotion in their rude meeting house, a party of Indians
suddenly approached the place, painted and armed
for the work of slaughter. They passed to and fro by
the open door of the house, looking inquisitively within and about the building, till having sufficiently re-
connoitred the quiet worshippers, they at length re-
spectfully entered and joined them. They were met
by the principal Friends with the outstretched hand
of peace, and shown to such seats as the house afforded, which they occupied in reverent silence till
the meeting was regularly dissolved. They were then
invited to one of the nearest dwellings by the leading
man of the Society, and hospitably refreshed. On
their departure the Indian chief took his host aside,
and pledged him and his people perfect security from

all the depredations of the red men. Said he, " when Indian come to this place, Indian meant to tomahawk every white man he found. But when Indian found white man with no guns, no fighting weapons, so still, so peaceable, worshipping Great Spirit, the Great Spirit say in Indian's heart—no hurt them, no hurt them !" So saying, he gave a final friendly grip and hastened off with his followers to find that sort of white man whose confidence in deadly weapons invited destruction.

THE CHRISTIAN TOWN IN THE TYROL.

The following is a beautiful extract from one of Lydia Maria Child's letters to the *Boston Courier*. I commend it not merely to a pleasant reading, which it will be sure to receive, but to a most serious consideration:

'To-day is Christmas. From East to West, from North to South, men chant hymns of praise to the despised Nazarene, and kneel in worship before his cross. How beautiful is this universal homage to the principle of love !—that feminine principle of the universe, the inmost centre of Christianity. It is the divine idea which distinguishes it from all other religions, and yet the idea in which Christian nations evince so little faith, that one would think they kept only to swear by that gospel which says, 'swear not at all.'

"Centuries have passed, and through infinite conflict have 'ushered in our brief day;' and is there peace and good will among men ? Sincere faith in the words of Jesus would soon fulfil the prophecy which angels sung. But the world persists in saying, 'this doctrine of unqualified forgiveness and perfect love, through beautiful and holy, cannot be carried into practice now; men are not prepared for it.' The same spirit says, 'it would not be safe to emancipate slaves; they must first be fitted for freedom.' As if slavery ever could fit men for freedom, or war ever lead the nations into peace ! Yet men who gravely utter these excuses, laugh at the shallow wit of that timid mother, who declared that her son should never venture into the water till he had learned to swim.

"Those who have dared to trust the principles of peace, have always found them perfectly safe. It can never prove otherwise, if accompanied by the declaration that such a course is the result of Christian principle, and a deep friendliness for humanity. Who seemed so little likely to understand such a position, as the Indians of North America? Yet how readily they laid down tomahawks and scalping knives at the feet of William Penn! With what humble sorrow they apologized for killing the only three Quakers they were ever known to attack ! 'The men carried arms,' said they, 'and therefore we did not know they were not fighters. We thought they pretended to be Quakers, because they were cowards.' The savages of the East, who murdered Lyman and Munson, made the same excuse. 'They carried arms,' said they, 'and so we supposed they were not Christian missionaries, but enemies. We would have done them no harm, if we had known they were men of God.'

"If a nation could but attain to such high wisdom as to abjure war, and proclaim to all the earth, 'we will not fight under any provocation ; if other nations have aught against us, we will settle the question by umpires mutually chosen ;' think you that any nation would dare to make war upon such a people?

Nay, verily, they would be instinctively ashamed of
such an act, as men are now ashamed to attack a
woman or a child. Even if any were found mean
enough to pursue such a course, the whole civilized
world would cry fie upon them, and, by universal consent, brand them as poltroons and assassins. And
assassins they would be, even in the common accepta·
tion of the term. I have read of a certain regiment
ordered to march into a small town (in the Tyrol, I
think,) and take it. It chanced that the place was
settled by a colony who believed the gospel of Christ,
and proved their faith by works. A courier from a
neighboring village informed them that troops were
advancing to take the town. They quietly answered,
'If they will take it they must.' Soldiers soon came
riding in with colors flying, and fifes piping their shrill
defiance. They looked round for an enemy, and saw
the farmer at his plough, the blacksmith at his anvil,
and the women at their churns and spinning-wheels.
Babies crowed to hear the music, and boys ran out
to see the pretty trainers, with feathers and bright
buttons, 'the harlequins of the nineteenth century.'
Of course, none of these were in a proper position to
to be shot at. 'Where are your soldiers?' they
asked. "We have none,' was the brief reply. 'But
we have come to take the town.' 'Well, friends, it
lies before you.' 'But is there nobody here to fight?''
'No we are all Christians.' Here was an emergency
altogether unprovided for by the military schools.
This was a sort of resistance which no bullet could
hit; a fortress perfectly bomb-proof. The commander
was perplexed. 'If there is nobody to fight with, of
course we cannot fight,' said he. 'It is impossible to
take such a town as this.' So he ordered the horses

heads to be turned about, and they carried the human animals out of the village, as guiltless as they entered, and perchance somewhat wiser.

"This experiment on a small scale indicates how easy it would be to dispense with armies and navies, if men only had faith in the religion they profess to believe. When France lately reduced her army, England immediately did the same; for the existance of one army creates the necessity of another, unless men are safely ensconced in the bomb-proof fortress above mentioned."

CAPT. BACK—THE QUAKERS—THE MALAYS.

I shall make no apology for adding to the foregoing the following extracts from another article, by the same fruitful and instructive pen.

"It is a mission worth living for, if I can give the least aid in convincing mankind that the Christian doctrine of overcoming evil with good, is not merely a beautiful sentiment, as becoming to the religious, as are pearls to the maiden's bosom, but that it is really the highest reason, the bravest manliness, the most comprehensive philosophy, the wisest political economy.

The amount of proof that it is so, seems abundant enough to warrant the belief that a practical adoption of peace principles would be always safe, even with the most savage men, and under the most desperate circumstances, provided there was a chance to have it distinctly understood that such a course was not based on cowardice, but on principle.

"When Capt. Back went to the Polar regions in search of his friend, Capt. Ross, he fell in with a band of the Esquimaux, who had never seen a white man.

The chief raised a spear to hurl it at the stranger's head; but when Capt. Back approached calmly and unarmed, the spear dropped, and the rude savage gladly welcomed the brother man, who had trusted in him. Had Capt. Back adopted the usual maxim, that it is necessary to carry arms in such emergencies, he would probably have occasioned his own death and that of his companions. "

Perhaps the severest test to which the peace principles were ever put, was in Ireland, during the memorable rebellion of 1798. During that terrible conflict the Irish Quakers were continually between two fires. The Protestant party viewed them with suspicion and dislike because they refused to fight or to pay military taxes; and the fierce multitude of insurgents deemed it sufficient cause of death, that they would neither profess belief in the Catholic religion nor help them fight for Irish freedom. Victory alternated between the two contending parties, and, as usual in civil war, the victors made almost undiscriminate havoc of those who did not march under their banners. It was a perilous time for all men: but the Quakers alone were liable to a raking fire from both sides. Foreseeing calamity, they had, nearly two years before the war broke out, publicly destroyed all their guns, and other weapons used for game. But this pledge of pacific intentions was not sufficient to satisfy the government, which required warlike assistance at their hands. Threats and insults were heaped upon them from all quarters; but they steadfastly adhered to their resolution of doing good to both parties, and harm to neither. Their houses were filled with widows and orphans, with the sick, the wounded and the dying, belonging both to the loyalists and the rebels. Sometimes, when the Catholic insurgents were victorious, they would be greatly enraged to find Quaker houses filled with Protestant families. They would point their pistols and threaten death, if their enemies were not immediately turned into the street to be massacred. But the pistol dropped, when the Christian mildly replied, "Friend, do what thou wilt, I will not harm thee, or any other human being." Not even amid the savage fierceness of civil war, could men fire at one who spoke such words as these. They saw that this was not cowardice, but bravery very much higher than their own.

On one occasion, an insurgent threatened to burn down a Quaker house unless the owner expelled the Protestant women and children who had taken refuge there. "I cannot help it," replied the Friend; "so long as I have a house, I will keep it open to succor the helpless and distressed, whether they belong to thy ranks, or those of thy enemies. If my house is burned, I must be turned out with them, and share their affliction." The fighter turned away and did the Christian no harm.

The Protestant party seized the Quaker schoolmaster of Ballitore, saying they could see no reason why he should stay at home in quiet, while they were obliged to defend his property. "Friends, I have asked no man to fight for me," replied the schoolmaster. But they dragged him along, swearing that he should at least stop a bullet. His house and schoolhouse were filled with women and children, who had taken refuge there; for it was an instructive fact, throughout this bloody contest, that *the houses of the men of peace were the only places of safety.* Some of the women followed the soldiers, begging them not to take away their friend and protector, a man who had expended more for the sick and starving, than others did for arms and ammunition. The schoolmaster said, "Do not be distressed, my friends. I forgive these neighbors; for what they do, they do in ignorance of my principles and feelings. They may take my life, but they cannot force me to do injury to one of my fellow creatures." As the Catholics had done, so did the Protestants; they went away, and left the man of peace safe in his divine armor.

The flames of bigotry were, of course, fanned by civil war. On one occasion, the insurgents seized a wealthy old Quaker, in very feeble health, and threatened to shoot him, if he did not go with them to a Catholic priest to be christened. They had not led him far, before he sank down from extreme weakness. "What do you say to our proposition?" asked one of the soldiers, handling his gun significantly. The old man quietly replied, "If thou art permitted to take my life I hope our Heavenly Father will forgive thee." The insurgents talked apart for a few moments, and then went away, restrained by a power they did not understand.

Deeds of kindness added strength to the influence of gentle words. The officers and soldiers of both parties had had some dying brother tended by the Quakers, or some starving mother who had been fed, or some desolate little ones who had been cherished. Whichever party marched into a village victorious, the cry was, "Spare the Quakers! They have done good to all, and harm to none." While flames were raging, and blood flowing in every direction, the houses of the peace makers stood uninjured.

It is a circumstance worthy to be recorded, that,

during the fierce and terrible struggle, even in counties where Quakers were most numerous, but one of their society fell a sacrifice.

That one was a young man, who, being afraid to trust peace principles, put on a military uniform, and went to the garrison for protection. The garrison was taken by the insurgents, and he was killed. "His dress and arms spoke the language of hostility," says the historian, "and therefore invited it."

A few years ago, I met an elderly man in the Hartford stage, whose conversation led me to reflect on the baseness and iniquity often concealed behind the apparent glory of war. The thumb of his right hand hung down, as if suspended by a piece of thread; and some of the passengers enquired the cause; "A Malay woman cut the muscle with her sabre," was the reply.

"A Malay woman!" they exclaimed. "How came you fighting with a woman?"

"I did not know she was a woman, for they all dress alike there," said he. "I was on board the U. S. ship Potomac, when it was sent out to chastise the Malays for murdering the crew of a Salem vessel. We attacked one of their forts, and killed some two hundred or more. Many of them were women; and I can tell you, the Malay women are as good fighters as the men."

After answering several questions concerning the conflict, he was silent for a moment, and then added, with a sigh:

"Ah, that was a bad business. I do not like to remember it; I wish I had never had any thing to do with it. I have been a seaman from my youth, and I know the Malays well. They are a brave and honest people. Deal fairly with them, and they will treat you well, and may be trusted with untold gold. The Americans were to blame in that business. The truth is, Christian nations are generally to blame, in the outset, in all the difficulties with less civilized people. A Salem ship went to Malacca to trade for pepper. They agreed to give the natives a stated compensation, when a certain number of measures full of pepper were delivered.

"Men, women and children were busy picking pepper and bringing it on board. The Captain proposed that the sailors should go on shore and help them; and the natives consented, with the most confiding good nature. The sailors were instructed to pick till evening, and then leave the baskets full of pepper around the bushes, with the understanding that they were to be brought on board by the natives in the morning. They did so, without exciting any suspicion of treachery. But in the night the baskets were all conveyed away, and the vessel sailed away, leaving the Malays unpaid for their valuable cargo. This, of course, excited great indignation, and they made loud complaints to the commander of the next American vessel that arrived on that coast. In answer to a demand of redress from the Government, they were assured the case should be represented, and the wrong repaired. But 'Yankee cuteness' in cheating a few savages, was not sufficiently uncommon to make any great stir, and the affair was soon forgotten. Some time after, another Captain of a Salem ship played a similar trick, and carried off a still larger quantity of stolen pepper. The Malays, exasperated beyond measure, resorted to Lynch law, and murdered an American crew that landed there about the same time. The U. S. ship Potomac was sent out to punish them for the outrage; and, as I told, we killed some two hundred men and women. I sometimes think that our retaliation was not more rational or more like Christians than theirs."

"Will you please," said I, "to tell me what sort of revenge *would* be like Christians?"

He hesitated and said it would be a hard question to answer. "I never felt pleasantly about that affair," continued he; "I would not have killed her if I had known she was a woman."

I asked why he felt any more regret about killing a woman than killing a man?

"I hardly know why myself," answered he. "I don't suppose I should, if it were a common thing for women to fight. But we are accustomed to think of them as not defending themselves; and there is something in every human heart that makes a man unwilling to fight in return. It seems mean and dastardly, and a man cannot work himself up to it."

"Then, if one nation *would* not fight, another *could* not," said I.

"What if a nation, instead of an individual, should make such an appeal to the manly feeling, which you say is inherent in the heart?"

"I believe other nations would be ashamed to attack her," he replied. "It would take away all the glory and excitement of war, and the hardiest soldier would shrink from it, as from cold-blooded murder."

"Such a peace establishment would be at once cheap and beautiful," rejoined I; and so we parted.

JONATHAN DYMOND—COLONY OF PENNSYLVANIA.

I shall relieve myself, and edify my readers, by concluding this chapter with a somewhat extended extract from the Essays of Jonathan Dymond. It is from that part of his third essay, headed, *"The probable practical effects of adhering to the moral law in respect to war."* It is exceedingly pertinent, lucid and convincing. He says:

"It is never to be forgotten that our apparent interests in the present life are sometimes, in the economy of God, made subordinate to our interests in futurity. Yet, even in reference only to the present state of existence, I believe that we shall find that the testimony of experience is, that forbearance is most conducive to our interests. There is practical truth in the position, that, 'When a man's ways please the Lord,' he 'maketh even his *enemies to be at peace with him.'*

"The reader of American history will recollect, that in the beginning of the last century a desultory and most dreadful warfare was carried on by the natives against the European settlers; a warfare that was provoked—as such warfare has almost always originally been—by the injury and violence of the [nominal] Christians. The mode of destruction was secret and sudden. The barbarians sometimes lay in wait for those who might come within their reach, on the highway or in the fields, and shot them without warning, and sometimes they attacked the Europeans in their houses, 'scalping some, and knocking out the brains of others.' From this horrible warfare the inhabitants sought safety by abandoning their houses, and retiring to fortified places, or to the neighborhood of garrisons; and those whom necessity still compelled to pass beyond the limits of such protection, provided themselves with arms for their defence. But amidst this dreadful desolation and universal terror, the

Society of Friends, who were a considerable portion of the whole population, were steadfast to their principles. They would neither retire to garrisons, nor provide themselves with arms. They remained openly in the country, whilst the rest were flying to the forts. They still pursued their occupations in the fields or at their homes, without a weapon either for annoyance or defence. And what was their fate? They lived in security and quiet. The habitation, which, to his armed neighbor, was the scene of murder and of the scalping knife, was to the unarmed Quaker a place of safety and of peace. *Three* of the Society were, however, killed. And who were they? They were three who abandoned their principles. Two of these victims were men who, in the simple language of the narrator, 'used to go to their labor without any weapons, and trusted to the Almighty, and depended on his providence to protect them (it being their principle not to use weapons of war to offend others, or to defend themselves), *but a spirit of distrust* taking place in their minds, they took weapons of war to defend themselves, and the Indians who had seen them several times without them and let them alone, saying they were peaceable men and hurt nobody, therefore they would not hurt them—now seeing them have guns, and supposing they designed to kill the Indians, they therefore shot the men dead. The third whose life was sacrificed was a woman, 'who had remained in her habitation,' not thinking herself warranted in going 'to a fortified place for preservation,' neither she, her son, nor daughter, nor to take thither the little ones: but the poor woman after some time began to let in a slavish fear, and advised her children to go with her to a fort not far from their dwelling. She went; and

shortly afterwards 'the bloody, cruel Indians, lay by
the way, and killed her.'

"The fate of the Quakers during the rebellion in
Ireland was nearly similar. It is well known the
Rebellion was a time not only of open war but of cold-
blooded murder; of the utmost fury of bigotry, and
the utmost exasperation of revenge. Yet the Quakers
were preserved even to a proverb; and when strangers
passed through streets of ruin, and observed a house
standing uninjured and alone, they would sometimes
point, and say, 'That, doubtless, is the house of a
Quaker.' So complete indeed was the preservation
which these people experienced, that in an official
document of the Society they say, 'no member of our
Society fell a sacrifice but one young man; and that
young man had assumed regimentals and arms.'

"It were to no purpose to say, in opposition to the
evidence of these facts, that they form an exception
to a general rule. The exception to the rule consists
in the *trial* of the experiment of non-resistance, not
in its *success*. Neither were it to any purpose to say,
that the savages of America, or the desperadoes of
Ireland, spared the Quakers because they were *previously* known to be an unoffending people, or because
the Quakers had *previously* gained the love of these by
forbearance or good offices. We concede all this: it
is the very argument which we maintain. We say,
that a *uniform, undeviating* regard to the peaceable
obligations of Christianity *becomes the safeguard of
those who practice it*. We venture to maintain that
no reason whatever can be assigned, why the fate of
the Quakers would not be the fate of *all* who should
adopt their conduct. No reason can be assigned why,
if their numbers had been multiplied ten-fold, or a

hundred-fold, they would not have been preserved. If there be such a reason, let us hear it. The American and Irish Quakers were, to the rest of the community, what one nation is to a continent. And we must require the advocate of war to produce (that which has never yet been produced) a reason for believing, that although individuals exposed to destruction were preserved, a nation exposed to destruction would be destroyed. We do not, however, say that if a people, in the customary state of men's passions, should be assailed by an invader, and should on a sudden choose to declare that they would try whether Providence would protect them—of such a people we do not say that they would experience protection, and that none of them would be killed. But we say that the evidence of experience is, that a people who habitually regard the obligations of Christianity in their conduct towards other men and who steadfastly refuse, through whatever consequences, to engage in acts of hostility, *will experience protection in their peacefulness.* And it matters nothing to the argument, whether we refer that protection to the immediate agency of Providence, or to the influence of such conduct upon the minds of men.

Such has been the experience of the unoffending and unresisting, in individual life. A *National* example of a refusal to bear arms, has only once been exhibited to the world; but that one example has proved, so far as its political circumstances enabled it to prove all that humanity could desire and all that skepticism could demand, in favor of our argument.

THE COLONY OF PENNSYLVANIA.

"It has been," says he, "the ordinary practice of

those who have colonized distant countries, to force a footing; or to maintain it with the sword. One of the first objects has been to build a fort, and to provide a military. The adventurers became soldiers, and the colony was a garrison. Pennsylvania was, however, colonized by men who believed that war was absolutely incompatible with Christianity, and who, therefore, resolved not to practice it. Having determined not to fight, *they maintained no soldiers* and *possessed no arms.* They planted themselves in a country that was surrounded by savages, and by savages who knew they were unarmed. If easiness of conquest, or incapability of defence, could subject them to outrage, the Pennsylvanians might have been the very sport of violence. Plunderers might have robbed them without retaliation, and armies might have slaughtered them without resistance. If they did not give a temptation to outrage, no temptation could be given. *But these were the people who possessed their country in security, whilst those around them were trembling for their existence.* Theirs was a land of peace, whilst every other was a land of war. The conclusion is inevitable, although it is extraordinary; they were in no need of arms, *because they would not use them.*

"These Indians were sufficiently ready to commit outrages on other states, and often visited them with desolation and slaughter; with that sort of desolation and that sort of slaughter which might be expected from men whom civilization had not reclaimed from cruelty, and whom religion had not awed into forbearance. 'But whatever the quarrels of the Pennsylvania Indians were with others, they uniformly respected and held, as it were, sacred, the territories of William Penn.' 'The Pennsylvanians never lost a man, woman or child by them; which neither the colony of Maryland nor that of Virginia could say, no more than the great colony of New England.'

"The security and quiet Pennsylvania was not a transient freedom from war, such as might accidentally happen to any nation. She continued to enjoy it 'for more than seventy years,' and 'subsisted in the midst of six Indian nations, without so much as a militia for her defence.'

"I cannot wonder that these people were not molested, extraordinary and unexampled as their security was. There is something so noble in this confidence in the Supreme Protector, in this utter exclusion of 'slavish fear,' in this voluntary relinquishment of the means of injury or of defence, that I do not wonder that even ferocity could be disarmed by such virtue. A people generously living without arms amidst nations of warriors! Who would attack a people such as this? There are few men so abandoned as not to respect such confidence. It were a peculiar and an unusual intensity of wickedness that would not even revere it.

And when was the security of Pennsylvania molested, and its peace destroyed? When the men who had directed its counsels, and *who would not engage in war, were outvoted in its legislature;* when *they who supposed that there was greater security in the sword than in Christianity, became the predominating body.* From that hour the Pennsylvanians transferred their confidence in Christian principles, to a confidence in arms; and *from that hour to the present they have been subject to war.*

Such is the evidence, derived from a national example, of the consequences of a pursuit of the Christian policy in relation to war. Here are a people who absolutely refused to fight, and who incapacitated themselves for resistance by refusing to possess arms; and these were the people whose land, amidst surrounding broils and slaughter, was selected as a land of security and peace. The only national opportunity which the virtue of the Christian world has afforded us of ascertaining the safety of relying upon God for defence, has determined that it is safe."

CHAPTER VI.

GENERAL OBJECTIONS ANSWERED.

1. Impracticable till the millennium—Principles of the millennium—Extracts from Professor Upham—2. Extremely difficult if not impossible—Hollowness of the objection—Battle at the passage of the Traun in Austria—3. More difficulty in small than large matters—Illustrations : The profane swearer reproved and subdued—The Christian slave and his enemy— How to overcome evil—Henry C. Wright and his assailant— The victorious little boy—Colony of Practical Christians— The avenger stayed—Conclusion.

The present chapter will be devoted to the consideration and removal of sundry common objections to the doctrine of Christian non-resistance.

OBJECTION I. IMPRACTICABLE TILL THE MILLENNIUM.

"Your doctrine may be true in its principles, and in its ultimate requirements; but it must be impracticable till the millennium. *Then,* when the whole human race shall have become regenerate, its sublime morality will be the spontaneous development of all hearts. Under existing circumstances, while there is so much depravity, and such multitudes of men are restlessly bent on aggression, it is obviously impracticable. The wicked would shortly exterminate the righteous were the latter to act on non-resistant principles."

ANSWER.—I affirm the exact contrary; viz., that the righteous would exterminate the wicked in the best sense of the word, were they to act on strict non-resistant principles. They would immediately usher in the millennium with all its blessings, were they to act on these principles in true and persevering fidelity. How else is it imaginable that any such state as the millennium should ever be developed among mankind? Is it to come arbitrarily and mechanically? Is it to come "with observation," the full grown production of some absolute miracle? Is not the kingdom of heaven "within" and "among" men, and thence, like leaven hid in three measures of meal, destined to ferment and rectify the whole mass? Ought not each true Christian's heart to be a germ of the millennium, and each Christian community a proximate miniature of it? If not, what is the evidence that men have been born again—that there is any such thing as *regeneration?* If professing to be disciples of Christ, they are unable, even by divine grace, to practice the precepts of their Lord and Master merely because the unregenerate around them are *so wicked,* what is their religion, their profession, their regeneration *worth?*

The objection before us involves such extreme incongruities, that it can be entertained only for a moment. Let us examine it. 1. It presupposes that Jesus Christ enjoined on his disciples, duties for the whole period preceding the millennium, which he knew they could not perform until the arrival of the latter period, and yet gave them no intimation of that fact. 2. It presupposes that Jesus enjoined many particular duties for which there will be no possible occasion in

the millennium, and which therefore can never be fulfilled. 3. It presupposes that the principles, dispositions and moral obligation of men in the millennium
will be essentially different from what the New Testament requires them to be now.

Is there any doubt in respect to these three statements? It is certain that Jesus apparently inculcates
his non-resistant precepts as *now* binding and practicable,—and that he gives no intimation of their *im-
practicability* till some remote future period. Was
this *design, chance or mistake!* In either case it
derogates from the honor of the Redeemer. It is not
to be presumed.

It is equally certain, on the objector's theory, that
Christ enjoined particular duties for which there can
be no possible occasion in the millennium. In the
millennium there will be no occasion to put in practice
the precept "Resist not evil;" for there will be no evil-
doers to forbear with. In that day there will be no
occasion for a man, when smitten on one cheek, to
turn the other; when distrained of his coat, to give up
his cloak; when persecuted and reviled, to bless; when
trespassed upon, to forgive; and no occasion to love
his enemy, do good to his hater, or pray for his injurer:
For there will be none to harm or destroy in all God's
holy mountain. There can be no occasion for non-
resistance where there is no aggression, injury or insult. So that the objector virtually makes the Son of
God appear in the highest degree ludicrous and absurd.
He makes him say, "Ye have heard that it hath been
said, An eye for an eye, and a tooth for a tooth; but
I say unto you that ye resist not evil," in the millennium when there will be none. "And if any man smite
thee on thy right cheek," in the millennium, when all

shall be love and kindness, "turn unto him the other also." "And whosoever will sue thee at the law" in the millennium, when the law of love shall be universally obeyed, "and take away thy coat, let him have thy cloak also." "Love your enemies," in the millennium, when you have no enemies; "bless them that curse you," when there are none to curse; "do good to them that hate you," when all love you; forgive offences "till seventy times seven," when offences shall be unknown; feed your foes, when all are friends; and "overcome evil with good," when no evil remains!

These are sublime virtues which you are to practice, not *now,* when there are so many occasions for them, and when they might exert such a powerful influence in favor of my religion as contrasted with the spirit of this world—*not now;* for they are *impracticable;* the unbelieving world is *too wicked* for such an exemplification of righteousness; but *in the millennium.* *Then* practice them, when you find no occasion for them, and when it will be absolutely impossible to fulfill them for want of an opportunity. "For then all shall know and serve the Lord, from the least unto the greatest!!" Is the great Teacher to be thus understood? Who will presume to say it?

The third statement is also true. The objection presupposes that the principles, dispositions and moral obligations of men in the millennium will be essentially different from what the New Testament requires them to be *now.* This is an error so fundamental and yet so common among professing Christians, that it ought to be thoroughly exploded. Professor Upham has done this so effectually, in his "Manual of Peace," that I cannot refrain from presenting my readers with the following excellent extract.

PRINCIPLES OF THE MILLENNIUM.

"' Are we to expect a new code, a new system of methods of operation? Are we to expect a new Saviour, a new crucifixion, a new and amended edition of the New Testament? Certainly not. The doctrines of the millennium are the doctrines of to-day; the principles of the millennium are the very principles which are obligatory on the men of the present generation; the bond which will exclude all contention and bind together all hearts, will be nothing more nor less than the gospel of Christ.

" The gospel is a book of principles—of great, operative, unchangeable principles. Men condemn it because they do not understand it; even Christians may be fairly charged with treating it with no small degree of disregard, because, in their worldliness, they have neglected to estimate its heights and depths. If heaven could be brought down to the earth—if Europe and America, and all other continents and parts of the world, could, at the present moment, be peopled with angels, and with seraphic natures,—the gospel, just as it stands, would be sufficient to guide and govern them. The blessed companies of the heavenly world, unlike the children of men, would ask no higher and better code. But can we regard it as allowable, under any assignable circumstances, for an angel to retaliate upon an angel, for a seraph to exercise hostility upon a seraph, for one of these holy beings to hold in his own hands the right of extinguishing the life of another? What sort of heaven would that be which should be characterized by the admission of such a principle? And we may ask, further, what sort of a millennium will that be which shall be characterized, either practically or theoretically, in the same way? When men are fully restored to the favor of God, whether in heaven or on earth, is there to be one code, one set of governmental principles for them, and another for other holy beings? Certainly not. In all the great matters of right and duty, the law of seraphs is the law of angels, and the law of angels is the law of men. If it is utterly and absolutely inconsistent with our conceptions of the heavenly world, that the power of life and death should be taken from the hands of Jehovah and that angels and seraphs should have the right to extinguish each other's existence, it is equally difficult to conceive of such a right in the millennium. And if it will not be right for the men of the millenium to exercise the power of life and death over each other, it is not right for them now. We have the same code of government now which we shall have then; we have the New Testament now and we shall have it then; and not only that, we shall understand it better and love it more. Nothing will be added to it; nothing will be taken from it. If it does not now consider human life inviolable, it never will; if it does not now proscribe all wars among the human species, it never will; the right of taking human life, if it exists now under the Christian code, will exist as a legal and authorized characteristic (painful and even horrible as the mere thought is) of the pure, blessed, and angelic state of the millennium. On the supposition, therefore, that life will be inviolable in the millennium, and that it will not be considered right for one man to put another to death for any possible reason, we argue that it is not right now. This form of reasoning is applicable to any other analogous case whatever. If it will not be right to steal in the millennium, it is not right to steal now; if it will not be right to be intemperate in the millennium, it is not right to be intemperate now; if it will not be right to hold slaves in the millennium, it is not right to hold slaves now; if it will not be right to take life and carry on war in the millennium, it is not right to take life and carry on war now. The principles which will be acknowledged as authoritative in the millennium, are the very principles which are prescribed, and are binding upon us at the present moment. No change in principles is required, but merely a change in practice. If the practice of men should to-morrow be conformed to the principles which the finger of God has written on the pages of the New Testament, then to-morrow would behold the millennium.

"We delight to linger upon this subject. There is a charm in the millennial name. *'Scribenti manum injicit, et quamlibet festinantem in se morari cogit.'* The wing of poetry flags under this great conception. Sometimes we see it under the type of a wilderness newly clothed with bud and blossom; sometimes we see it under the type of a city descending from heaven, prepared as a bride adorned for her husband; sometimes we behold it as a great temple arising out of the earth, and capacious enough to contain all nations. This temple is not built of earthly materials that will perish with the using, but is supported on immutable columns. Every great moral and religious principle is a pillar in the millennial temple. The principle of total abstinence from intoxicating liquor is one pillar; it suddenly arose, fair and beautiful, and even now is enveloped with some rays of millennial glory; the doctrine that all slaveholding is a sin is another pillar, standing firm, awfully grand and immoveable; the doctrine of the absolute inviolability of human life is another—this is in a state of preparation, but it will soon ascend and stand brightly and majestically in its place; and thus principle after principle will be established, column after column will be erected, till the spiritual house of the Lord shall be established in the tops of the mountains, and shall expand upon the eye of the beholder far more beautiful than the Parthenon. And what then will be wanting? Only that the nations in the language of prophecy, shall flow into it ; only that the people should occupy it and rejoice in it; and this is millennial glory. But, unless you have firm, unchangeable, immutable principles, it will be like a certain house that was built upon the sand; 'and the rain descended and the floods came, and the winds blew, and beat upon that house; and it fell, and great was the fall of it.' "

OBJECTION II. EXTREMELY DIFFICULT IF NOT IMPOSSIBLE.

"The practice of non-resistance, if not impossible for the majority of Christians, is certainly extremely difficult, even for the most advanced. It seems like overstraining duty. It is urging on men so much more than they feel able to perform, that multitudes will faint under the burden and abandon Christianity altogether, as a system wholly beyond their reach. It is unwise to require what must discourage so many thousands from attempting anything at all, as avowed disciples of Christ."

ANSWER.—Who is to be the judge of what is possible ? God, or man ? Who is to judge what and how much shall be required ! Jesus Christ, or his disciples ? Are we to set at nought a duty because it seems to us difficult of performance? Are we to doubt that God's grace is sufficient for the weakest of his trusting children, to enable them to perform any duty He may lay upon them? Are we to accommodate divine truth and duty to the convenience of our fellow men, in order to multiply superficial disciples? Are we to pare down and fritter away the requirements of our heavenly Father, for fear of discouraging and driving off half-hearted professors? Who is it that presumes to daub with such untempered mortar? He must be a most dangerous latitudinarian. Is this the way in which Christ and his apostles built up the Church amid the violence of a contemptuous and persecuting world? Would it be any great misfortune to Christianity, if nine-tenths of its present worldly minded professors, convinced of the truth of the non-resistance doctrine, should honestly declare to the world, "Since this is Christianity, we cannot consistently profess to adhere to it, as its cross is greater than we are willing to bear?" Would not the world at that moment be nearer its conversion than now?

But why need we hold this language? God reigns and not man. He declares the law of perfect rectitude through his Son. That Son is the head of every man—the Lord and Master of all true disciples. He has enjoined the practice of non-resistance on his professed followers as their indispensable duty. He has promised to be with and aid them to the end of the world. If so, let us say at once whether we believe in Christ or not. Whether we will endeavor to follow him and keep his sayings or not. Whether we will try to do our duty, confiding in the proffered strength of Heaven, or not. If we will be Christian, let us try with all our might to do our duty, and see how far we

shall be left to fall short. Let men earnestly try to
carry out Christian non-resistance with this full purpose of heart, and though they may experience the
pain of the cross sometimes, they will soon rejoice in
a crown of triumph. It is difficult always to do
right in this, as it is in respect to other departments
of duty; and no more so. There is no virtue which
does not involve some painful and almost overwhelm-
ing trials. If we were to cast off all obligations that
ever required the hazard of mortal life, we should reject every single commandment of the living God.
For there is not one that has not had its martyrs, and
also its apostates under great temptation. But to the
faithful how blessed is even death itself—if duty
obliges the sacrfice ? And to the obedient, the willingly cross-bearing, how true is it that Christ's "yoke
is easy and his burden light !" It is only for us to resolve that we will TRY. All things are then found
possible, if they are right.

And what is there so discouraging to the humble
and upright soul ? Did not Jesus live and die the
glorious exemplar of his own non-resistant precepts ?
Did not his apostles ? Did not the primitive Christians for more than two centuries ? Have I not
brought up a host of witnesses, practically illustrating that under the most adverse circumstances it was
generally even safer to carry out non-resistance principles than their opposite ? Behold robbers looked
out of countenance and actually converted; ferocious
banditti rendered harmless; wild savages inspired
with permanent kindness; and all manner of evil overcome with good ! Am I to be asked after all this—
"What would you do if a robber should attack you ?
If an assassin should threaten your life ? If a mob

should break forth upon you? If a tribe of savages should beset your dwelling? If a foreign army should come against your land? If lawless soldiers should deal death and rapine about your neighborhood?" What would I do? If I did right—if I acted the Christian part—the wise and noble part, I should adhere to my non-resistance principles, and ten to one experience the most signal deliverance, and achieve the most glorious of all victories, in the conquest of my own passions and those of my assailants!

HOLLOWNESS OF THE OBJECTION.

But the extreme hollowness of the objection before us becomes at once obvious, when I turn the tables and demand whether the practice of injurious resistance offers immunity from extreme trial, danger, hardship and suffering? How happens it that human beings enough to people from eighteen to forty such globes as ours have perished in war? How happens it that blood enough has been shed by the sword to fill a harbor that would embosom at quiet anchor the combined navies of the world? Do these tremendous facts indicate that resistance is sustained without hardships, distresses and mortal agony? Let us contemplate the scenes of a single battle.

PASSAGE OF THE TRAUN.

"In 1809, in the campaign of Aspern and Wagram, Massena added to his former renown, and was one of the firm props of Napoleon's empire on those fiercely fought battle-fields. Previous to the battle of Aspern, after the battle of Eckmuhl, while Bonaparte was on the march for Vienna, chasing the Archduke before him, Massena had command of the advance guard. Following hard after the retreating army of

the Archduke, as he had done before in Italy, he came
at length to the river Traun, at Ebersberg, or Ebers-
dorf, a small village on its banks just above where it
falls into the Danube. Here, for a while, an effectual
stop seemed put to his victorious career; for this
stream, opposite Ebersberg, was crossed by a single
long, narrow, wooden bridge. From shore to shore,
across the sand-banks, islands &c., it was nearly half
a mile, and a single narrow causeway traversed the
entire distance to the bridge, which itself was about
sixty rods long. Over this half mile of narrow path
the whole army was to pass and the columns to charge;
for the impetuous torrent could not be forded. But a
gate closed the further end of the bridge, while the
houses filled with soldiers enfiladed the entire opening, and the artillery planted on the heights over it
commanded every inch of the narrow way. The high
rolling ground along the river was black with the
masses of infantry, sustained by terrific batteries of
cannon, all turned on that devoted bridge, apparently
enough in themselves to tear it in fragments. To
crown the whole, an old castle frowned over the
stream, on whose crumbling battlements cannon were
so planted as to command the bridge. As if this were
not enough to deter any man from attempting the passage, another row of heights, over which the road
passed, rose behind the first, covered with pine trees,
affording a strong position for the enemy to retire to
if driven from their first. Thus defended, thirty-five
thousand men, supported by eighty cannon, waited to
see if the French would attempt to pass the bridge.
Even the genius of Massena might have been stag-
gered at the spectacle before him. It seemed like
marching his army into the mouth of the volcano to

advance on the awful batteries that commanded that long, narrow bridge. It was not like a sudden charge over a short causeway; but a steady march along a narrow defile through a perfect tempest of balls. But this was the key to Vienna, and the Marshall resolved to make the attempt—hoping that Lannes, who was to cross some distance further up, would aid him by a movement on the enemy's flank. The Austrians had foolishly left four battalions on the side from which the French approached. These were first attacked, and being driven from their positions, were forced along the causeway at the point of the bayonet, and on the bridge followed by the pursuing French. But the moment the French column touched the bridge, those hitherto silent batteries opened their dreadful fire on its head. It sank like a sand bank that caves under the torrent. To advance seemed impossible; but the heroic Cohorn, flinging himself in front, cheered them on, and they returned to the charge, driving like an impetuous torrent over the bridge.

"Amid the confusion and chaos of the fight between these flying battalions and their pursuers, the Austrians on the shore saw the French colors flying, and fearing the irruption of the enemy with their friends, closed the gate and poured their tempest of cannon balls on friend and foe alike. The carnage then became awful. Smitten in front by the deadly fire of their friends, and pressed behind with the bayonets of their foes, those battalions threw themselves into the torrent below, or were trampelled under foot by the steadily advancing column. Amid the explosion of ammunition wagons in the midst, blowing men into the air, and the crashing fire of the enemy's cannon, the French beat down the gate and palisades and rushed with headlong speed into the streets and village. But here, met by fresh battalions in front, and swept by a destructive cross-fire from the houses, while the old castle hurled its storm of lead on their heads, these brave soldiers were compelled to retire, leaving two-thirds of their number stretched on the pavement. But Massena ordered up fresh battalions, which, marching through the tempest that swept the bridge, joined their companions, and regaining the village, stormed the castle itself. Along the narrow lanes that led to it the dead lay in swaths, and no sooner did the mangled head of the column reach the castle walls, than it disappeared before the dreadful fire from the battlements as if it sunk into the earth. Strengthened by a new reinforcement, the dauntless French returned to the assault, and battering down the doors, compelled the garrison to surrender. The Austrian army, however, made good their position on the pine-covered ridge behind the village, and disputed every inch of ground with the most stubborn resolution. The French cavalry, now across, came on a plunging gallop through the streets of the village, trampling on the dead and dying, and amid the flames of the burning houses, and through the smoke that rolled over their pathway, hurried on with exulting shouts and rattling armour to the charge. Still the Austrians held out, till threatened with a flank attack they were compelled to retreat.

"There was not a more desperate passage in the whole war than this. Massena was compelled to throw his brave soldiers, whether dead or wounded, into the stream, to clear a passage for the columns. Whole companies falling at a time, they choked up

the way and increased the obstacles to be overcome. These must be sacrificed or the whole shattered column that was maintaining their desperate position on the farther side be annihilated. It was an awful spectacle to see the advancing soldiers, amid the most destructive fire, themselves pitch their wounded comrades, while calling out most piteously to be spared, by scores and hundreds into the torrent. Le Grand fought nobly that day. Amid the choked-up defile and deadly fire of the batteries, he fearlessly pressed on, and in answer to the advice of his superior officer, deigned only the stern reply, ' Room for the head of my columns—none of your advice;' and rushed up to the very walls of the castle. The nature of the contest, and the narrow bridge and streets in which it raged, gave to the field of battle the most horrid aspect. The dead lay in heaps and ridges, piled one across the other, mangled and torn in the most dreadful manner by the hoofs of the cavalry and the wheels of the artillery which were compelled to pass over them. TWELVE THOUSAND men thus lay heaped, packed and trampled together, while across them were stretched burning rafters and timbers which wrung still more terrible cries and shrieks from the dying mass. Even Bonaparte, when he arrived, shuddered at the appalling sight and turned with horror from the scene. The streets were one mass of mangled, bleeding, trampled men, overlaid with burning ruins."
—*American Review.*

Such was one of the world's ten thousand bloody conflicts. Suppose all the courage and endurance displayed on this horrible occasion could be brought into the service of peace and non resistance ! Should we hear any more of the extreme difficulty, if not im-

possibility, of carrying out the doctrine? Suppose
these soldiers to have been devoted Christian non-resistants, scattered over the whole earth; and suppose
them exposed to all the robberies, assaults and batteries, abuses, injuries and insults by any means
likely to fall to their lot; and then, let our objector
tells us how much harder their service would be, in
the army of the Prince of Peace, than that of the
Prince of murderers! The truth is, men can endure
almost any thing they choose. What they have endured as the servants of sin is a proof of what they
are capable of enduring for righteousness' sake. The
latter service requires not a thousandth part of the
physical and mental suffering of the former. How
flimsy then is the objection we are considering! Let
it never be repeated by any man calling himself a
Christian. A true heart, a sound principle of action
and a conscientious will, can never find Christian
non-resistance either an unattainable or an unsupport-
able virtue.

OBJECTION III.—MORE DIFFICULT IN SMALL THAN
LARGE MATTERS.

"The practice of non-resistance is more difficult in
small than large matters. It is not in abstaining from
war and battle, or in enduring great and notorious injuries with forbearance, that non-resistance imposes
the heaviest burdens. Men gather strength in such
cases from the consciousness of public admiration and
sympathy,—and even from the magnitude of the conflict and the consequent glory of a triumph. Extraordinary events and occasions inspire an extraordinary enthusiasm, power and firmness of purpose. But
in every-day life, where people pass through a thous-

and trials, consuming to the vital spirits of their being, unnoticed, unsympathized with, unpitied and un-
cared for, it is by no means so easy to endure the
mean, vexatious aggressions, wrongs and insults of
petty injurers. But your doctrine obliges the abused
wife of a brutal husband, and the insulted and smitten
victim of insolent scoundrelism, to refrain from defensive violence, and even from prosecutions at law,
at least under the existing type of human government. It does not appear that you would allow even
a mob to be repelled with military force, or so much
as a demand to be made on the government for the
protection of one's property, family or life. It is this
extreme and intolerable nicety of your doctrine to
which I object, as much as to anything about it."

ANSWER.

There is truth in the assertion that a practical exemplification of non-resistance in the small matters of
every-day life, is more difficult than in great matters
on extraordinary occasions. And is not this true of
all the great virtues enjoined in Law or Gospel? It
may be easier to eschew idolatry, adultery, fornication, murder, robbery, theft, falsehood, covetousness,
&c., in the open gaze of public scrutiny and public
opinion, even under the mightiest temptation, than
in private unobserved life. It may be easier to suffer
the martyrdom of death before a gaping and amazed,
perhaps admiring, multitude, than the petty martyrdom of a taunt, a kick, a cuff, or a wrung nose, of
which the multitude know nothing and for which they
might care as little. Be it so. Does this change
principle or abrogate duty? What is right? What
ought we all to do in small as well as large matters?

These are the questions to settle.   Not what may
chance to be most convenient, or easy, or comfortable,
or self-indulgent under momentary temptations.   We
have already settled them, so far as respects the duty
never to resist injury with injury.   Is indulgence
asked for the commission of daily violations of this
duty, or occasional violations of it in what are called
small matters?   Go demand indulgence to commit
violations of the ten commandments in small matters.
Plead how difficult it is in every-day life not to lie a
little, deceive a little, defraud a little, extort a little,
hate your neighbor a little, steal a little, be murderous a little, idolatrous a little and lascivious a little.
Get your indulgence from Heaven for all this, and
then doubtless an indulgence will not be withheld to
resist injury with injury a little, and to render evil
for evil a little, in ordinary matters.   Till then, the
law and standard of righteousness must not be relaxed
to suit human convenience.   Duty must be insisted
on without abatement, and whoever exhibits weakness, imperfection, frailty or sin, must bear   the
shame and condemnation.

It is in these small matters that every virtue suf-
fers its greatest betrayal.   A continual dropping
wears the hardest stone.   A continual unscrupulous-
ness in little things undermines all moral principle.
The ocean is made up of drops.   Righteousness is an
aggregate of the littles of life.   He that is faithless
habitually in small matters is not to be depended on
in great matters.   He may, or may not do right.   A
principal reason why public institutions, laws and
measures are so repugnant to justice and humanity is
that the individual consciences of the people, in the
small matters of ordinary life, are habitually un-

scrupulous. If, then, non-resistance is to be insisted on at all, as a duty, it is to be insisted on in small matters as well as large.

And after all that may be said of the difficulty of practising it, we know that it has been and can be practised. Nothing is wanting but the will to try. I will add to the numerous illustrations already given, a few others relating chiefly to individual affairs and the so-called small matters of life

THE PROFANE SWEARER REPROVED AND SUBDUED.

Mr. Deering, a Puritan minister, being once at a public dinner, a gallant young man sat on the opposite side of the table, who, besides other vain discourse, broke out in profane swearing, for which Mr. Deering gravely and sharply reproved him. The young man, taking this as an affront, immediately threw a glass of beer in his face. Mr. Deering took no notice of the insult ; but wiped his face and continued eating as before. The young gentleman presently renewed his profane conversation, and Mr. Deering reproved him as before,—upon which, but with more rage and violence, he flung another glass of beer in his face. Mr. Deering continued unmoved, still showing his zeal for the glory of God by bearing the insult with Christian meekness and humble silence. This so astonished the young gentleman that he rose from the table, fell on his knees, and asked Mr. Deering's pardon ; and declared, that if any of the company offered him similar insults, he would stab them with his sword. Here was practically verified the New Testament maxim : "Be not overcome of evil but overcome evil with good."—Rom. 12 : 21.— *Anonymous.*

THE CHRISTIAN SLAVE AND HIS ENEMY.

The following was first published in the *London Christian Observer*:—

A slave in one of the West Indies, who had origi-nally come from Africa, having been brought under the influence of religious instruction, became singu-larly valuable to his owner, on account of his integ-rity and general good conduct. After some time his master raised him to a situation of some consequence in the management of his estate: and on one occasion, wishing to purchase twenty additional slaves, em-ployed him to make the selection, giving him in-struction to choose those who were strong and likely to make good workmen. The man went to the slave market and commenced his scrutiny. He had not long surveyed the multitude offered for sale, before he fixed his eye upon an old decrepit slave, and told his master that he must be one. The poor fellow begged that he might be indulged; when the dealer remarked, that if they were about to buy twenty, he would give them that man in the bargain. The pur-chase was accordingly made and the slaves were con-ducted to the plantation of their master; but upon none did the selecter show half the attention and care that he did upon the poor old decrepit African. He took him to his own habitation and laid him upon his own bed; he fed him at his own table and gave him drink out of his own cup; when he was cold, he carried him into the sunshine; and when he was hot, he placed him under the shade of the cocoa-nut tree. Astonished at the attention this confidential slave be stowed upon a fellow-slave, his master interrogated him upon the subject. He said, "You could not take so much interest in the old man but for some special

reason: he is a relation of yours; perhaps your father?''
''No, massa,'' answered the poor fellow, ''he no my
fader.''   ''He is then an elder brother?'' ''No, massa,
he no my broder !''   ''Then he is an uncle, or some
other relation ?''   ''No, massa, he no be my kindred
at all, nor even my friend !''   ''Then,'' asked the
master, ''on what account does he excite your interest ?'' ''He my enemy, massa,'' replied the slave;
''he sold me to the slave dealer ; and my Bible tell
me, when my enemy hunger, feed him, and when he
thrist, give him drink.''

HOW TO OVERCOME EVIL.

''I once had a neighbor, who, though a clever man,
came to me one hay day, and said, 'Esquire White, I
want you to come and get your geese away.' 'Why,'
said I, 'what are my geese doing?' 'They pick my
pigs'ears when they are eating, and drive them away,
and I will not have it.'   'What can I do?' I said.
'You must yoke them.'   'That I have not time to do
now,' said I, 'I do not see but they must run.'   'If
you do not take care of them, I shall,' said the clever
shoemaker in anger. 'What do you say, Esq. White?'
'I cannot take care of them now, but I will pay you
for all damages.' 'Well,' said he, 'you will find that
a hard thing, I guess '

''So off he went and I heard a terrible squalling
among the geese. The next news from the geese was,
that three of them were missing. My children went
and found them terribly mangled and dead and
thrown into the bushes.

'Now,' said I, 'all keep still and let me punish
him. ' In a few days, the shoemaker's hogs broke into my corn. I saw them but let them remain a long

time. At last I drove them all out, and picked up the corn which they had torn down, and fed them with it in the road. By this time the shoemaker came in great haste after them.

'Have you seen any thing of my hogs?' said he. 'Yes, sir, you will find them yonder, eating some corn which they tore down in my field.' 'In your field?' 'Yes sir,' said I, 'hogs love corn, you know—they were made to eat.' 'How much mischief have they done?' 'O, not much,' said I.

"Well, off he went to look, and estimated the damage to be equal to a bushel and a half of corn.

'Oh, no,' said I, 'it can't be.' 'Yes,' said the shoemaker,' 'and I will pay you every cent of damage.' 'No,' replied I, 'you shall pay me nothing. My geese have been a great trouble to you.'

The shoemaker blushed, and went home. The next winter, when we came to settle, the shoemaker determined to pay me for my corn. 'No,' said I, 'I shall take nothing.'

After some talk, we parted; but in a day or two, I met him in the road, and fell into conversation in the most friendly manner. But when I started on he seemed loath to move, and I paused. For a moment both of us were silent. At last he said, 'I have something laboring on my mind.' 'Well, what is it?' 'Those geese. I killed three of your geese and shall never rest until you know how I feel. I am sorry.' And the tears came in his eyes. 'Oh well,' said I, 'never mind, I suppose my geese were provoking.'

I never took any thing of him for it; but whenever· my cattle broke into his field after this, he seemed glad—because he could show how patient he could be.

'Now,' said the narrator, 'conquer yourself, and

you can conquer with kindness where you can conquer in no other way.'"—*Anonymous.*

HENRY C. WRIGHT AND HIS ASSAILANT.

The following incident in the life of Henry C. Wright shows his admirable consistency and the salutary influence of non-resistance on the offender. He was in a hotel in Philadelphia, and there engaged in a conversation on non-resistance. An officer present became enraged and struck him. Mr. Wright took no notice of the assault but proceeded with his remarks. In a few moments the officer struck him again. Friend Wright still preserved his equanimity and continued the conversation. His assailant struck him a third time and nearly knocked him down. He recovered himself, and though much injured by the blows of his opponent, took him by the hand and said, " I feel no unkindness towards you and hope soon to see you at my house." He then left the company and returned home. Mr. Wright saw his assailant much sooner than he expected, for he was called up at dawn next morning, by the very man who had struck him the previous evening. He exclaimed, as he entered the house, "can you forgive me? I have been in agony all night. I thought you would strike again or I never should have struck you." "He that is slow to anger is better than the mighty; and he that ruleth his spirit than he that taketh a city."

"He that, unshrinking and without a groan
Bears the first wound, may finish all the war
With mere courageous silence, and come off CONQUEROR."
— *Watts.*

—*McCree.*

THE VICTORIOUS LITTLE BOY.

I had the following anecdote from a gentleman of
veracity. A little boy in Connecticut, of remarkably
serious mind and habits, was ordinarily employed
about a mechanic's shop where nearly all the hands
were addicted to the common use of intoxicating
liquors. The lad had imbibed temperance principles,
and though often invited could never be induced to
partake with any of the shop's crew. At length his
teacher in the Sunday School, in conversation on certain non-resistant texts of scripture, had awakened
his mind to that subject, and he very conscientiously
avowed his determination to try to live in accordance
with this great Christian doctrine. Three or four of
the harder drinkers in the shop, somewhat piqued at
such precocious piety and scrupulousness of conscience, resolved to humble the lad, or at least put
his new notions to the test. They resolved to force a
dram of rum down his throat by some means. Seizing an opportunity when he was left alone in the shop
with themselves, they invited him to drink. He refused. They then told him they should compel him.
He remained calm and unmoved. They threatened
him with violence. Still he neither seemed angry
nor attempted to escape nor evinced the least disposition to yield; but insisted that it was wicked and he
could not do it. They then laid hold of him, a man
at each arm, while the third held the bottle ready to
force it into his mouth. Still their victim remained
meek and firm, declaring that he had never injured
them and never should, but that God would be his
friend and protector, however they might abuse him.
The man who held the fatal bottle, up to that moment resolute in his evil purpose, was so struck by

the non-resisting dignity and innocence of the lad, that, as he afterwards confessed almost with tears, he actually felt unable to raise his hand. Twice he essayed to lift the bottle, as he placed the nose of it in the child's mouth, but his arm refused to serve him. Not the least resistance was made in this stage of the proceeding otherwise than by a meek protesting look; yet the ringleader himself was overcome in his feelings and gave over the attempt, declaring that he could not and would not injure such an innocent, conscientious, good hearted boy. Such is moral power. Such is the strength by which evil may, sometimes at least, be overcome with good.

COLONY OF PRACTICAL CHRISTIANS.

The following is another extract from the writings of Lydia M. Child. It needs no commendation. It will speak to the better feelings of the soul and leave its sweet odor there.

"The highest gifts my soul has received during its world pilgrimage, have often been bestowed by those who were poor, both in money and intellectual cultivation. Among these donors, I particularly remember a hard working, uneducated mechanic, from Indiana or Illinois. He told me he was one of thirty or forty New Englanders, who, twelve years before, had gone out to settle in the western wilderness. They were mostly neighbors, and had been drawn to unite together in emigration from a general unity of opinion on various subjects. For some years previous, they had been in the habit of meeting occasionally at each others' houses, to talk over their duties to God and man, in all simplicity of heart. Their library was the Gospel, their priesthood the inward light. There

were then no anti-slavery societies; but thus taught
and reverently willing to learn, they had no need of
such agency to discover their duties to the enslaved.
The efforts of peace societies had reached this secluded
band only in broken echoes; and non resistance societies had no existence. But with the volume of the
Prince of Peace and hearts open to his influence
what need had they of preambles and resolutions ?

" Rich in God-culture, this little band started for
the far West. Their inward homes were blooming
gardens; they made their outward ones in a wilderness. They were industrious and frugal, and all
things prospered under their hands. But soon wolves
came near the fold in the shape of reckless, unprincipled adventurers; believers in force and cunning,
who acted according to their creed. The colony of
practical Christians spoke of their depredations in
terms of gentlest remonstrance and repaid them with
unvarying kindness. They went farther—they openly
announced, 'You may do us what evil you choose; we
will return nothing but good.' Lawyers came into
the neighborhood and offered their services to settle
disputes. They answered, ' We have no need of you.
As neighbors, we receive you in the most friendly
spirit; but for us your occupation has ceased to exist.'
' What will you do, if rascals burn your barns and
steal your harvests ? ' ' We will return good for evil.
We believe this is the highest truth, and therefore
the best expediency. '

" When the rascals heard this, they considered it a
marvellous good joke, and said and did many provoking things, which to them seemed witty. Bars were
taken down in the night and cows let into the corn-
fields. The Christians repaired the damage as well as

they could, put the cows in the barn, and at twilight drove them gently home; saying, 'Neighbor, your cows have been in my field. I have fed them well during the day, but I would not keep them all night lest the children should suffer for their milk.'

"If this was fun, those who planned the joke found no heart to laugh at it. By degrees, a visible change came over these troublesome neighbors. They ceased to cut off horses' tails and break the legs of poultry. Rude boys would say to a younger brother, 'Don't throw that stone, Bill! When I killed the chicken last week, didn't they send it to mother, because they thought chicken-broth would be good for poor Mary! I should think you'd be ashamed to throw stones at their chickens.' Thus was evil overcome with good; till not one was found to do them wilful injury.

"Years passed on, and saw them thriving in worldly substance beyond their neighbors, yet beloved by all. From them the lawyer and the constable obtained no fees. The sheriff stammered and apologized when he took their hard earned goods in payment for the war-tax. They mildly replied, "Tis a bad trade, friend. Examine it in the light of conscience and see if it be not so.' But while they refused to pay such fees and taxes, they were liberal to a proverb in their contributions for all useful and benevolent purposes.

"At the end of ten years, the public lands, which they had chosen for their farms, were advertised for sale at auction. According to custom, those who had settled and cultivated the soil were considered to have a right to bid it in at the government price; which at that time was $1.25 per acre. But the fever of land speculation then chanced to run unusually high.

Adventurers from all parts of the country were flocking to the auction; and capitalists in Baltimore, Philadelphia, New York and Boston were sending agents to buy up western lands. No one supposed that custom or equity would be regarded. The first day's sale showed that speculation ran to the verge of insanity. Land was eagerly bought in at seventeen, twenty-five and forty dollars an acre. The Christian colony had small hope of retaining their farms. As first settlers, they had chosen the best land; and persevering industry had brought it into the highest cultivation. Its market-value was much greater than the acres already sold at exorbitant prices. In view of these facts, they had prepared their minds for another remove into the wilderness, perhaps to be again ejected by a similar process. But the morning their lot was offered for sale, they observed with grateful surprise that their neighbors were everywhere busy among the crowd, begging and expostulating: 'Don't bid on these lands! These men have been working hard on them for ten years. During all that time, they never did harm to man or brute. They are always ready to do good for evil. They are a blessing to any neighborhood. It would be a sin and a shame to bid on their land. Let it go at the government price.'

"The sale came on; the cultivators of the soil offered $1.25; intending to bid higher if necessary. But among all that crowd of selfish, reckless speculators, not one bid over them ! Without one opposing voice, the fair acres returned to them ! I do not know a more remarkable instance of evil overcome with good. The wisest political economy lies folded up in the maxims of Christ.''

THE AVENGER STAYED.

I will add one more impressive illustration, and close. I copy from the |*Advocate of Peace* for April, 1845, which appears to have quoted from the History of Danish Missions:

"The history of the Danish missions in Greenland is well known. Hans Egede, a man of apostolic benevolence and zeal, was the pioneer in those efforts to Christianize the wild and savage wanderer of the frozen north; and among his|successors was his grandson, Hans Egede Saabye, from whose interesting diary we select the following tale of vengeance sternly purposed, but graciously turned into love by the power of the gospel.

"The law or custom of Greenland requires every murder, especially that of a father, to be avenged by the nearest of kin   Some twenty years before the arrival of Saabye, a man was murdered under circumstances of great atrocity, in the presence of his own son.   The boy, only thirteen years old, was too young to defend his father, but he did not forget the debt of vengeance due to his murderer.   Fleeing for his own safety into a remote part of the country, he there fanned in his bosom the secret flame for twenty-five years, and waited only for an opportunity to let it burst forth in full and fierce revenge.   The murderer was a man of so much influence, and surrounded with so many adherents ready for his defence, that the son feared to attack him; but having persuaded a number of his own relatives to accompany him, he started at length on his long cherished purpose of vengeance, and came in quest of his victim near the residence of Saabye.   The houses in Greenland are a species of common property. The people quit them during their short summer, and on returning the next winter, take possession of any one they may chance to find unoccupied. Winter was now beginning to stretch his icy arms over the north; but the avenger found no shelter for himself and his associates in the work of vengeance. Only one was vacant, and that belonged to the preacher of peace and forgiveness; but Saabye, though well apprized of his purpose, let him have the house, and treated him with his wonted courtesy and kindness. These attentions touched the avenger's heart; and he came to thank Saabye, and repeated his visits so often, that he apologized at length for their frequency by saying, 'You are so amiable that I cannot keep away from you.' After a lapse of several weeks, he said, 'I should like to know something of that great Lord of Heaven, about whom you say so much; and some of my relations wish to learn too.' Saabye granted his request, and found ten or twelve of the company anxious for instruction. He sent a catechist to live with them, and was much gratified at their progress, especially that of the avenger, who frequently left his fishing to hear instruction, and who at length resolved to ask for baptism.

In the month of May, Kunnuk came to Saabye, and said, 'Teacher, will you baptize me? You know I'm obedient. I know God; and my wife, as well as I, wishes to become a believer.' 'Yes,' replied the preacher, 'you know something of God. You know he is good; you see how he loves you and desires to make you happy; but he desires also to have you obey him.' 'I do love him,' earnestly rejoined the avenger; 'I will obey him.' 'But,' answered Saabye, 'if you wish to obey him, you must kill nobody. You have often heard his command, thou shalt not kill.'

"Kunnuk shook his head in great emotion, and only said, half to himself, 'hard doctrine; hard doctrine!' —'Hear me, good Kunnuk,' continued the man of God. 'I know you have come to avenge the murder of your father; this you must not do if you wish to become a believer.' 'But,' retorted the avenger with a flash of indignation gleaming from his eye, 'he murdered my father, my own father! I saw it but could not help him; and now I must punish the murderer.' —'You grieve me!' said the man of peace. 'How?' asked the avenger. 'Because you seem resolved to murder.' 'Only him who deserves to die.'—'But the great Lord of Heaven says, thou shalt not kill.' 'I will not—only him.'—'But you must not kill even him. Have you forgotten how often during the winter, you heard this command: 'Avenge not thyself, but rather give place unto wrath; for vengeance is mine, I will repay, saith the Lord.'—'But,' asked the avenger, 'shall the wicked murder with impunity?'— 'No; he shall not; God will punish him.' 'When?'— 'Perhaps in this world; but certainly at the day of judgment, when he will reward every one according to his deeds.'— 'That is so long,' replied Kunnuk; 'my countrymen and relations will blame me if I do not myself avenge my father now.'—'If you did not know the will of God, I should say nothing; but now I must not be silent.' 'This is hard!' said the avenger. 'What shall I do?'—'You must not kill him; you must even forgive him.' 'Forgive him!' exclaimed the avenger. 'Your doctrine is very strange and difficult.'—'The doctrine,' replied the preacher, 'is not mine, but Christ's.'

"Kunnuk sighed deeply, but made no reply; and

Saabye continued, 'perhaps your father was not innocent; he too may have killed somebody.' 'As to
that,' replied Kunnuk, 'I do not know. I only know
that this man deserves to die.' 'Well,' answered
Saabye, turning to leave the avenger, 'I have done.
Kill him, if you will; but remain an unbeliever, and
expect his children one day to kill you in turn.' 'You
are amiable no longer,' retorted the man of blood,
'you speak hard words.' 'No, Kunnuk,' replied the
man of peace, 'I love you still, and therefore wish you
not to sin against God, who will do justice both to
you and your adversary.' Saabye turned to go;
but Kunnuk cried after him, 'Stay, teacher: I will
speak to my relations.'

"His relations urged Kunnuk day after day to revenge, and threatened him with the curses of his kindred and the scorn of his countrymen, if he shrunk
from avenging his murdered father. The bosom of
the son seemed a theatre of conflicting emotions. The
preacher, in his visits to him, perceived the struggle,
and, without taking any notice of the particular subject, read such portions of Scripture and such hymns
as led to peaceful and forgiving thoughts. Some days
after, Kunnuk returned to the preacher. His countenance, his manner, every thing about him, indicated
a violent struggle. 'I will,' said he, 'I will not; I
hear, and I do not hear. I never felt so before.'
'What will you,' asked the preacher, 'and what will
you not?' 'I will forgive him, and I will not forgive
him; I have no ears, and yet I have ears.' 'When
you will not forgive, answered Saabye, 'then your
unconverted heart speaks, and would dissuade you;
and when you will forgive, then your better heart
speaks. Which will you obey?' 'I was so moved,'

said the avenger, when you spoke yesterday, that my heart wished to obey.' 'See, then, ought you not,' said Saabye, 'to feel that it is the voice of your Heavenly Father speaking in your heart; he bids you be like him; and he giveth sunshine and showers to his foes as well as his friends. Think of your Saviour, too, and strive to resemble him. Did he ever hate his enemies or return their curses on their own heads? When smitten, did he smite back? When persecuted from city to city, did he return evil upon his persecutors? When led to the cross like a lamb to the slaughter, did he open his mouth? Yes; but it was to pray for his murderers: Father, forgive them; for they know not what they do.'

"This appeal touched the avenger's heart; a tear stood in his eye; and earnestly he replied, 'Yes, yes, that was praiseworthy; but he was better than we.' 'Yes, infinitely better,' rejoined Saabye; 'but, if we have a good will, God will give us strength. Hear how a man like you and me can pray for his murderers.' The preacher then read the martyrdom of Stephen; and Kunnuk, drying his eyes, said, 'Wicked man! but he is happy; he is certainly with God in heaven. My heart is so moved; but give me a little time; and, when I have brought my other heart to silence, I will come again.'

"Soon Kunnuk returned with an altered countenance that spoke the peace and joy of his heart. 'Now,' said he, 'I am happy. I hate no more; I have forgiven; my wicked heart shall be silent. Did you not see how moved I was when you read about him on the cross praying for his murderers? Then I vowed in my heart, I will forgive; I have forgiven. Now I hope I and my wife, who has never hated, may be

baptized.' His request was granted; and when the
day arrived for the ceremony, he gave a simple and
touching account of his faith; tears streamed from
his eyes, as he knelt for baptism; and, at the close of
the service, he said, 'Receive me. now as a believer;
I will hate no more; we will love each other, and all
men.' To the murderer of his father, he soon after
sent a message, saying, 'I am now a believer; you
have nothing to fear.' He even invited the murderer to his house, and received him in a most friendly
manner. Being invited to return the visit, he went
alone; but to show the heathen murderer in contrast
with the Christian, Kunnuk found on his way back, a
hole cut in his kajak, or boat, for the purpose of
drowning him. He soon stopped out the water, and
said with a smile, 'Ah! he is still afraid; but I'll
never harm him. Vengeance is no longer mine; I
leave him to God, and pray that he may see his sins
as I have seen my own.' "

CONCLUSION.

Who can contemplate such practical exemplifica-
tions of Christian non-resistance as these, and not be
ravished with the excellence and loveliness of the
sublime doctrine! Can we turn around and gaze on
the battle field, the hospital of mangled mortality, the
gaudy military parade, the pomp of blood-stained
chieftains; or into the more ordinary affairs of life,
on the scuffles, retaliations, resentments, duels,
litigations and endless quarrels of a world infatuated
with resisting violence;—can we look on these things
without heart-sickness and disgust? How base, despicable and abhorrent are they all, compared with
the spiritual heroism, the moral bravery, the glorious

self sacrifice, the life-preserving, heart-reforming, soul-redeeming works of genuine Christianity! "O, my soul, come not thou into their secret; unto their assembly, mine honor, be not thou united."

And shall those who ought to be "the light of the world" and "the salt of the earth," dishonor their high calling, and defile their garments, by engaging in the conflicts of human ambition, violence and revenge? Shall they lust after the dainties of cannibalism, admire the splendors of martial idolatry, and delight themselves in the acts of mortal cruelty! If risen with Christ, ought they not to seek the things of Christ, inhale the perfumes of his Spirit, follow in his footsteps, and make it their supreme satisfaction to do the will of the Father? Is it for them to fly from the dangers of Gethsemane to look with despair from afar on the non-resistant cross, and to make themselves one with a mutually defiant and destructive world! Shall they see lions in the way, and fear to go forth? Shall they stand shivering like the sluggard because it is cold, and so neglect to plow? Does it become them to complain that the duties of love are hard, that non-resistance is impracticable, impossible or extremely difficult; when its principle is so god-like; its spirit so heavenly, its exemplification so beautiful, its fruits so refreshing, and its achievements so glorious! What if it demand a strict discipline; what if it require some severe exertions; what if it impose some manly endurance; what if it offer an opportunity to perform some exploits of moral heroism; shall it therefore be unattractive to great souls? Nay, rather let it seem the more worthy of a holy and generous enthusiasm. Let its calls for volunteers appeal more thrillingly to a noble ambition—an ambition to be and do something worthy of our divine Parentage— worthy ot the Love that has purchased our redemption with the tears and groans and blood of the cross—worthy of immortality—worthy of living and dying for. To save one life, to recover one lost brother, to make one heart holy and happy—or even to qualify ourselves by self-denial for the indwelling Spirit of the Highest—is infinitely more worthy of a whole life's cares and vigils, than all the wealth, pomp and splendor which the world's favorite destroyers ever acquired by the sword. "God forbid that we should glory in any thing save the cross of our Lord Jesus Christ.''

"How hardly man this lesson learns,
To smile and bless the hand that spurns;
To see the blow—to feel the pain,
But render only love again.
This spirit not to earth is given;
ONE had it—HE came from heaven.
Reviled, rejected and betrayed,
No curse he breathed, no plaint he made,
But when in death's deep pang he sighed,
Prayed for his murderers and died."—*Edmiston.*

CHAPTER VII.

Non-Resistance In Relation To Government.

Is Non-Resistance for or against human government?—Human government *de facto*—Objection— Answer –Constitutions of Massachusetts and the United States—extracts —Why not participate to reform?—Cannot lie and commit perjury—Delegated power to declare war—Letters of marque and reprisal, piracy—Legal and political action—How to reform government—Injurious force not essential to government—Under what circumstances this country might have a non-resistant government—View of the present order of things, and remedy—Extract from M. Guizot's Lectures—Conclusion.

IS NON-RESISTANCE FOR OR AGAINST HUMAN GOVERNMENT?

I propose to occupy the present chapter in treating on the relation of non-resistance to human government. Is non-resistance, as defined and expounded in this work, for or against human government *per se?* This depends on what sense is given to the adjective human when joined to the noun government. If human government be understood to imply or presuppose an inherent, original, ABSOLUTE power in man to make laws and exercise discretionary control over man, non resistance is against it. It denies any such inherent, original, absolute power in man, and refers it to God only. In this sense all rightful government is essentially divine; man being ever a subject—not a governor. And whenever he assumes to require any thing repugnant to the divine law, he is a rebel against

God, and a usurper over his co-equal fellow-man. Man cannot rightfully legislate or govern insubordinately to his Creator. He can only govern under and with the divine sanction. If this position needs any defence, non-resistants are prepared to maintain it against the world. None, however, but atheists and would-be Deicides—[God-killers]—the genuine no-governmentists, can be reckless enough to controvert it.

But if human government be understood to imply only divine government clothed in human forms and administered by human organizations, with merely incidental human imperfections, non-resistance is for it *per se.* It has no necessary opposition to it whatever. It recognizes man as by nature a social being. It sees the ties and dependencies of husband and wife, parent and child, friend and neighbor, smaller and larger community; and is essentially friendly to all social organizations founded on love to God and man. Human government in this sense would be an organization of society constitutionally deferential to the highest known law of God. It would disclaim and denounce all assumption of power to set up and enforce any law, regulation or usage in violation of the natural equality and brotherhood of mankind. It would inscribe on its main pillars, no resistance of injury with injury no rendering of evil for evil—evil can be overcome only with good! It would pledge its entire religious, intellectual, moral, physical, industrial and pecuniary resources to the maintenance of the right education, good conduct, comfortable subsistence and general welfare of all its population. It would declare and treat all its officers as servants of their brethren, entitled to no other remuneration than an equal subsistence and dividend of general profits with the mass of unofficials. It would know no such thing as government craft, and have no separate interests of its functionaries to be fattened at the expense of their constituents. It would disclaim all authority of its own, and rest all its legislation, its judicial decrees, and its executive proceedings on their intrinsic rectitude and fitness to promote the public good. It would put off all external display, pomp, parade and childish insignia, and be a plain simple business concern, provided with all things decent and convenient for its necessary use and nothing more. It would incur no expense for distinction's sake—for show and dazzle. Man would make no wicked and foolish attempt to appear a god to his fellow-worms. The most exalted servant of the people would need to dwell in no better house, eat no better food, drink no costlier liquids, wear no richer livery, ride in no better carriage, under a wise and righteous government than would be proper for every common citizen. He would be ashamed to wish anything better. "He that will be chief among you shall be as he that doth serve." This is the pattern for the head of a Christian republic. Such a government would verify the prophetic prediction: "I will also make thy officers peace, and thine exactors righteousness. Violence shall no more be heard in thy land, wasting nor destruction within thy borders." Such a government there will yet be throughout the earth. It is coming in the dim distant future. Christian non-resistance is its forerunner, and will hail its arrival amid the welcome shouts of an enlightened world. Men will then look back on our present semi-barbarous government, much as a philosopher now does on the picture of an Indian Sachem, smeared with paint, ornamented with feathers and wampum and resting on his war club or tomahawk. Understanding then by human government only divine government humanized in its forms, applications and details, non-resistance is decidedly for it *per se.*

HUMAN GOVERNMENT DE FACTO.

But is it for human government as it is *de facto*? This is now the practical question. No. Why not? Because it cannot be both for and against itself. Non-resistance cannot be for war, capital punishment, slavery and all sorts of penal injury. Nor can it be for any government which is fundamentally for these things. These things are not reconcilable with non-resistance. Its adherents cannot therefore be voluntary participators in existing governments. Not because they are opposed to government *per se*; but because they are utterly opposed to these fundamental evils, with which all that is good in existing governments is inseparably interwoven. They demand a removal of these anti-Christian articles from our national and state constitutions before they can voluntarily participate in the government. Are they right in assuming this stand?

OBJECTION.

"No," says the objector, "you are not clearly right, to my apprehension, in charging our national and state constitution with being necessarily for war, capital punishment, slavery and penal injury. But if you are right in this, you are positively wrong in refusing to participate in the government till these things are expunged. If you will neither hold office, vote nor bring actions at law under the government, how do you expect these evils are to be eradicated ! You ought to take part in the government, if for nothing else. to effect the necessary amendments in our constitutions. Who is to remove these evils, if you, who see and feel them, refuse to lift a finger to dislodge them? Stay in the government and reform it. You frustrate your own aims by non-participation."

ANSWER.

War, capital punishment, slavery and many penal injuries have prevailed in the United States. They still prevail. Are they contrary to the fundamental law? Do they not flourish under its positive sanction? I shall not go far out of my way to establish facts naked to universal observation. Without meddling with fine spun arguments, designed to show that the federal constitution is an anti-slavery instrument, or anticipating any ingenious plea which might be offered to demonstrate its consonance with Christianity in respect to capital punishment, I shall content myself with presenting an extract from the Constitution of Massachusetts, (a state in the vanguard of human improvement,) and two or three from that of the United States. These will show whether non-resistance can endorse even republican constitutions—not to mention the written and unwritten ones of the old world.

EXTRACT FROM THE CONSTITUTION OF MASSACHU-
SETTS.

"The Governor of this Commonwealth, for the time being, shall be the commander-in-chief of the army and navy, and of all the military forces of the State, by sea and land; and shall have full power, by himself, or by any commander, or other officer and officers, from time to time, to train, instruct, exercise and govern the militia and navy; and for the special defence and safety of the Commonwealth, to assemble in martial array, and put in warlike posture, the inhabitants thereof; and to lead and conduct them, and with them to encounter, repel, resist, expel, and pursue, by force of arms, as well by sea as by land, within or without the limits of this Commonwealth, and also to KILL, SLAY AND DESTROY, if necessary, and conquer, by all fitting ways, enterprizes and means whatsoever, all and every such person or persons as shall, at any time hereafter, in a hostile manner, attempt or enterprise the destruction, invasion, detriment or annoyance of this Commonwealth; and to use and exercise, over the army and navy, and over the militia in actual service, the law martial, in time of war and invasion, and also in time of rebellion declared by the Legislature to exist, as occasion shall necessarily require; and to take and surprise, by all ways and means whatsoever, all and every such person or persons, with their ships, arms, ammunition, and other goods, as shall, in a hostile manner, invade, or attempt the invading, conquering, or annoying this Commonwealth; and that the Governor be entrusted with all these and other powers, incident to the offices of captain general and commander-in chief and admiral, to be exercised agreeably to the rules and regulations of the Constitution, and the laws of the land, and not otherwise."

EXTRACTS FROM THE U. S. CONSTITUTION.

"The Congress shall have power—to define and punish piracies and felonies committed on the high seas, and offences against the laws of nations.

"To declare war; grant letters of marque and re-prisal: and make rules concerning captures on land and water.

"To raise and support armies.

"To provide and maintain a navy.

"To provide for calling forth the militia to execute the laws of the union, suppress insurrections and in-vasions.

"To provide for organizing, arming and disciplin-ing the militia, &c.

"The President shall be commander-in-chief of the army and navy of the United States, and of the mi-litia of the several States, when called into actual ser-vice.

"His oath shall be:—I do solemnly swear (or affirm) that I will faithfully execute the office of President of the United States; and will, to the best of my ability, preserve, protect and defend the Constitution of the United States.

"This Constitution, and the laws of the United States which shall be made in pursuance thereof, and all treaties made, or which shall be made, under the authority of the United States, shall be the SUPREME LAW of the land.'"

These extracts ought to make it clear to every man's apprehension that our State and National Con-stitutions authorize, provide for and sanction war, preparations for war and all the abominations inci-dent to or consequent upon the murderous military system. The objector has no ground to stand on here.

WHY NOT PARTICIPATE IN ORDER TO REFORM?

But to come to the second part of the objection. If

the non-resistants are right, as to the fundamental, military and penal character of the government, the objector declares they are positively wrong in refus ing to participate in the government till these things are expunged. He wishes to know how, or by whom, we expect these evils to be eradicated, if we will neither hold office, vote nor bring actions at law. He bids us stay in the government to reform it; and tells us we frustrate our own aims by non-participation.

This will pass current with the mass of people for sound common sense; but I shall show it to be more specious than substantial. If our scruples related solely to minor details and incidental defects in the existing governments, the objector's reasoning would be conclusive. For we do not exact absolute per fection, either theoretical or practical, in constitutions of government, as a condition of our participation in them. We can readily conceive of a radically Chris tian government with minor errors and defects in its details, and certainly with incidental abuses of ad ministration arising out of human imperfection. In such governments we could conscientiously partici pate, and should feel bound to do so for the purpose of purifying them entirely; if possible, from errors and abuses.

But the governments now under notice are radi cally, fundamentally ANTI-CHRISTIAN. "The whole head is sick, and the whole heart faint." Military and injurious penal power is their very life blood— the stamina of their existence. They are as repugnant to non-resistance, as pride is to humility, wrath to meekness, vengeance to forgiveness, death to life, destruction to salvation.

These Constitutions have the double character of

declarations and covenants. They declare what is to be considered truth and duty, and are a solemn mutual covenant of the people with each other, as to what may or shall be done in their name. They are written out with great clearness and precision, so that no one may misunderstand them. When a man assents to them, or swears to support them, or acknowledges himself a party to the compact established by them, they become to all intents and purposes declarations of what he regards as truth and duty, and a pledge on his part that he will faithfully co-operate in carrying them into full effect. If they do not declare his sentiments, he makes himself a liar by endorsing, subscribing or assenting to them. If he does not honestly mean to co-operate in giving them practical efficacy, he perjures himself by solemnly engaging to support the compact.

CANNOT LIE AND COMMIT PERJURY

Am I advised to lie and commit perjury in order to reform an anti-Christian government? If I accept any office of destinction, I must swear or affirm to support the Constitution: not in parts, but entire. In fact, I cannot vote, without either actually taking such oath or affirmation, or at least virtually acknowledging myself to be under the highest obligations of allegiance. Government in this country is vested in the voters. They are leagued together by their common declaration of sentiments and mutual covenant—the Constitution—to conduct the government in a certain way, and to maintain its authority by military force. It seems to have been universally taken for granted that military force would be indispensable.

It is therefore a gross fraud and imposition for any man to appear at the ballot-box as a voter, who is at heart false to the Constitution, who does not mean in good faith to abide by and support it, and just as it is, till it can be constitutionally amended. This is what a non-resistant cannot do, without treason to the divine government; without trampling under foot the precepts of Jesus Christ.

Would the objector have me join an association of persons who covenant that their governor shall be "commander in chief of their army and navy, and of all their military forces by sea and land?" Whose army, navy and military? Mine? Am I, a non-resistant, in company with a combination who have armies, navies and military forces? And do I agree that our chief servant shall command these? That he may lead them forth to "KILL, SLAY AND DESTROY" our enemies! Am I to vote for such an officer, and agree to have him put under oath to do such things! A most exemplary non-resistant indeed! Should I not speedily convince the common mind that I was amazingly opposed to war and all its kindred deeds!

DELEGATED POWER TO DECLARE WAR.

Will the objector insist that I shall proclaim to all the world my assent and agreement as a co-governing citizen of the United States, that "Congress shall have power to DECLARE WAR?" My representatives have power to do this wicked thing, in my name at their discretion! Power to turn the whole nation into impious robbers, murderers and desolators of the earth! Power to authorize the perpetration of all the crimes and cruelties of war! Never. I will not agree or consent to any such thing. It is an abomination.

I will hold office on no such conditions, I will not be a voter on such conditions, I will join no church or state, which hold such a creed or prescribes such a covenant for the subscription of its members.

LETTERS OF MARQUE AND REPRISAL, PIRACY.

Much less will the objector persuade me to authorize any Congress of mine ever to grant those piratical commissions, called "letters of marque and reprisal." Defensive war on the home soil, to repel murderous invaders, though the most excusable of all war, is forbidden by Christianity. How much more these seven-fold abominations, called "letters of marque and reprisal?" What are they? Nothing but commissions to unprincipled buccaniers to rob, plunder and murder defenceless people on the high seas. Their victims may be individually the most peaceable and honest people in the world; but if they belong to a certain nation, against which, for some foollish or wicked reason, Congress has declared war, their goods are made lawful plunder, and themselves the prey of sharkish voracity. Is a common high-wayman to be held in universal abhorrence and hung up by the neck on a gibbet, and yet are Christian people to authorize their Congress to grant letters of piracy! And will a man after agreeing that such things shall be perpetrated in his name, presume to go about preaching peace and non-resistance? Does the objector wish me to make myself supremely ridiculous, as well as wicked?

And yet, notwithstanding all this, I must be a member of the national organization, which is bound by this political creed and covenant. I must be a voter. I must vote for the President of the United States to be "commander-in-chief of our army and navy." I must agree to have him put under oath, faithfully to execute this office. I must myself be ready to accept of this, that and the other office, prefaced by an obligation to support the entire Constitution, war, slavery and all, as "the SUPREME LAW of the land!" And if IDOLATRY were a fundamental prescription of the compact, I must support that too! All this for the sake of wielding the necessary influence to reform the government! Unless I lie, perjure myself, and sacrifice every particle of my non-resistant principle for the time being, in order to participate in the government as it is, I can never hope to see a Christian government established! I happen to see "a more excellent way," FIDELITY TO PRINCIPLE.

LEGAL AND POLITICAL ACTION.

Many people seem to take for granted that legal and political action afford to good men indispensable instrumentalities for the promotion of moral reform, or at least for the maintenance of wholesome order in society. Hence we hear much said of the duty of enforcing certain penal laws, of voting for just rulers, and of rendering government "a terror of evil doers." Now I make no objection to any kind of legal or political action which is truly Christian action. Nor deny that some local and temporary good has been done by prosecutions at law, voting in our popular elections and exercising the functions of magistracy, under the prevailing system of human government. But I contend that there is very little legal and political action under this system, which is strictly CHRISTIAN action. And I deny that professedly good men do half as much to promote as they do to subvert

moral reform and wholesome order in society by
legal and political action. The common notions respecting these matters are extremely superficial,
delusive and mischievous. Look at facts.

1. Is it not a fact, that men strenuous for legal
coercion, who devote themselves to the prosecution of
lawbreakers as an important duty, generally become
incapable of benevolent, patient, suasory moral
action? Do they not become disagreeable to human
minds, and objects of defiance to the lawless? Is not
this generally the case? I am sure it is. Reliance on
injurious penal force costs more than it comes to, as
an instrumentality for the promotion of moral reform.
It works only a little less mischievously in morals
than in religion.

2. Is it not a fact, that equally good men are
divided among all the rival political parties, and
that, under pretence of doing their duty to God and
humanity, they vote point blank for and against the
same men and measures, mutually thwarting, as far
as possible, each others' preferences? Every man
knows this. Does God make it their duty to practice
this sheer contradiction and hostility of effort at the
ballot-box! Does enlightened humanity prompt it?
No; there must be a cheat somewhere in the game.
The Holy Ghost does not blaspheme the Holy Ghost;
nor Satan cast out Satan. Either the men are not
good, or their notions of duty are false.

3. Is it not a fact that the most scrupulously moral
and circumspect men in all the rival political parties
are uniformly found, with very rare exceptions, either
among the rank and file of their party, or in the inferior offices? Are our wisest and best men of each
party put forward as leaders? Are not the managers

—the real wire-pullers—generally selfish, unscrupulous men? Whatever may be the exceptions, is not this the general rule? We have all seen that it is. How then is it to be accounted for, on the supposition that political action is so adapted to moral reform and wholesale order in society? The good men in political parties are not the leaders, but the led. They do not use political action to a noble end, but are themselves the dupes and tools of immoral managers—put up or put down, foremost or rearmost, in the centre or on the flank, just as they will show and count to the best advantage. All they are wanted for is to show and count against the same class in the other party. Their use is to give respectability, weight of character and moral capital to their party. They are the "stool pigeons," the "decoy ducks," the take-ins of their managers. The way they are used and the game of iniquity played off, are the proofs of this. Yet this is what many simple souls call having influence.

4. Is it not a fact that of the very few high-toned moral men who happen to get into the head quarters of political distinction, not one in ten escapes contamination or utter disgust? And now what do all these facts prove? That under the present system of government, legal and political action is generally anti-Christian. That political good men are influential chiefly as tools for mischief. And that non-political good men are the most likely to render legalists and politicians DECENT in the affairs of government.

HOW TO REFORM GOVERNMENT.

Existing governments have their merits. They

might be worse than they are. They are as good as the great mass of the people demand, or are capable of appreciating. If full grown Christian constitutions were proffered to them, they would vote them down with contempt. If we could cheat them into the reception of one, they would not know how to live under it. Governments are correct exponents of the aggregate religious light, moral sentiment and intellectual developement of the people living under them. People with a false and low religion, a false and low morality, a low and undeveloped intellect, will have a corresponding false and low organization of society, false and low government ! An Esquimaux, Hottentot, or New Hollander, would desire and administer an Esquimaux, Hottentot, or New Holland government. The reason why we have not a Christian government is, that our people are not in the aggregate a Christian people. The aggregate religion is far below the Christian standard. The aggregate conscience and moral sentiment of the people is semi-barbarous. And their aggregate intellect is not yet sufficiently improved by knowledge and discipline to see how low their religion and morality is. They are, therefore, not even ashamed of war and slavery. They do not see that these gross abominations are their disgrace and curse. We have got to enlighten them, expand their intellects, purify their moral sentiment, quicken their conscience and reform their religious ideas. This is not to be done by voting at the polls, by seeking influential offices in the government and binding ourselves to anti-Christian political compacts. It is to be done by pure Christian precepts faithfully inculcated, and pure Christian examples on the part of those who have been favored to receive

and embrace the highest truths. They must hold up
the true standard, let their light shine and patiently
persevere in the great work of creating a new heart
and a new spirit in the people. They must do nothing to disparage or hinder whatever is good in the existing order of society and government. Still less
must they do anything to hinder their own pure testimony; either by seditious opposition to government
or by voluntary participation in its sins. They must
not falsify their principles by going with the government to do evil, nor in going against its wrongs by
anti-Christian means, nor by contemning any thing in
which is right and good *per se*. Thi: is the strait and
narrow way of Christ.

When a considerable portion of the people have
been enlightened and won over to Christian non-resistance, the tide of public sentiment will begin to
set with such force against war and the whole injury-
inflicting system, that the less enlightened and less
conscientious portion will insensibly yield to the current, and the relics of barbarism, one after another,
be "cast to the moles and bats." Thus, ultimately,
government will be christianized, and the most scrupulous disciples of the non-resistant Saviour feel at liberty to perform any service in it which the public
good may require.

What a work is to be performed! It has commenced, and will progress much faster than either
faint-hearted friends or unbelieving scoffers antici-
pate; though doubtless its consummation is at a great
distance. In this view of the case, how supremely
silly would it appear for a handful of non-resistants
to run a tilt of politics and harness themselves to the
car of Juggernaut, in the hope of influencing the mis-

guided multitude to renounce their idolatry! It would be treason to their cause and ridiculous infatuation, for them to play such antics. Their mission is to "have no fellowship with the unfruitful works of darkness, but rather reprove them;" to *teach,* not *number* the people; to show forth a model of what *ought to be*—not conform to what *is;* to testify against spiritual wickedness in high places, and to cause the popular abominations of the land to be properly appreciated and utterly loathed; to scatter light and call the people to repentance; to reform our thirty-thousand religious teachers, so that instead of patronizing, inculcating, apologizing for, consenting to, and pronouncing benedictions on military power and display, they may view and speak of it with the same abhorrence they now do *idol worship;* to convert our hundreds of thousands of church members to that primitive Christianity, which nerved up the ancient disciples to say, in the face of threatened death—"I am a Christian, and can not fight!" When we have done all this we will begin to think about voting and accepting office in the government. We believe we shall then no longer be obliged to subscribe Constitutions which make our governors and presidents *"commanders-in-chief of the army,"* or which invest Congress with discretionary power "to declare war, grant letters of marque and reprisal"—those flagrant crimes against God and humanity. If we *should,* we would still ply our axe to the root of the tree, and *non-participate* till a better day had dawned on the world. Such is the method by which true Christianity teaches its disciples to reform government. True, it is not according to "the wisdom of this world, which is foolishness with God;" but it is according to "the wisdom that cometh down from above, which is first pure, then peaceable, gentle, easy to be entreated, full of mercy and good fruits, without partiality, and without hypocrisy."—James 3: 17.

INJURIOUS FORCE NOT ESSENTIAL TO GOVERNMENT.

I shall now be told by the opposer that I am a Utopian, a dreamer, a chimerist, to imagine any such thing as a government without a war power in the last resort—without the power of deadly compulsion to suppress individual crime and mobocratic violence. That such a government would be a body without a soul—a house without a foundation—a powerless non-resistant abstraction; a something which can never have existence on earth, at least so long as human imperfection remains. I know that this is the common opinion respecting government. But it is false, the spawn of ignorance—a sheer delusion. A little reflection will show how utterly groundless it is. It derives all its plausibility from the exhibitions of past and remaining barbarism. Because men have been barbarous, and their laws and penalties barbarous, it is taken for granted that they *can not* be otherwise; just as the African, in the center of the Torrid Zone, assumed that there could be no such thing as ice because he had never seen any; and just as all ignorant people assume that nothing can exist unlike what has come under their own observation.

Suppose one should confidently assert that there could be no such thing as a man, actually living and transacting business among mankind, without a military chapeau on his head, a sword dangling by his side or a musket over his shoulder, or at least pistols or bowie knife about his person; that no man could live in the world without either *actually* fighting, or *threat-*

ening to fight, or at least *being armed* for a fight. Who would not see the absurdity of the assertion? The man and the man's means of preserving his life do not necessarily belong together. The Christian non-resistant is as much of a man as your sword and dagger character, and much less of a *brute;* and the former stands a much better chance of long life, civil treatment and substantial happiness in the world, than the latter. Suppose some one should assert that there could be no such thing as a family or good family government, without guns and dogs to defend them against marauders, and plenty of *switch-sticks* to wear up over the children's backs. Would it show any thing more than the ignorance and low moral development of the asserter? Suppose another should affirm that there can be no such thing as a church of Christ without the *Inquisition* and *auto da fe?* Men of intelligence, reflection and Christianized moral feeling, know the contrary.

UNDER WHAT CIRCUMSTANCES THE COUNTRY MIGHT HAVE A NON-RESISTANT GOVERNMENT.

Let us have two-thirds of the people of the United States (including that portion who *are,* or would be *thought,* Christians, philanthropists, people of intelligence and orderly citizens) once firmly committed to non-resistance, as explained and illustrated in this work, with even a large share of imperfection still lingering about them, and the government might triumphantly dispense with its army, navy, militia, capital punishment, and all manner of *injurious* inflictions. Under the light necessary to effect so general a change of public sentiment, a considerable portion of the people would have reconstructed neighborhood society by voluntary association, in such a manner as nearly to do away intemperance, idleness, debauchery, miseducation, poverty and brutality, and to insure the requisite inducements, means and opportunities for great self-improvement and social usefulness. The consequence would be that very few poor creatures would remain without a strong moral guardianship of wise and true friends to look after their welfare. Wholesome cure would be applied with vast success to the ignorant and vicious, and at the same time powerful preventives beyond estimation applied to the new-born generation. Under such circumstances, suppose a truly Christian government to administer the general affairs of the several states and of the nation. How little would they have to do, how well might they perform that little, and how trifling would be the burdens of it either to officers or people? It would hardly require *hundreds of millions* of dollars to carry such a government through a single year. They would not expend eighty per cent. of all their receipts on ships of war, forts, arsenals, troops, &c., &c. If they expended half this sum on the reformation of the few remaining vicious, the right education of youth, and the encouragement of virtue among the whole people, their work would be cut short in righteousness. If here and there a disorderly individual broke over the bounds of decency, the whole force of renovated public sentiment would surround and press in upon him like the waters of the ocean, and slight *uninjurious* force would prevent personal outrage in the most extreme cases. And every day the causes of such extreme cases would be undergoing the process of annihilation. Meantime England, and the other great nations, between whom and ourselves there is such a frequent and increasing familiarity of intercourse, would vie with ours, not which should have the strongest army and navy, and be able to do the most mischief, but which should lead off in the glorious work of reforming, improving and blessing the human race. Patriotism would then no longer strut in regimentals, recount its ruffian exploits, and provoke quarrels with fellow men for the crime of having been born over sea or on the other side a mountain or river. It would glory in superior justice, forbearance, meekness, forgiveness—*charity*. O glorious era, I see thee coming to smile on my country and the world. Thou art advancing in silent majesty on the remote verge of the blue horizon. Clouds of dust intervene between thee and the uncouth present. They conceal thee from the gaze of the boisterous and bustling multitude. The prophets even can but dimly discern thy beautiful outline. But thou art drawing nearer. Angels are thy heralds. The morning stars are singing together in thy train, and the sons of God shout for joy. In due time the heaven shall kiss the earth in thy presence, and the earth shall be restored to the bliss of heaven!

VIEW OF PRESENT ORDER OF THINGS, AND REMEDIES.

But we must turn back from this vision and listen again to the scoffs of skepticism, the growls of frowning bigotry, and the jargon of Babylon the great. We must hear those who make the sword, the gibbet and the dungeon their gods, denounce the doctrines of mercy, and extol the efficacy of cruelty. "The world is full of criminals," say they, "horrid criminals, ravening like wolves for the prey, and it is presumption to think of trusting to love, mercy, forbearance and uninjurious restraints. The wicked must be slain. The unprincipled must be threatened with destruction. The lawless must be held at bay by the terrors of the halter and the cell. Mankind are too depraved to be held and treated as brethren." This is the language of many professedly wise and upright men in what are falsely supposed to be the first ranks of society. But it is the language of men who need to be born again before they can enter into the kingdom of God—Pharisees and Sadducees, haughty religionists and moralists, who know not their own hearts, nor "what manner of spirit they are of." They look not into the causes of crime. They feel not for their fellow creatures, who were born and have lived under the worst possible circumstances. They see not that nine-tenths of the crimes of those whom they glory in bringing to punishment, might have been prevented, had good people, so called, been *good enough* to care for others beyond the precincts of their own blood relationship. They themselves are great sinners and need great mercy; yet they have little compassion on their fellow sinners of a lower grade. They live in a sort of conventional decency and imagine it to be true morality. They are clothed with the fashionable garments of a superfine selfishness, and vainly imagine themselves acceptable to God. They are supremely covetous of this world's goods and revel in the midst of extravagance, yet think only of the guilt and deserved punishment of *thieves* and *robbers*. Let them spare their maledictions against the punishable class of their fellow creatures. Let each one of them seriously ask the following questions:

"How much better am I by nature than these murderers, robbers, thieves, and wretched culprits whom I so much detest? Had I been born of their parents, been brought up as they were brought up, been neglected by the better classes as they were neglected, been tempted as they have been tempted, and been treated as they have been treated, should I have been at this moment what I am? Should I not have been one among them, hated and hunted down as a hopeless reprobate? How much attention have I given, in my whole life, to the consideration of the causes which make one person to differ from another? How much time have I spent in earnest endeavors to prevent my fellow creatures from falling into these crimes, in educating them while children, providing them a good home of industry and comfort in youth and in inducing them in mature age to lead orderly lives? How much *thought,* how much *affection,* how much *time,* how much *money,* have I devoted to such purposes? Have I considered these things, and brought up my family to consider them? Have I proposed them to my neighbors? Have I brought them before my religious or literary associates? Have I tried by precept, persuasion and example to unite my friends in preventing pauperism, vice and crime? Or have I thought chiefly of deterring and punishing crime? Have I been spending nearly all my attention and efforts on *myself* and my own family, to obtain wealth, distinction, fame, self-aggrandizement and self-indulgence? Have I not been living all this time to *myself,* and for my own little circle of relations and friends? What has my religion done towards making me a Christian after the pattern of Jesus? What has my morality amounted to but worldly decency? And have I not done some things, in secret, in spite of all my religion and morality, which if known to the world would plunge me into the depths of disgrace? What have I to boast of? Why am I so intent on punishing instead of forgiving and reforming my less fortunate fellow sinners!" Would not such a self-examination as this essentially humble and chasten many a self-righteous soul?

The truth is, if one-hundredth part of what the better classes of society now acquire contrary to the law of love and expend on themselves to their positive *hurt,* were faithfully devoted to the prevention and reformation of crime, scarce an offender would remain in society. If no more than what is expended in detecting, trying and punishing criminals, were judiciously applied to this work of prevention and reformation it would accomplish ten times more for society than it now does. But alas, as *undertakers* live and flourish by burying the dead, so there are not a few in the present organization of society who live by hunting and punishing criminals. And yet many of the worst offenders luxuriate in perfect impunity, fortified by bulwarks impregnable to the penal laws. At the same time the ordinary acquisition of property by what are called the better classes, the criers out for "punishment, punishment," is only a fashionable species of gambling and extortion, in which the cunning, the fortunate and the unscrupulous carry off the stakes amid the perpetual grumblings of the unlucky losers. Besides this, intemperance and licentiousness are permitted to allure millions through their *licensed* portals to the chambers of hell; and slavery shakes her whips and chains over a sixth portion of a professedly free people, under the protection of our star-spangled banner! Is it any wonder that such a state of things, such a religion, such a morality, such unbridled acquisitiveness, such selfishness, and such oppression of the *governing portion,* should breed, foster and perpetuate all manner of vice and crime in the *under classes of society?* Not at all.

Therefore, Christian non-resistance protests against

the wickedness of the *punishing* as well as the *punished* classes. It proposes and insists on a radical reform. And when this reform shall have gone forward to a certain point, a government untainted by military power or penal injury will be both practicable and certain. To show that such a government is possible, I will now present a clear, discriminating, irrefutable extract from M. Guizot, prime minister of France.

EXTRACT FROM M. GUIZOT'S LECTURES.

"Is it not forming a gross and degrading idea of government to suppose that it resides *only,* to suppose that it resides *chiefly,* in the force which it exercises to make itself obeyed in its coercive element?

"Let us quit religion, for a moment, and turn to civil government. Trace with me, I beseech you, the simple march of circumstances. Society exists. Something is to be done, no matter what, in its name and for its interest; a law has to be executed, some measure to be adopted, a judgment to be pronounced. Now, certainly, there is a proper method of supplying the social wants; there is a proper law to make, a proper measure to adopt, a proper judgment to pronounce. Whatever may be the matter in hand, whatever may be the interest in question, there is, upon every occasion, a truth which must be discovered, and which ought to decide the matter, and govern the conduct to be adopted.

"The first business of government is to seek this truth; is to discover what is just, reasonable and suitable to society. When this is found, it is proclaimed: the next business is to introduce it to the public mind; to get it approved by the men upon whom it is to act; to persuade them that it is reasonable. In all this, is there anything coercive? Not at all. Suppose now

that the truth which ought to decide upon the affair
(no matter what;) suppose, I say, that the truth being
found and proclaimed, all understandings should be at
once convinced; all wills at once determined; that all
should acknowledge that the government was right,
and obey it spontaneously. There is nothing yet of
compulsion, no occasion for the employment of force.
Does it follow, then, that a government does not exist?
Is there nothing of government in all this? To be sure
there is, and it has accomplished its task. Compulsion
appears not till the resistance of individuals calls for it
—till the idea, the decision which authority has adopted,
fails to obtain the approbation or the voluntary submission of all. Then government employs force to make
itself obeyed. This is a necessary *consequence* of human imperfection; an imperfection which resides as
well in power as in society. There is no way of entirely
avoiding this; civil governments will always be obliged
to have recourse, in a certain degree, to compulsion.
Still it is evident they are not made up of compulsion,
because, whenever they can, they are glad to do without it, to the great blessing of all; and their highest
point of perfection is to be able to discard it and trust
to means purely moral, to their influence upon the understanding; so that, in proportion as government can
dispense with compulsion and force, the more faithful
it is in its true nature, and the better it fulfils the purposes for which it is sent. This is not to shrink, this is
not to give way, as people commonly cry out; it is
merely acting in a different manner, in a manner more
general and powerful. Those governments which employ the most compulsion perform much less than those
which scarcely ever have recourse to it. Government,
by addressing itself to the understanding, by engaging

the free will of its subjects, by acting by means purely intellectual, instead of contracting, expands and elevates itself; it is then that it accomplishes most and attains to the greatest objects. On the contrary, it is when a government is obliged to be constantly employing its physical arm that it becomes weak and restrained —that it does little and does that little badly.

"The essence of government then by no means resides in compulsion, in the exercise of brute force; it consists more especially of a system of means and powers, conceived for the purpose of discovering upon all occasions what is best to done, for the purpose of discovering the truth which by right ought to govern society, for the purpose of persuading all men to acknowledge this truth, to adopt and respect it willingly and freely. Thus I think I have shown that the necessity for, and the existence of a government, are very conceivable, even though there should be no room for compulsion, even though it should be absolutely forbidden."—*History of Civilization in Europe, Lecture 5.*

CONCLUSION.

Is this satisfactory? Is this conclusive? It ought to be so. It is not the language of a non-resistant enthusiast—a Utopian dreamer—but of Monsieur Guizot, the intelligent and accomplished prime minister of Louis Phillipe. Let the arrogant contemners of the idea of a pure Christian government revolve the matter, and consider whether their skepticism arises out of knowledge or *ignorance?* To a sound mind the case admits of little doubt. The great prerequisite to the establishment of such a government has already been pointed out. It is religious, moral and intellectual reform among the people, superinducing in them a more Chris-

tian faith, a more Christian conscience, a more enlightened intellect, and a purer morality. This noble work
non-resistance espouses and will unfalteringly prose-
cute to its blessed consummation. To carry it forward
the faithful will lay aside pecuniary, political, military
and all worldly ambition—every weight that encumbers
—and press forward to the mark for the prize of their
high calling in Christ Jesus.; despising the cross and enduring the shame, till they enter into his glory and partake of the true majesty of his kingdom. He is King
of kings, and Lord of lords; and the kingdoms of this
world shall at length become his in *righteousness and
peace.*

> "I've thought at gentle and ungentle hour,
>   Of many an act and giant shape of power;
>   * * * * Of bruised rights, and flourishing bad men,
> And virtue wasting heavehwards from a den:
> Brute force, and fury, and the devilish drouth
> Of the foul cannon's ever gaping mouth;
> And the bride-widowing sword; and the harsh bray
> The sneering trumpet sends across the fray;
> And all which blights the people-thinning star
> That selfishness invokes—the horsed war,
> Panting along with many a bloody mane:
> I've thought of all this pride, and all this pain,
> And all the insolent plentitudes of power;
> And I declare by this most quiet hour,
> * * * that power itself has not one half the might
> Of *Gentleness.* 'Tis want to all true wealth;
> The uneasy madman's force to the wise health;
> Blind downward beating, to the eyes that see;
> Noise to persuasion, doubt to certainty;
> The consciousness of strength in enemies,
> Who must be strained upon, or else they rise;
> * * * Or as all shrieks and clangs, with which a sphere
> Undone and fired, could rake the midnight ear,
> Compared with that vast dumbness nature keeps
> Throughout her starry deeps,
> Most old, and mild, and awful, and unbroken,
> Which tells a tale of Peace beyond what'er was spoken."
>   —*Leigh Hunt.*

PART I

APPENDIX

BIOGRAPHICAL SKETCH OF THE AUTHOR.

Adin Ballou, author of the foregoing treatise, belonged to a family widely known and somewhat distinguished in the religious history of this country during the nineteenth century, especially in its relation to the so-called Universalist Church, one of his distant cousins, Hosea Ballou, being generally regarded as the most prominent exponent and leading champion in his day of the distinctive form of faith which that church represents, while quite a number of his other kinsmen have been and still are much esteemed and highly honored members, as ministers or laymen, of the same fellowship, one of whom, Hosea Ballou, 2d, a man of superior ability, rare culture and noble character, was the first president of Tufts College, honored not only by his immediate associates and friends, but also by Harvard University, which conferred upon him the degree of M.A. and D.D. and which he served for many years as a member of its Board of Overseers.

Adin Ballou was a descendant in the fifth generation of Maturin Ballou, the immigrant ancestor of all bearing the family name in America, a French Protestant, it is said, who came to this country about 1640 and was associated with Roger Williams in the founding of Providence, R. I., and the son of Ariel and Edilda (Tower) Ballou, of Cumberland, R. I., where he was born, April 23, 1803. He grew up after the common manner of high-minded farmer's sons of those days (his father being a typical New England yeoman), with plenty of work suited to his age, and few educational advantages of any sort. His mind was active and thoughtful from early childhood, and a thirst for knowledge seemed to be innate with him. In his youth he earnestly desired a liberal education, but circumstances restricted him to the limited privileges of the ordinary public school. These he sedulously improved, endeavoring to make up for his privation by diligently searching for knowledge wherever he thought it might be found, and by subjecting himself to a careful discipline of his mental powers—a practice he followed through life.

He was naturally disposed to religious emotions and impressions, and when eleven years of age was the subject of an experience of that sort the influence of which upon his character and life was most salutary and continuous, even to the end of his mortal pilgrimage. A year later he was baptized by immersion and received into a church in his neighborhood belonging to the so-called "Christian Connexion," a small division of the general Baptist ecclesiastical body located mostly in Rhode Island and Connecticut. When he was about eighteen he had a spiritual vision, as he termed it, requiring him imperatively to preach the gospel. From this he shrank most decisively as thwarting his fondly-cherished worldly plans, but at length reluctantly consented from an overmastering sense of duty, preaching his first sermon from the text "Necessity is laid upon me; yea, woe is unto me if I preach not the gospel." He had received no training for such service and spoke chiefly from inward inspiration. But so impressed were the multitudes who heard him, and especially those of the church to which he belonged, that he soon after accepted a formal call to the ministry of that church, an arrangement which continued for about a year. It was one of the dogmas of that communion that all who died out of Christ or "the finally unpenitent," as the saying went, would be sentenced at the judgment to a punishment ending at length in their destruction or utter annihilation; and to this dogma he gave his unqualified assent. But the reading of a work on the doctrine of the ultimate restoration of all souls to holiness and happiness, and the profound study of the subject induced thereby, led him to abandon the former belief for the latter, which brought him into very close sympthy with the then growing Universalist movement, to which he had been previously most strongly, not to say bitterly, opposed. Being strictly honest and true to his convictions he openly avowed his change of opinion upon the subject. Whereupon his church associates, his own father being foremost among them, rose in protest against him, at length ejecting him from the ministerial office after having served in it scarcely a year. His newly-accepted views and the sympathies engendered by them inclined him strongly towards the Universalists in spite of his former repugnance to them, and he was soon drawn almost irrestibility into their followship. They very naturally hailed the accession to their numbers with unbounded delight.

But while in happy accord with his new coadjutors in regard to the great question of the final destiny of all souls—of the ultimate outcome of things in the moral and spiritual universe under the government of an infinitely powerful, wise and good God, to wit, *universal holiness and happiness,* he found that he was quite at variance with many of them, and especially with their leaders in respect to the doctrine of future retribution—

a doctrine which he regarded as of very great importance in its bearing upon human character and conduct,
and which he therefore proclaimed in his public min-
istrations, but which many of his brethren repudiated
with something like contempt of it and of its advocates.
This soon caused friction between the subject of this
sketch and them, which increased as time went on and
which, with the dogmatism and intolerance of those
opposed to him, who seemed to dominate the great body
of the Denomination, at length led him, in fidelity to his
deep-rooted convictions of truth and duty, to sever his
ecclesiastical relations at the expiration of about ten
years of nominal fellowship, and in co-operation with
a dozen or more others of similar views and feelings,
to organize what was called "The Massachusetts Association of Independent Restorationists." The members
of this organization sympathized and fraternized with
a section of the Unitarian denomination, with which
they ultimately become organically affiliated, the Res-
torationist Association having been dissolved.

About this time the subject of this sketch became
very deeply interested in the practical nature of Christianity and especially in its bearing upon human character and human life in its various relations and manifestations. This prepared and predisposed him to examine and, after examination, to recognize the claims
made by their advocates in behalf of the great, leading
reforms of the day, temperance, anti-slavery, the rights
of woman, peace and, finally, social reform, each and
all of which he at length heartily espoused, becoming a
consistent exponent and an earnest and eloquent champion of them all. As time went on his interest and
thought seemed to center in and fasten upon the matter
of social reorganization, which he was pleased to name

"Practical Christian Socialism," deeming it inclusive of all other needed reforms and regarding it as the effective way by which the divine kingdom was to come into the world and the will of God to be done "on earth as it is in heaven." So fully persuaded was he of this and so strong was his faith in the beneficent results to humanity that would follow the exemplification of the principles of Practical Christian Socialism in actual life, that he projected and, as leader of a goodly number of others—men and women—of like faith, founded in the town of Milford, Mass., "The Hopedale Community," which was designed under the general system of reconstructed society formulated by him, to be the forerunner and the inspirer of an indefinite number of similar enterprises scattered here and there throughout the land, and possibly all over the globe.

This experiment failing of the success that was anticipated, its characteristic industrial feature being abandoned some fifteen years after it was started, while its moral and religious interests were at a later day merged in what was termed "the Hopedale Parish," a constituent of the Unitarian branch of the Christian church. Mr. Ballou received and accepted a call to the pastorate of the parish. In that position he remained till 1880, when failing health and the infirmities of age induced him to resign his position and retire from the active duties of his profession, only as occasional calls for ministerial services, which he did not feel obliged to decline, were made upon him. And these occurred almost to the end of his days.

After the dissolution of the Community at Hopedale, he spent most of the time that could be spared from professional duties in literary pursuits. He prepared several works for the press, notably among which was a "History of the town of Milford," a royal octavo volume of 1,150 pages, and an elaborate "History of the Ballous in America," a similar work of 1,325 pages. He also wrote a "History of the Hopedale Community," an autobiography, and Volumes II and III of a work entitled "Primitive Christianity and its Corruptions" (the first volume of which had been published in 1870) to be put in print after his decease, which has been accordingly done, the books having been widely distributed in theological and college libraries throughout the United States. He was at an earlier day the author of several published works, among which were "Christian Non-resistance," "Spirit Manifestations," "Memoir of his son, Adin Augustus Ballou," also a large volume of 650 pages entitled "Practical Christian Socialism," an exposition of the principles involved in that science, and a presentation of methods by which this principle could be illustrated in the actual life of communities, states and nations. He was also the compiler of "The Hopedale Hymn Book" and the author of "The Monitorial Guide" to be used in social religious meetings and elsewhere, as an aid to devotion and the higher life of the sons and daughters of men. The number of tracts, pamphlets, etc., of a religious and reformatory character that came from his pen at irregular intervals, as occasion or inclination suggested, beginning early in life and continuing almost to the end, was large and not easily estimated, no record of them having been preserved.

Adin Ballou was twice married. First to Abigail Sayler, of Smithfield, R. I., in 1822. She bore him two children, a son who died in childhood, and a daughter still living, the wife of Rev. William S. Heywood, a Unitarian minister of Dorchester, Mass. The mother died in 1829, and the husband married, second, Lucy Hunt, of Milford, Mass. She had two children, sons, the older of whom, Pearly Hunt, died when two years and three months old; the other, Adin Augustus, richly endowed by nature with qualities of mind, heart and character, which, as he grew in years, won the love, the confidence and the admiration of all who knew him, and gave promise of eminent usefulness and a most honorable career in the world, was in the bloom of opening manhood stricken with a fatal disease which, in a few days, put an end to his mortal existence, to the unutterable sorrow of his family and a host of devoted and appreciative friends.

Mr. Ballou passed away on the 5th of August, 1890, at the advanced age of eighty-seven years, three months and fifteen days. His wife, with whom he had lived in tender, sacred companionship more than sixty years, survived him but a year and two days, dying August 7, 1891, aged seventy years, nine months and eight days.

Mr. Ballou's faith in non-resistance, or radical peace principles, never gave way nor faltered as long as he lived, but grew stronger and more assured with every passing year; and, while health and strength permitted, he expounded, defended and promulgated those principles, as far as possible, by the agency of the printing press and in public addresses, whenever opportunity offered or occasion seemed to require. In 1865 he presided over the meeting in Boston at which "the Universal Peace Union" was organized; and, though feeling obliged to decline the permanent presidency of the new association, made an able, eloquent and most admirable speech in support of its declared principles and objects, with which he was in most hearty

sympathy and accord; as he continued to be to the
end of his days: retaining his membership in it, speaking from time to time at its meetings, contributing to
its funds, and otherwise giving it the countenance and
support which he felt it so richly deserved. He appreciated the grand and noble work it was doing, under
the direction of its honored president, his valued
friend, Mr. Alfred H. Love, and efficient Board of
Managers, for the advancement of the cause in which
he had such profound interest, and for the promotion
of which he had labored with untiring devotion and
zeal during the greater portion of his long and constantly active life.

PART II
APPENDIX

THE HIGHER PATRIOTISM AND ITS RE-
LATION TO THE CAUSE OF
UNIVERSAL PEACE.

By Rev. William S. Heywood,

DORCHESTER, MASS.

"It is not that I love country less but humanity more that . . . I plead the cause of a higher and truer Patriotism."—*Charles Sumner.*

"There is no Patriotism so coherent and mighty as that which stands conformed to the boundless Brotherhood of the Gospel. That Gospel makes all human slaughter fratricidal."—*Bishop F. D. Huntington.*

The essentially wicked and reprehensible character of the great War System of the world, as it has existed and displayed itself in all past ages, is revealed not only in the more open and violent manifestations of its devastating power but in the subtle, malarious influence it has diffused through almost every department of human experience. While it has disturbed the otherwise quiet and orderly processes of domestic, social and civil life, destroyed the fruits of human genius and toil accumulated through long generations, laid waste cities and provinces without number, armed men with deadly weapons and sent them forth to mangle and destroy their fellow-men, strewn fair and fertile fields with the ghastly bodies of the dying and the dead, drenched the earth again and again with human blood, and multiplied many fold the agonies and tears of mankind, it has also woefully perverted the better instincts of the human heart, demoralized most grievously both private and public character, corrupted the fountains of human thought, and vitiated the very airs that nourish and renew the vital energies of the world. The pages of literature, which is the proper treasure-house of culture, refinement, virtue and piety, have been debased and polluted by it, and history, which should be a trustworthy record of humanity's progress from the earliest known date and the causes thereof, with the method of their operation, has, for the most part, been one long-drawn-out book of Chronicles, telling of the marshaling and going forth of armies and navies, of battles and sieges, of defeats suffered and victories won, while the great intellectual, moral and spiritual forces and agencies, ordained of God for the enlightenment, elevation and redemption of the race, have been either wholly unrecognized and unrecorded or remanded to a subordinate place in the classification.

Moreover, under the satanic enchantment of the iniquitous system, the ordinary forms of human speech have been grossly perverted or robbed of their highest meaning, words and phrases being misused or interpreted by the light of its baleful fires, and so made to beguile the unthinking mind and minster to its own unhallowed purposes and aims. Thus courage, heroism, honor, patriotism, words of intrinsic worth and power, are not infrequently disassociated from the common virtues or duties of life where they justly belong, forming as they do an essential part of a well-balanced character, and where they find ample field for laudable and even glorious exemplification, and are employed to represent distinctively soldierly attributes,

martial prowess and valor, as their chief and most
signal if not *only* worthy mode of expression. That is,
with many people, blinded by the deceitful glamor of
militarism to the true significance of the terms named,
the qualities they stand for are of little account, save
as displayed mid scenes of mortal combat and drip
with the blood of wounded and slaughtered men. Even
such grandly important words as *right, duty, responsi-
iblity,* are often despoiled of their intrinsic moral quality by the same deceitful sorcery and given a merely
conventional or political meaning, expressive only of
fealty to the existing civil order or system of government, irrespective of its form, character or requirements, be they just or unjust, righteous or wicked,
when tested by the eternal standards of ethics and
religion. In this way an idol of purely human manufacture is "exalted above all that is called God," and
made an object of supreme allegiance in place of the
infinite One whose right it is to rule and to whom all
such allegiance is forever due—an act of gross impiety
if not of blasphemy. It is to rescue these terms from
the misconception and abuse to which they have thus
been subjected in popular estimation that I take the
last and chiefest of them, Patriotism, which in some
proper sense may be understood as representing the
others, and make it the special theme of consideration
on the present occasion.

What we dignify by the name Patriotism, defined in
our dictionaries as love of country, is, I take it, a
native instinct or sentiment of the human heart, the
spontaneous outcome of impulses or affections that
antedate all nurture and training, of whose beginning
memory preserves no record, and of whose existence
philosophy offers no explanation, except that it is an

original part of the constitution of man. It is natural for one to feel the pulsations of this instinct or sentiment in the breast; and so, being of an elementary character and not a creation of art or tradition, it has the merit of universality, is not of local or temporary manifestation, characterizes no one class or condition of people, knows no distinction of race, color or nationality. It exists more or less active among the rude tribes of the forest; it is found a ruling motive among the most civilized of the children of men. It manifested itself in the remotest periods of history; it was never more in evidence than it is today, under all skies, wherever human beings dwell.

> "Man, through all ages of revolving time—
> Unchanging man, in every varying clime,
> Deems his own land of every land the pride
> Beloved by heaven o'er all the world beside."

The ancient Jews thought that Canaan was most highly favored of Jehovah and Mt. Zion, around which their history and their piety revolved, nearest His throne. The Greeks of old regarded their Olympus the dwelling place of the gods, and hence the choicest spot beneath the stars. So the early Romans felt that their great empire was nobler than all others and their capital city the grandest in the world. In more modern times the German sings praises to his fatherland; the Frenchman exults in the charms of his native valleys and vine-clad hills, under whatsoever government he lives; the storm-swept mountains of Switzerland have an unsurpassed grandeur for those dwelling perpetually in their presence; and the subjects of Victoria's widely extended rule, consider their own Albion, as they do her Majesty, worthy of profound esteem. The Laplander, whose home is amid scenes of never-failing

snow and ice, can with difficulty be lured to more genial
latitudes, while the American Indian, driven from the
wilds of his childhood and youth by the white man's
greed or otherwise, sighs and pants for his familiar
hunting grounds and the regions, desolate as they may
be, where the bones of his ancestors are laid. And are
you and I lacking this same impulsive sentiment? Do
we pay no spontaneous tribute of the heart to the land
in which we were born and within whose boundaries it
is our privilege to live, to work, to share the manifold
blessings of existence, to serve our Maker and our
fellow-men—

"Land of the Pilgrim's pride, land where our fathers died,"

and so on? Who does not feel an honest delight at the
thought of this country of ours, vast in extent, wonderful in the variety, beauty and grandeur of its scenery,
rich in resources and possibilities; with its marvelous
history, its sublime ideals of liberty, justice and humanity, its institutions of religion, education and charity;
with its great and good men and women who have lived
and are living to make the world better and to bring
in the kingdom of heaven? Despite her errors, follies
and sins, her inhumanities and perfidies—not few nor
far between, God knows; notwithstanding these things,
not to be justified, condoned or palliated, who does not
feel impelled when thoughts of his country and all it
represents come trooping through his mind, to exclaim
in grateful gladness, "O land of mine, America, with
all thy faults, I love thee still."

Regarding Patriotism in the light thus thrown upon
it, as a native instinct of the human heart, and therefore to be not only innocently but joyfully exercised
and employed, I am free to confess that I can not sym-

pathize with the distrust which some over-scrupulous peace men and women cherish towards it, and certainly not with that feeling of opposition and reprobation with which it is contemplated by the great Russian reformer, Count Tolstoy, who characterizes it as "a terrible evil and supersition." "The great sorrow of my old age," he says, "is that I have not succeeded in communicating to my brethren the truth, which I feel with the same evidence that I feel the light of the sun, that Patriotism must lead to lies, violence and murder; and not only to the loss of material well-being, but to the grossest moral depravation." "I think it is one of the most dreadful delusions of the world."

For reasons already indicated, I count this a distorted view of the subject, as unphilosophical and false to human nature and to history as it is unsatisfactory and misleading. It is based, it seems to me, not upon a comprehensive study of the subject, but upon some of its lowest and most reprehensible manifestations; upon those acts of deceit, oppression and cruelty which, in the name and under the guise of Patriotism, have been perpetrated in his own and other lands, in times of both peace and war. Just as Dr. Johnson, beholding the chicanery, fraud, corruption and iniquity practiced in his day with the same pretext, was moved to declare that "Patriotism is the last refuge of a scoundrel."

And not only is Patriotism to be regarded as an innate impulse or endowment of human nature, but as one of the strongest and most commanding of its capabilities, urging to the greatest sacrifices, to the most heroic endeavors, to the grandest achievements. What have not men dared, what have they not done under the inspiration and motive power of this inborn passion, roused from its constitutional lethargy to energetic

action, for the accomplishment of some real or sup-
posed-to-be lofty purpose or object! This has been
illustrated in times of war, when, at the sound of the
trumpet, men, under a sense of loyalty to their country,
have rushed forth at the risk of life and of all that
made life dear to them, to defend her against a foreign
foe or maintain her standing before the world. It has
been illustrated no less in times of peace, when other
men, who never doffed a soldier's garb or wore
shoulder-straps, like Sir Thomas Moore, Milton, Wil-
berforce and Gladstone across the sea, and Adams,
Sumner, Giddings and Phillips in our own land, have
foregone a thousand delights and suffered obloquy,
detraction, poverty, and sometimes imprisonment and
death, for freedom's sake and the perpetuity of those
ideas and institutions upon which the well-being of
their county and of its people depended.

But while this love of country is a native and divinely
appointed instinct or force of human nature it is not
necessarily self-regulative and praiseworthy in its
diversified promptings and manifestations, as already
intimated. In common with all other human capabilities it needs guidance, restraint, wise and righteous
control. Like a mountain stream, which may be pure,
healthful, invigorating at its source, it is liable to
become so devitalized, so charged with deleterious,
foreign elements in its onward flow as to hinder rather
than help the truer life of men—as to become a bane
and not a blessing to society and the world. Channing,
one of the earliest and most clear-sighted champions of
the cause of peace in the United States, speaking of
Patriotism, says, "It is a natural and generous impulse
of human nature to love the country that gave us
birth." "But this sentiment often degenerates into a

narrow, partial, exclusive attachment, alienating us from other branches of the human family and instigating to aggression on other States. In ancient times this principle developed with wonderful energy and sometimes absorbed every other sentiment." And he might have added that it not infrequently has overmastered and trampled in the dust every consideration of justice and the eternal right, the most imperative dictates of reason and humanity.

"Patriotism as existing among certain of the Greeks," says the brilliant essayist and statesman, Macaulay, "turned kingdoms into gangs of robbers, whom mutual fidelity rendered more dangerous, gave a character of peculiar atrocity to war, and generated the worst of political evils, the tyranny of nation over nation." To the Roman of the time of the Cæsars the empire was the most important, as it was in a material sense the most powerful of dynasties, and it claimed the right as it made the attempt to subjugate and absorb all other nations, vanquishing their armies on the field of battle and bringing commanders and chieftains, potentates and kings home to the imperial city as trophies of its victorious might. These other nations in his estimation were of no account, save as they could be made to increase its wealth, extend its dominion, add to its glory. In many of the so-called Commonwealths of antiquity and of the medieval ages, in which there was some professed regard for liberty, Patriotism, like liberty itself, was often made à pretext for assaults upon the inborn rights of mankind, for adopting and enforcing measures that stifled thought and free discussion, corrupted the administration of justice, sacrificed the well-being of the many to the ambition of the few, and crushed the hopes of aspiring multitudes under the iron heel of arbitrary power.

This same spirit is, alas, still abroad in the world, carrying on its direful work under the same alluring disguise. It is to be found, not among ignorant, degraded, so-called heathen nations alone, but among nations claiming to be pre-eminently civilized and Christian. Ay, sometimes in the name of civilization and Christianity as well as of Patriotism does that fell spirit sound the tocsin of aggressive war, summon minions from the peaceful and beneficent pursuits of life, equip them and send them forth by land and sea to engage in the work of human butchery; showing thereby how closely allied the foremost of nations in our own time may be to those benighted peoples of bygone days whose tyrant chieftains, impelled by the greed of empire or of gain, were every ready

> "To wade through slaughter to a throne
> And shut the gates of mercy on mankind."

This was signally illustrated in the case of the war between this country of ours and Mexico occurring within the memory of some of us here present, as needless, as unjustifiable and wicked a conflict at arms as was ever waged since time began, inaugurated, as it was, and carried through for the indisputable purpose of strengthening the slave power in the national councils and of thereby perpetuating on American soil a system of oppression and outrage, "one hour of which," Thomas Jefferson said," was fraught with more misery than whole ages of that which our fathers rose in rebellion to oppose." And yet it was a war waged ostensibly for the purpose of promoting the honor and glory of the country and therewith also the welfare and happiness of mankind. The Governor of my own State, an honored deacon of an evangelical (?) church, issued a proclamation calling upon the young men of the Commonwealth to enlist as volunteers in the country's service and go forth across the continent to kill or to be killed, in the name of "Patriotism and Humanity"—words easily suborned to beguile the common mind and to soften, if not sanctify, the enormities incident to the systematic slaughter of man by the hands of his fellowman.

The devout Governor, who personally believed the conflict with Mexico to be wrong, was deluded and thrown off his moral base, by the often prevailing fallacy that when a country is engaged in a war all loyal citizens are bound to render it free and hearty support, whatever may be the merits or demerits of the strife; and that under such circumstances Patriotism can be shown in no other way. As was said by a soldier of the Civil War, prominent afterward in public affairs: "It is conceit for any man to think he can serve his country in any way but in the ranks." In other words, no one can be a true lover of his country while an armed conflict is going on, except he approve, uphold and aid the government under whose auspices it is waged. And this the real patriot will cheerfully do, irrespective of any scruples he may have concerning the rightfulness of war in general or the particular war in hand. Under the same prepossession the *New York Independent,* a religious journal of advanced views, soon after the opening of hostilities with Spain two years or more ago, besought those of its readers who believed "the war wicked and unnecessary to join with us in support of the government in fighting it quickly to the end." That is, fling your ideas of right

and wrong to the winds, abandon your principles, trample conscience under foot, and unite with others in
what you believe to be a scheme of iniquity, if so be it
a foolish or sinful administration of public affairs
demands it.   From all such counselors, religious or
otherwise, we may say in the words of the Liturgy,
"Good Lord, deliver us."   Such Patriotism, I have no
hesitation in pronouncing both false and immoral, and
such loyalty to country, treason to God, as I shall show
later on.

And not only is that Patriotism false and misleading
which thus seeks to hide, palliate or justify the evils
of the great war system, or of some special war—a war
perchance of invasion and conquest inaugurated by
unscrupulous leaders and urged on by the baser elements of the political arena and by morally deceptive
religious teachers, on the ground that it is the work
of the government and that the patriot will stand by
the government in such a case—but that Patriotism
also is false and misleading, yea, and dangerous as well,
which is blinded by the glamour of military display and
achievement to various forms of personal vice and
crime existing beneath a soldier's uniform or within an
army encampment; or which by some impious leger-
demain converts a man of unclean and disorderly life
into a hero or a saint upon enlisting as a soldier in his
country's service—his enlistment papers being counted
a sufficient passport to the realms of bliss, and an
honorable discharge from military duty the guarantee
of an abundant entrance into the heavenly kingdom.

The distinguished orator at Harvard University a
few weeks ago, Hon. William Everett, LL.D., in a
brilliant and brave address upon the subject I am now
discussing, speaks of the immorality which is often

lost to sight or duly atoned for by assuming a military costume, in terms worthy of remembrance. "If a monarch," he says, "a statesman, a soldier, stands forth pre-eminent in exalting the name or extending the boundaries of his country, he is a patriot, and that is enough. Such a leader may be as perjured and blasphemous as Frederic or as brutal and stupid as his father; he may be as faithless and mean as Marlborough or as dissolute and bloody as Julius Cæsar; he may trample on every right of independent nations and drive his countrymen to the shambles like Napoleon; he may be as corrupt as Walpole or as wayward as Chatham; he may be destitute of every spark of culture, or prostitute the gifts of the Muses to the basest ends; he may have, in short, all manner of vices and defects, but if he is true to his country, if he is her faithful standard-bearer, if he strives to set her and keep her high above her rivals, he is right, a worthy patriot. And if he seem lukewarm in her cause, if, however wise and good he may be in all other relations, he fails to work with all his heart and soul to maintain her position among the nations, he must be stamped with failure if not with a curse."

Such conceptions of Patriotsim and all of kindred nature are gross perversions of the true meaning of the word—a prostitution of it to base and unhallowed uses. Readiness to enlist in the army of a country and to go forth and help fight her battles is no proof or token of patriotism. Thousands of men are thus ready and eager to enlist and to fight, whose hearts never felt one honest throb of real love for their country, whose minds never cherished one earnest purpose to further their country's well-being, who never spent one solitary moment in striving to know in what their country's real honor consisted or how they could most effectively promote it.   And thousands there are in every army corps of such ignoble, degraded, shameless lives, that it might be truly said that the best service they could personally render their country would be to go out of it on some hazardous venture in far-away lands, where they could work the least possible harm to the common weal.   Patriotism in any proper sense can not be made a shield for criminality and guilt or an expiation for offenses of any sort against the moral law.   Nor is it to be identified with bellicosity or the fighting spirit, whatever form it may assume.   "Patriotism," said Starr King, "is not that pugilistic passion which estimates glory by battlefields, weighs national worth by vigor of muscle, and culls the anthology of its bloody traditions into a sort of pirate's own book, by which its brutal appetite is nourished."   Yet it is by multitudes of people so regarded. "The fighting man," it has been truly remarked, "the man of desperate deeds, the captain of the bloody deck and riddled rigging, is the patriot of popular song," as it is of many a favorite story.   From the martial standpoint—the standpoint of war—Patriotism that is of any account must drip with human blood.

"But it is sometimes said," observes the before quoted Channing, "that war kindles patriotism"; that "by fighting for his country one learns to love it."   But he adds, "the patriotism which is cherished by war is ordinarily false and spurious, a vice and not a virtue, a scourge to the world, a narrow, unjust passion, which aims to exalt a particular State on the humiliation or destruction of other States."   And if we may judge by the history of the war system, as it has existed from time immemorial, and by the influence of the military spirit wherever it has prevailed to any extent, the patriotism engendered and nurtured amid scenes of violence and carnage has wrought more harm than good to national welfare, and been, as a rule, a menace rather than a protection to the higher interests of the people.

And while Patriotism in its better aspects derives no significance nor force from the spirit of belligerence with which it is so often associated and is never to be confounded with mere militarism in any of its manifestations, it is not, on the other hand, what is represented by the flamboyant rhetoric and spread-eagle oratory frequently displayed on the Fourth of July and like occasions, nominally observed for a patriotic purpose. It is more than this—more than a glorification of the fathers, more than a rehearsal of heroic deeds, more than fulsome praise of national resources, wealth, power, achievement, or possibility. It is more than pronouncing the Shibboleth of some political party, manipulating conventions, ratifying nominations, or celebrating any victories of election day. Let us take heed lest we be led astray by the clangor of mere words or by the false meaning that popular opinion or the excitement of an hour or a day or any form of sophistry may put into words; lest "we crown that which is only a blind passion as a lofty emotion and clothe with the robes of duty what is little more than a superstition."

True Patriotism, as distinguished from that which is false and deceitful, is love of country for what it really stands for, in its own distinctive character and in the life of the world. As an enlightened, refined sentiment, flavored, so to say, with morality and religion, it is love of country for that in it which is worthy of

regard and commendation; for that which makes it a
living factor in the development, elevation, and perfect-
ing of humanity. In this land of ours, true Patriotism,
while recognizing and appreciating its material resources, advantages, blessings of whatever sort, will
prize it, rejoice in it, and honor it chiefly for its intellectual, moral, social, civil, and religious characteristics:
for the tokens of Providential favor that illumine so
many pages of its history, for the lofty character of the
brave adventurers, who, as the representatives of an
advancing civilization, first peopled its shores and laid
the foundation of its various and manifold institutions,
for the great ideas of justice, equity, and freedom
promulgated to the world from its high places, for
what ·has been accomplished within its borders in the
way of realizing a better domestic, social, and civil
order for all classes and conditions of people, for what
has here been done through the agency of its more
Christlike men and women and in other ways to build
up the kingdom of heaven on the earth.

And such a Patriotism will manifest itself, not so
much in the politician's arts, in the resolutions of cau-
cuses and conventions, in glowing sentences, or idle
boasting or impassioned appeals, or noisy demonstra-
tions of any sort, as in personal integrity, in fidelity to
the great trusts of life, in a noble type of manhood and
womanhood, in loyalty to that law of eternal rectitude
which alone can honor, adorn, and save a State as it
can an individual soul. It will display itself in purified
homes and the right ordering of domestic life, in a
cherished spirit of conciliation and brotherhood, in the
maintenance of kindly and helpful relations with all
sorts and conditions of people, in practical endeavors to
uplift, benefit and redeem the more dependent, unfor-

tunate and needy classes of society—to remedy the abuses, harmonize the differences, lessen the inequalities, and overcome the evils of the existing social order, in striving to exemplify in all the affairs and relations of life the principles, precepts, and spirit of the gospel of Christ. It will show itself in independence of thought and action upon all important concerns, in refusing to be the tool or the victim of tricksters and demagogues, in exposing the chicaneries and iniquities of unscrupulous aspirants for office, in protesting against the wrongs of public as well as private life, in resisting all solicitations to go with the multitude to do evil, in disobeying unrighteous requirements even though made by the government itself, and in maintaining the supremacy of the right, good and true over all legislative enactments, State policies, and national decretals whatsoever.

But passing from these generalizations, I am moved to make certain affirmations based upon the divine order of the world which a true and enlightened Patriotism will recognize and be governed by as essential to a proper and rightful development or expression of national life.

1. The first is that the well-being, prosperity and happiness of a nation is indissolubly associated with the well-being, prosperity and happiness of all classes of its population and their corresponding unity, harmony and kindly co-operation. There can be no well-assured national good, no ideal national life, no unsullied national honor, where any considerable number of people are subject to the evils of ignorance, poverty, vice and crime, or are enslaved by bad habits and besotted by debauchery and excess. And no nation is really worthy of admiration in which gross and start-

ling inequalities of circumstance, condition and opportunity exist; as between the rich and poor, the educated and uneducated, the refined and the vulgar, the so-called higher and lower elements of society. Nor can a nation be ideally prosperous and happy, or free from threatening ills, in which class distinctions assume a hostile and virulent form, or where envy, jealousy, ill-will or other spirit of alienation and distrust disturbs otherwise harmonious relations and engenders bitterness and wrath between man and man or between party and party; in social circles, in industry, business, politics or religion. Differences of opinion and of action there may be, there must be, except the individuality of men be destroyed, which would be a dire calamity—but all differences must be shared and exercised in the spirit of true liberty, without intolerance and persecution, each granting to others the rights claimed for himself, and all striving together for the common good of all. Fraternity, co-operation, harmony, are the watchwords of an orderly, happy community, town, State, nation, world.

2. A second important consideration regulating the expression or overt action of true Patriotism is that one's country is but a single member of an extended brotherhood of countries, each and all having a place in the Providential plan of the world and a part to play in the great drama of human life on the earth. As a legitimate deduction from this proposition, it follows that the several countries constituting this brotherhood, like the different classes or circles in any one of them, have certain common interests and rights entitled to mutual respect, and certain common obligations to be sacredly regarded and faithfully met; and that between those countries there should be nurtured the feeling of fra-

ternal sympathy, helpfulness and goodwill. This makes all international jealousy, enmity, wrath and war not only derogatory to the character of the particular nations concerned, but perilous to the higl est good of the entire fraternity of nations. The scorr, contempt, hostility, sometimes shown by citizens of one country towards those of another is no proof of pure Patriotism but of the lack of it; as a man who hates his neighbor's children can have no pure love for his own. Such scorn, contempt, hostility, is but the outcome of national conceit, egotism, bigotry, as offensive to a profound sense of justice and honor in a Commonwealth or empire as in an individual, and as full of mischief and peril. National selfishness, like personal selfishness, is the grave of all true nobleness and renown; it festers with the germs of decay and death.

And the practical recognition of this fact of the brotherhood of nations opens out naturally into the larger fact of the brotherhood of the human race; the special love of one's country under divine tuition growing into that love for all men, without which we are told upon good authority there can be no real love of God. So that without depreciating or limiting one's affection for the land in which he lives or his desire or ability to serve its highest good, he may say in all honesty, as did one of America's noblest philanthropists, "My country is the world and my countrymen are all mankind." In the spirit of this broader, more inclusive interpretation of the word Patriotism may men and nations dwell together in unity, in friendliness and in peace, mutual helpers of each other in all things pertaining to their enduring progress and glory, each striving with all and all with each for the universal good, the ultimate "federation of the world."

3. And once more I observe that Patriotism of the higher order recognizes and regards the great fundamental fact of the universe that there is a law superior to all human enactments or decrees—a moral government of the world, supreme over all human interests and concerns, to which not alone the common personal affairs of men must be made subject, but all social, civil, national and international affairs as well; the greatest no less than the least of them. A nation without the consciousness of such a law, "whose seat is the bosom of God and whose voice is the harmony of the world," without a living sense of loyalty to such a government, on the part of its rulers and the great mass of its people, is a nation doomed, a nation rushing upon the thick bosses of the buckler of the Almighty. It is a dictum not from the Scripture records alone, but from the council chamber of the eternities, that comes ringing through all the corridors of time, saying, "Righteousness exalteth a nation, but sin is a reproach to any people." How slow are men to learn the sacred lesson that "whatsoever a man (or a nation) soweth that shall he (or it) also reap;" that no one individual, though he be King or President, and no body of men, though it be a Legislature or Parliament, can annul the statutes of the great Framer of all worlds, make a wrong thing right, or stay the operations of that retributive Justice which holds all rational, responsible beings in all possible conditions under all possible relations amenable to its own solemn, unescapable operations and behests.

These things being so, the intelligent patriot shapes his thought and conduct accordingly. True to its permanent interests he refuses to be a party or lend support to whatever he sees or believes to be wrong in his country's counsels, in its governmental policy, or in any department of the public service. The younger Pitt, whom Macaulay termed "the greatest master of parliamentary government the world has ever seen," resigned his place as Prime Minister of England, rather than violate his conscience in breaking faith with the Catholics of Ireland. Granville Sharpe, the patriarch of British Abolitionists, gave up his position in the government of the kingdom rather than lend support in any way to the war against the American colonies in 1776, deeming it unjust and therefore detrimental to the public welfare. It was no lack of Patriotism that prompted the action of these men, but the impulse of the highest type of Patriotism. They were better patriots by far than the monarch and members of Parliament whose policy they opposed. Who were the more worthy to be called patriots in this country before the Civil War, the Abolitionists, who, seeing the giant iniquity that was destroying the liberties of the people and threatening the life of the nation, sought to have it put away by legitimate means and without violence and the effusion of blood, or their proslavery detractors, in and out of office, who, by a blind and wicked policy, brought on the strife at arms, causing the Republic to totter in her accustomed seat and the Southland to be strewn with the dead bodies of more than half a million of her sons?

No true patriot shuts his eyes to his country's follies, crimes, abominations, or withholds his testimony against them, whatever be the sacrifice or risk. Much less does he palliate them, apologize for them, or seek to shield them from the rebuke and condemnation which are their righteous due. Nor does he adopt or give currency, repute and weight to such maxims as

"My country, however bounded," "My country, right or wrong," "My country, my whole country, and nothing but my country," maxims born of the war spirit, and employed chiefly in war time to pervert the judgment of men and help on war's bloody work. No thoughtful, high-minded patriot is deceived and led astray by them. They are morally indefensible, wicked, atheistic. They dethrone God; they ignore, set at naught, bring into contempt, the everlasting law; they deserve only censure and unqualified reprobation at the hands of all who reverence truth, justice and the eternal right.

And now let us consider what relation true Patriotism sustains to the great cause of Peace, whose interests this gathering represents, and whose triumph it is designed to advance. That it is exceedingly cordial and intimate has been already indicated. Every consideration offered in exposition of such Patriotism, of its essential nature and character, of its workings in human history, of what it suggests, inspires and seeks to accomplish, is in singular and happy accord with the principles, purposes, methods and hopes of the friends of Peace, appeals directly to their sympathy and judgment, and commends itself to their approval, confidence and regard. The cause of Peace is emphatically the cause of the Republic; and the welfare of the Republic is largely dependent upon the development and ascendency among its citizens of that type of personal character and the prevalence of that spirit of friendliness, co-operation and harmony which it is the special purpose of the Peace movement to engender and make dominant in public as well as in private life.

As a matter of fact, true Patriotism and the Peace cause operate along similar lines to one and the same transcendent end; along lines of justice, mercy, love, towards mutual good will, unity, solidarity in the state and nation, and towards the final enfranchisement and pacification of the world. There is ample room for illustrating in detail this likeness of the two to each other—of showing their many points of correspondence, if not their absolute identity; and even that in many particulars. Certainly the Peace cause recognizes and emphasizes the three fundamental truths or principles of civic order just now stated, the acknowledged supremacy of which has been declared to be essential to true and enlightened Patriotism—truths or principles that need no further elaboration or enforcement.

True Patriotism and the cause of Peace correspond in desiring and seeking to enhance the enduring greatness of a country and in the conception of what that greatness is—of its real nature and character. And this has never been set forth in more eloquent and impressive language than by the distinguished philanthropist and statesman, Charles Sumner, in his splendid oration upon "The True Grandeur of Nations." "War," he says, "is utterly and irreconcilably inconsistent with true greatness." "That consists in imitating as near as possible for finite man the perfection of an infinite Creator; above all, in cultivating those highest perfections, Justice and Love." "The true greatness of nations is in those qualities which constitute the greatness of the individual. It is not to be found in extent of territory, nor in vastness of population, nor in wealth; not in fortifications, nor armies, nor navies; not in the phosphorescent glare of fields of battle, nor in Golgothas, though covered with monuments that kiss the clouds. For all these are creatures

and representatives of qualities in our nature unlike
anything in God."

"Nor is the greatness of nations to be found in the
triumphs of the intellect alone—in literature, learning,
science or art. These may widen the sphere of its
influence; they may adorn it, but they are only its
accessories. The polished Greeks—the world's masters
in language and thought, and the commanding Romans,
overawing the earth with their power, were little more
than splendid savages; and the age of Louis XIV.,
spanning a long period of worldly magnificence, was
degraded by immoralities that can not be mentioned
without a blush, and by deeds of injustice not to be
washed out by the tears of all the recording angels of
heaven. The true grandeur of humanity is in moral
elevation, sustained, enlightened and decorated by the
intellect of man. And the truest tokens of this
grandeur are the diffusion of the greatest happiness
to the greatest number, and that Godlike justice which
controls the relations of the State to other States and
to all the people under its care." It is national greatness
thus delineated that the true patriot and the friend of
Peace conjointly seek to honor and enhance.

Such greatness will command the approval and admiration of all noble souls, not alone by the sublime
qualities that characterize it, but by the extent and
splendor of its achievements. It will be not simply
a latent and inappreciable force in the world—an
abstract idea for the student of political economics—
but an active energy in human life and history, making
the nation, illustrating it a mighty factor in the problem
of human uplifting and redemption. We are hearing
just now a great deal about the part which the United
States is coming to play in the great drama of human

affairs by reason of her recent military and naval exploits. "The war with Spain," says Governor Adams, of Colorado, "makes our country *a world power.*" Other purblind politicians and half-fledged patriots are saying the same thing, and the responding populace rend the air with shouts of applause thereat. To such persons, ignorant of the philosophy of history as they are of ethical principles and agencies, this great American nation was of little account in the world until within two or three years. But now, since San Juan and Manila, we, her people, are somebody; we can take our place among other nations and defy them all; we can whip all creation; no foreign, old-time dynasty will henceforth dare to tread on the toes of our venerable Uncle Sam or insult the dignity of his imperial majesty. The watchwords henceforth are to be, "Hands off" and "Beware."

So some people talk. But such talk is cheap—too cheap for serious consideration, and as vicious as it is cheap. It is the glorification of brute force and national pugilism. It is the exaltation of might over right, of military prowess over justice and humanity. It is the boast of the braggart, the swaggerer, the prize-fighter; not an expression of true valor, of lofty statesmanship, of clear-seeing philosophy. It makes the United States the chief bully among the nations—a distinction not to be proud of and not to be coveted. This vain and shameful braggardism was so well stated and elucidated a year or more ago by Rev. Dr. Jefferson, of Broadway Tabernacle, New York City, in a sermon from the text "And the devil taketh him up into an exceedingly high mountain," etc., that I venture to quote a brief passage:

"Men are everywhere exulting in the notion that we,

as a nation, have become a great world-power. We amounted to nothing before the victory at Manila. He is a Rip Van Winkle of an American who had to be aroused from sleep by a cannon shot to learn that the United States has been a world-power for years. How did she become such? By her army? No. By her navy? No. By dabbling in diplomacy? No. By colonies and dependencies? No. But by the culture of the arts of peace, by building schools, colleges, churches; by developing free institutions. . . . We have not fooled away our time in drilling men to kill each other. We have not squandered our money on armies and navies." "America is not isolated. Her spirit for years has walked up and down the earth. Where is there a land her influence has not reached? . . . Her ideas have touched the hearts of men under every sun. . . . She is a power already in the evolution of the race. And yet some men never knew it till a gun was fired at Manila. . . . A great naval power—a great military power! In many a circle these are phases to conjure with. A great *Christian power* to my ears sounds much better!" As it does, I apprehend to the ears of both peace men and true patriots—to the ear of God and his holy angels. A great power for justice, righteousness, brotherhood, peace, throughout the earth. So may she be.

So indeed let us hope and pray that she may be. For it is in the way suggested that our beloved country is to act a noble part on the stage of history and serve humanity's highest good in the years to come. Not like Rome of old by making other nations tremble at the mention of her name, not by conquests at arms on distant battle-fields, not by subjugating weaker provinces and compelling them to bow to her imperial sway.

Not by elevating her standards on foreign soil and refusing to take them down again, however unrighteously they may have been set up; but by her proclamation of the principles of civil and religious liberty, by her championship of the inborn rights of mankind, by her ideals of freedom made real within her own borders, by the light of her example of righteous self-government shining forth to illume the benighted portions of the globe, by the contagion of an honorable, just, humane national life, by the prosperity, virtue and happiness of all classes of her population, by her institutions of learning, charity and religion, by her sympathy for and hospitality to down-trodden and oppressed peoples struggling after liberty and a better life, by her missionaries and heralds of Christian faith going forth in the spirit of the Master into all the world to preach the Gospel of love to God and man and to wage holy warfare against human folly, ignorance, sin and shame, not with carnal weapons but with spiritual, which are mighty through God to the pulling down of the strongholds of the adversary and to the achievement of a final victory for the true, the beautiful and the good throughout the earth.

True Patriotism in this land of ours supplements and reinforces the cause of Peace in vigorously resisting the growing militarism which is dominating to a large extent the policy of the national government, corrupting the high standards of public life and exalting brute force to the place in common esteem which properly belongs to reason, the judicial sense, and the spirit of brotherhood. Two and a half years ago, under the pretext of delivering the inhabitants of the island of Cuba from the cruel tyranny of Spain, the baser elements of the political arena and the jingoists of the press throughout the country roused the latent war-spirit of the people at large from the repose of a generation to an intensity that overruled their calmer judgment and more humane feeling and that inaugurated a new regime in the administration of national affairs full of mischiefs and portents of coming ill. As a result the army of the United States has been multiplied fourfold, with a fair prospect of indefinite increase under the infatuation created by the widely prevailing greed of gain and of empire in our borders. An army is in its very nature a despotism, and, extended beyond the limits of a national police force, a menace to the Republic and to that freedom and independence for which the Republic, true to its ideals and the principles of its founders, stands; a menace to all forms of popular government. This is shown in the history of the ancient and mediæval Commonwealths, as it is in the experience of the French nation since it last assumed the name and form of Democracy. Again and again has the government established by Thiers, Hugo, Favre, and other actors in the revolution of 1870 come near to shipwreck by reason of the arbitrary spirit, and the imperialistic tendencies, the malign influence of the army. Washington clearly apprehended danger from this source to the political edifice he helped to raise, and in his Farewell Address warned his fellow-countrymen against "overgrown military establishments, which," he said, "under any form of government are inauspicious to liberty, and which are to be regarded as particularly hostile to Republican liberty." True Patriotism to-day, among wise, prophetic men, as in the person of the "Father of his country," views the rapid increase of these liberty-imperilling establishments with deep solicitude and even alarm, and protests against them accordingly. Moreover, such establishments and their accessories are highly prejudicial to the well-being of the great mass of the people of a country, especially of the industrial classes—the honest yeomanry. We have but to look at continental Europe for indisputable proof of this. The army equipments there, which have doubled within thirty years, are maintained at immense cost, necessitating a system of taxation which reduces the populace to a condition of extreme poverty and degradation, a condition provocative of unrest and disorder, and well calculated to generate Nihilism, Anarchism, and all forms of violent upheaval and bloody outbreak. If our land is to avoid social and civil tumult and convulsions in days to come, she must guard assiduously against the causes that produce them, chiefest of which is an oppressive militarism, as experience in the countries alluded to demonstrates. Clear-seeing, high-minded patriots among us see the impending peril, and join must heartily with the friends of Peace, in demanding a halt in the military activities of the time, a suppression of the prevailing war spirit for the sake of the Republic, of the people generally, and of the cause of freedom in the world at large.

In conclusion, I am moved to affirm that true Patriotism and the Peace Cause are singularly coincident in deprecating and condemning unqualifiedly the war now (1900) being carried on by the United States government against the people of the Philippine Islands, and the policy of the national administration in respect to the same. The latter bases its verdict upon those fundamental principles of morality, justice, brotherhood, love, of which it is the practical expression; the former upon those fundamental principles of civil and religious liberty on which the American Republic was founded and for which it has ever stood before the nations. Those principles are distinctly set forth in the Declaration of Independence, the Magna Charta of that type of national life which this country represents. The issuance of that instrument marked an epoch in the social and civil evolution of the race; it was a new departure in the march of humanity to its final earthly destiny. On that instrument and on the great truths it enunciated the national edifice has been built; by it has the national character been shaped, and under its inspiration and guidance whatever is most signal and praiseworthy in the national career has been achieved.

But the governmental policy in regard to the Philippine war is in open contravention of the spirit and affirmations of the Declaration; a denial of its claims, an abandonment of what has been most distinctive in the national life. It is a virtual repudiation of the work of the nation's founders; a return to old world ideals, doctrines, practices, methods of administration. It is a surrender of America and the West to Europe and the East. It is a re-adoption of the statecraft which the pilgrim and the Puritan dared the perils of the sea and the greater perils of the wilderness to escape. It is playing the part of George III. and Lord North over again in their dealings with the American colonies one hundred and twenty-five years ago; attempting to subjugate and render submissive to a foreign power a people who, like our revolutionary fathers, are striving for liberty and independence. It may be called the onward march of democratic ideas, but it bears all the insignia of imperialism and what that term stands for in the philosophy of government and the history of nations. It may be called "benevolent assimilation," but it is of the same nature and character as "criminal aggression," and no shuffle of words can make it otherwise. It is practically a war of invasion and conquest, such as has been waged from time immemorial under the barbarous, tyrannical assumption that "might makes right." It puts the nation into the same category and reduces it to the same plane with the dynasties of the old world, enabling them to say to it in scornful derision, "Aha! thou didst set thyself up as vastly wiser and better than we were, and so our light and our example; but now, how art thou fallen and become as one of us!" Wise statesmen see this and deplore it, while the demoralized politician, the devotee of brute force, and the unthinking multitude, drunk with the wine of militarism or infatuated with the lust for dominion, are oblivious to the gravity of the situation and to the direful consequence which it assuredly portends.

But there is a moral and humanitarian aspect of the case, more serious, if possible, than the political. How did this war with the Filipinos come to be? Two years ago they were our friends and we were theirs. Now the two are deadly enemies. Two years ago we solicited their aid as allies in overcoming the forces of Spain at Manila with the assurance, if not open promise, that, if successful, they should have their independence. They gladly acceded to our request. Yet no sooner was Spain conquered, and conquered by their help, than our arms were turned against them, under the demand of absolute subjection to our authority to which they owed no allegiance, with no regard for their inborn rights, but with scornful refusal to listen to their repeated appeals in behalf of such rights. And from that day to this the United States government has been fighting and attempting to conquer them as miscalled rebels and insurgents. The treatment of them is as gross, unjustifiable and base an act of perfidy as the annals of nations records. Rev. Mr. Chadwick, of Brooklyn, says: "The colonial history of Spain contains no such atrocious piece of treachery as the Filipinos have suffered at the hands of this country." It is to be believed that they have been subjected to more outrage, cruelty, loss of blood and life under eighteen months of United States domination in and about Manila than under eighteen years of Spanish misrule; to the nation's lasting dishonor and unutterable shame.

Such being the case, both Patriotism and the cause of Peace enter a solemn protest against the whole proceeding, and demand an immediate cessation of hostilities. They cry aloud, amid the impending gloom and clash of resounding arms, for a return to the principles of the Declaration of Independence, to the principles of justice and humanity, upon which the safety, prosperity and glory of the Republic rests, and in which lies the hope of the downtrodden and oppressed of all lands and climes to the ends of the earth.

Unfortunate, however, and deplorable as is the condition into which our beloved country has been brought at this period of her history, and forbidding as is the outlook in many directions, yet may we not despair. A way out of the encompassing darkness will, in the good providence of God, be opened, and new light will in due time, I doubt not, illumine the pathway of the Republic and gladden all our hearts. "The wrath of man shall praise Him, and the remainder of wrath will He restrain." Recovering from this fearful lapse towards barbarism and escaping the perils incident thereto; instructed it may be and purified by the experience and invested with new power of accomplishment, the nation will go forward more rapidly than before to the attainment of that destiny which I can but believe is her inalienable birthright—a destiny worthy of her origin, of her lofty ideals, of her history, of her opportunities and of her possibilities; sublime in itself and unspeakably beneficent for mankind. A destiny it is, as I contemplate it, of universal liberty, not of license; of justice to all men, not of oppression and outrage to any; of noble ideas, not of barbarous maxims and immoral sophistries; of healthful growth and normal development of resources and character, not of foreign invasions and enforced annexations; of peace and good will, and not of war. A destiny of lifting up fallen races, of educating benighted tribes, of regenerating sinful peoples, of leading other nations and the world in the grand march of humanity to its divinely ordained, ultimate estate of universal liberty, righteousness, brotherhood, harmony and happiness. In the faith and hope that such is the transcendently glorious mission of this country of ours in the years to come, the part she is to hereafter play in the great drama of human existence upon the earth, we can most sincerely salute her in the inspiring verse of the elder President Dwight, of Yale College:

"Columbia, Columbia, to glory arise,
Thou queen of the world and child of the skies!
Thy genius commands thee: with rapture behold,
While ages on ages thy splendors unfold.
Thy reign is the last and noblest of time,
Most fruitful thy soil, most inviting thy clime;
Let the crimes of the East ne'er encrimson thy name,
Be freedom and virtue and knowledge thy fame.

"To conquest and slaughter let Europe aspire,
Whelm nations in blood and wrap cities in fire;
Thy heroes the rights of mankind shall defend,
And triumph shall crown them and glory attend.
A world is thy realm; for a world be thy laws
Enlarged as thine empire and just as thy cause;
On freedom's broad basis that empire shall rise,
Extend with the years and dissolve with the skies.

"Thy fleets to all regions thy power shall display,
The nations admire thee and ocean obey;
Each shore to thy glory shall tribute unfold,
And the East and the South yield their spices and gold.
As the dayspring unbounded thy splendor shall flow,
And earth's smaller kingdoms before thee shall bow,
While the ensigns of union, in triumph unfurled,
Hush the tumult of war and bring peace to the world."